Genocide Lives in Us

WOMEN IN AFRICA AND THE DIASPORA

Series Editors

STANLIE JAMES
AILI MARI TRIPP

Genocide Lives in Us

Women, Memory, and Silence in Rwanda

Jennie E. Burnet

The University of Wisconsin Press

Publication of this book has been made possible,
in part, through support from the University of Louisville's
University Committee on Academic Publication.

The University of Wisconsin Press
1930 Monroe Street, 3rd Floor
Madison, Wisconsin 53711-2059
uwpress.wisc.edu

3 Henrietta Street
London WC2E 8LU, England
eurospanbookstore.com

Printed in the United States of America

Library of Congress Cataloging-in-Publication Data

Burnet, Jennie E.
Genocide lives in us : women, memory, and silence in Rwanda / Jennie E. Burnet.
p.   cm.—(Women in Africa and the diaspora)
Includes bibliographical references and index.
ISBN 978-0-299-28644-6 (pbk.: alk. paper)
ISBN 978-0-299-28643-9 (e-book)
1. Women—Rwanda—Social conditions.   2. Women in public life—Rwanda.
3. Rwanda—History—1994-   4. Rwanda—History—Civil War, 1994—Atrocities.
5. Genocide—Rwanda.   I. Title.   II. Series: Women in Africa and the diaspora.
DT450.44.B87   2012
967.57104′31—dc23
2011045391

For

my Rwandan mothers and sisters

In memory of

Alison Des Forges
Elise Nimugire
Alvera
Verdianne
Aloys Rumanzi
Dieudonné Ndatimana
François Mutama

Contents

Illustrations

Figures

Tables

Preface

In April 1994 I was finishing my last semester as an undergraduate at Boston University. Preoccupied with a senior thesis, coursework, and a job search in the midst of a recession, I barely noticed the horrific events going on in Rwanda. Then in June of the same year the *Boston Globe* headlines began grabbing my attention each morning as I bought my coffee and boarded a commuter train bound for my new job. By July the images of desperate mothers and dying babies in refugee camps in eastern Zaire had made an impression on me. I wanted to know more about how the situation had evolved. Internal Amnesty International briefing papers on the genocide explained that "Hutus" had killed "Tutsis" in Rwanda because of "ancient tribal hatred." The descriptions of the violence focused on the cutting off of Tutsis' legs because the Hutu killers wanted to "cut them down to size." As a human rights activist deeply involved with Amnesty International, I was quite familiar with the many ways that humans had devised to torture and kill each other; yet this explanation of the 1994 genocide in Rwanda did not ring true for me.

In my activism I met refugees from Rwanda and the former Yugoslavia who were being resettled in the Boston area. Although many refugees also explained the wars in their home countries in terms of ethnic hatred, my interactions with them suggested that people in these faraway places were not much different from my neighbors and coworkers in Boston. Knowing what I did about human motivations, such simplistic explanations left me increasingly dissatisfied. My determination to find better answers eventually led me into a doctoral program in anthropology, studying war, genocide, and human rights violations at the microlevel.

When I undertook fieldwork in Rwanda beginning in April 1997, a very tense time due to the forced repatriation of nearly two million refugees and the ongoing war in Zaire, I began to confront the stark realities of poverty, immiseration, and powerlessness with which average Rwandans lived on a daily basis. In collaboration with AVEGA-Agahozo, an organization for widows of the genocide, I met with grassroots women's groups and interviewed survivors. From these initial experiences grew the research project that resulted in this book, which examines the challenges and complexities of life faced by women in the aftermath of war and genocide. While this book focuses primarily on women in postgenocide Rwanda, its overarching story and lessons apply to the general human condition.

Rwanda's story is also a story about how Europeans and Americans perceive Africans and Africa's problems. Students often arrive in my courses thinking that genocide and ethnic/racial conflict are problems faced by other people in distant times and places. Particularly when students perceive these places as being premodern and underdeveloped, students imagine that these faraway problems have little to do with their own lives in North Carolina or Kentucky. One of this book's implications, however, is that genocide lives in all of us, for we are all capable of perpetrating great evil on others. The relationships between Hutu, Tutsi, and Twa in Rwanda are not inherently different from those between European American, African American, American Indian, Asian American, and Hispanic American in the United States; however, the social, economic, and political contexts that structure these relationships are different.

Acknowledgments

While I accept full responsibility for the ideas and analysis presented in this book, the intellectual work herein would not have been possible without the contributions of numerous people and institutions over the years. I will attempt here to thank many of them, but I am sure to miss some, and there are still others who prefer to remain anonymous.

For their intellectual and moral support of this project over the years, I would like to thank Bob Daniels, Catharine Newbury, and David Newbury. Several regional specialists and scholars mentored me during my field-work in Rwanda, believed in my project, and encouraged me to continue, including Timothy Longman, Simon Gasibirege, Villia Jefremovas, Déogratias Mbonyinkebe, Jean Rugagi Nizurugero, Danielle de Lame, Johan Pottier, and Peter Uvin. During my dissertation fieldwork, Alison Des Forges offered useful advice, helpful contacts, and moral support; after fieldwork, she offered critical feedback as well as encouragement. Her wisdom and deep knowledge of Rwandan history, culture, and politics as well as her courage are deeply missed. Thanks and gratitude go to Lee Ann Fuji, Ann Porter Rall, Lars Waldorf, Susan Thomson, and Peter Verwimp for their mutual moral support in research and exchange of ideas. During my graduate work at the University of North Carolina at Chapel Hill, Cathy Lutz, Judy Farquhar, Michael Lambert, Don Nonini, Julius Nyangoro, Patricia Sawin, and Alphonse Mutima helped me grow into a scholar. At the Joan B. Kroc Institute for International Peace Studies, Scott Appleby, David Cortright, John Darby, Larissa Fast, and Rashied Omar introduced me to peace studies as a discipline instead of a topic. My colleagues in the Department of Anthropology at the University of Louisville have given helpful feedback and encouragement along the way. They have all influenced this book in ways difficult to measure.

I would like to acknowledge the hard work, patience, and strength of my Rwandan research assistants: Bernadette Mumukunde, Dancille Mukarubibi, and Elise Nimugire. During the years of my fieldwork, their insights and translation skills were invaluable. I hope Elise's children will grow up to know the true courage of the mother they never knew. My gratitude goes to Father Irenée Jacob as well as his assistant Thérèse, who initiated me in Kinyarwanda and gave me the best pronunciation advice ever: "Kinyarwanda is sung, not spoken." I would also like to thank the many people in Rwanda who have provided logistical support, housing, and, most important, friendship to me over the years, including Odette, Veneranda, Norah, Cressence, Yvette, the Rugangura family, Veronique, Priscille, Frédéric and Jeanne Jacquet, Jean-Pierre Dalfau, Michel Campion, Father Romain, Klaas de Jonge, Sara Rakita, Judith Registre, Anne Morris, Ruth and Charles, and the many others I have neglected to mention.

Thank you to Anne Welschen, Sabine Cornelis, Danielle de Lame, and Nancy Vanderlinden of the Musée royal de l'Afrique centrale in Tervuren, Belgium, for their assistance locating the colonial era image of Tutsi, Hutu, and Twa of Rwanda (figure 3). Many thanks to Julia Besten, executive manager of the Archives and Museum Foundation of the United Evangelical Mission, who provided a high-resolution scan of and licensing rights for the same image in a very short time. Jacob Noel and Carie Hersch, former undergraduates in the Department of Geography at the University of Louisville, created the maps for this book. I also appreciate the assistance of Nancy Williams with research and organization for the past two years.

At the University of Wisconsin Press, I would like to thank Gwen Walker, acquisitions editor, and Aili Tripp, series editor, for their unwavering support and patience as I reshaped this project into a publishable book. The two anonymous reviewers provided detailed feedback and constructive criticism that substantially improved the final product. The University of

Wisconsin Press faculty board provided insightful commentary to help finalize the manuscript.

This research would not have been possible without the authorization and support of the Government of Rwanda. Several ministries facilitated my project, including the Ministry of Gender and Women in Development (MIGEPROF) and the Ministry of Local Governance. In particular, I would like to acknowledge the assistance of Vincent Karega, former director in the Ministry of Gender and Women in Development; Aloisea Inyumba, minister of gender and women in development and former executive director of the National Unity and Reconciliation Commission; Fatuma Ndangiza, former executive director of the National Unity and Reconciliation Commission; and the many other regional and local government administrators and representatives of the Ministry of Gender and Women in Development who facilitated my research in communes throughout Rwanda.

Numerous local and international NGOs in Rwanda aided me in this research by providing information, contacts, and logistical support. I would like to thank the *équipes de vies* of Karama Parish, Père Masinzo, Sœur Teya, Père Romain, and the Catholic Diocese of Butare. Many Rwandan women's organizations showed me the incredible resilience of human beings, including Réseau des femmes œuvrant pour le développement rural, AVEGA-Agahozo, Duterimbere, Pro-femmes Twese-Hamwe, and Duhozanye as well as many grassroots groups. Annie Kairaba and the Rwanda Initiative for Sustainable Development (RISD) proved to be energizing research partners on women's land rights. The personnel of several international NGOs provided logistical and other support during various stages of the project, although they did not have an official role in the project, including Médecins du monde, CARE-Rwanda, Africare, Human Rights Watch, and Amnesty International.

Many organizations, foundations, institutions, and US government agencies helped fund the research and the writing of this book. A Rockefeller Visiting Fellowship at the Joan B. Kroc Institute for International Peace Studies at the University of Notre Dame allowed me to develop and write the first draft of this book. Fieldwork in Rwanda was supported by a Fulbright-Hays Dissertation Research Abroad Grant from the United States Department of Education; a Jennings Randolph Dissertation Fellowship from the United States Institute of Peace; a research grant from the Institute for the Study of World Politics of the Fund for Peace; a democracy studies traineeship from the National Science Foundation and the University Center for International Studies at the University of North Carolina at Chapel Hill; travel grants from the Patrick Stewart Human Rights Fellowship of Amnesty International and from the University Center for International

Studies at the University of North Carolina at Chapel Hill; Foreign Language Area Studies Fellowships from the United States Department of Education; and research grants from the Department of Anthropology, the Commission for the Status of Women, the Anne Braden Institute for Social Justice, the College of Arts & Sciences, the Muhammad Ali Institute for Peace and Justice, and the Office of the Vice President at the University of Louisville. A dissertation completion grant from the Graduate School of the University of North Carolina at Chapel Hill allowed me to complete my dissertation, which later developed into an earlier version of this manuscript.

I would like to thank the many people who gave me feedback on my writing over the years, including Kimberly Abels, Karen Britt, MaryAnne Gobble, Alison Greene, Hager el Hadidi, Krizsti Fehevary, Matthew Hull, Eric Karchmer, Sharon Kowalsky, Linus Owen, and Jon Wallace. Their critical yet kind feedback has been indispensable in finishing this project.

Finally, I would like to acknowledge the unflagging support of my family during the fifteen years that passed from the conception of this book to its final fruition. My parents, Sarah and Hazen Burnet, have always had faith in my intellectual abilities and tolerance for my adventurous spirit. Their encouragement and assistance have been indispensable. My husband, Theogene Manzi, and our children, Hazen and Rene-Yves, have brought bountiful joy into my life and have endured my periodic absences and frequent distractions. Thank you for making life worth living.

A version of chapter 7 first appeared as "The Injustice of Local Justice: Truth, Reconciliation, and Revenge in Rwanda," *Genocide Studies and Prevention* 3, no. 2 (August 2008): 173–93, copyright © *Genocide Studies and Prevention*, reprinted with permission from University of Toronto Press (www .utpjournals.com). Another version of chapter 7 appeared as "(In)justice: Truth, Reconciliation and Revenge in Rwanda's Gacaca," in *Transitional Justice: Global Mechanisms and Local Realities after Genocide and Mass Violence*, edited by Alexander Laban Hinton (New Brunswick, NJ: Rutgers University Press, 2010), 95–118, copyright © Rutgers, the State University, reprinted with permission of Rutgers University Press.

Abbreviations

AFDL	Alliance des forces démocratiques pour la libération du Congo-Zaïre (Alliance of Democratic Forces for the Liberation of Congo-Zaire)
AMI	Association modeste et innocent (Modeste and Innocent Association)
AVEGA	Association des veuves du génocide de l'avril 1994 (April 1994 Genocide Widows Association)
CDR	Coalition pour la défense de la république (Coalition for the Defense of the Republic)
CND	Conseil national du développement (National Development Council)
ECHO	European Community Humanitarian Office
FAR	Forces armées rwandaises (Rwandan Armed Forces)
FARG	Fonds d'assistance aux rescapés du génocide (genocide survivors' assistance fund)

FAZ	Forces armées zaïroises (Zairian Armed Forces)
HRW	Human Rights Watch
ICRC	International Committee of the Red Cross
ICTR	International Criminal Tribunal for Rwanda
IDP	internally displaced person
IJR	Institute for Justice and Reconciliation
IOM	International Organization for Migration
IPJ	*inspecteur de police judiciaire* (judicial police inspector)
IRIN	Integrated Regional Information Network, UN Department of Humanitarian Affairs
LIPRODHOR	Ligue Rwandaise pour la Promotion et la Défense des droits de l'Homme (League for the Promotion and Defense of Human Rights in Rwanda)
MDR	Mouvement démocratique républicain (Republican Democratic Movement)
MIGEPROF	Ministère du genre et de la promotion de la femme (Ministry of Gender and Women in Development)
MRND(D)	Mouvement révolutionnaire national pour le développement, renamed Mouvement républicain national pour la démocratie et le développement (Revolutionary Movement for National Development, renamed Republican Movement for Democracy and Development)
MSF	Médecins sans frontières (Doctors without Borders)
NPR	National Public Radio
NURC	National Unity and Reconciliation Commission
PARMEHUTU	Parti du mouvement de l'émancipation hutu (Hutu Emancipation Movement Party)
PDR-Ubuyanja	Parti démocratique de renouveau-Ubuyanja (Democratic Party for Renewal-Ubuyanja)
PL	Parti libéral (Liberal Party)
PSD	Parti social démocrate (Social Democratic Party)
RDF	Rwandan Defense Forces
RPA	Rwandan Patriotic Army
RPF	Rwandan Patriotic Front
RTLM	Radio-télévision des mille collines
TIG	*travaux d'intérêt general* (works of general interest)
UNAMIR/MINUAR	United Nations Assistance Mission for Rwanda (Mission des nations unies d'assistance au Rwanda)
UNAR	Union nationale rwandaise (Rwandan National Union)

UNDP	United Nations Development Program
UNHCHR	United Nations High Commissioner for Human Rights
UNHCR	United Nations High Commissioner for Refugees
UNHRFOR	United Nations Human Rights Field Operation in Rwanda
UNICEF	United Nations Children's Fund
UNIFEM	Fonds de développement des Nations unies pour la femme (United Nations Development Fund for Women), now part of UN Women
UNREO	United Nations Rwanda Emergency Office
WFP	World Food Program, United Nations
WHO	World Health Organization, United Nations

Note on Kinyarwanda Usage and Spelling

In general, I have used current spellings for Kinyarwanda throughout the text. Thus spellings do not indicate long and short vowels or high and low tones. Words are cited with their prefix and augment, elements that change between the singular and plural (e.g., *umurima*, sing., "field," and *imirima*, pl., "fields"). The sequence *-li-* is always written *-ri-* except for a few proper names.

For names of groups or categories of people, I have retained the Kinyarwanda prefixes *umu-/aba-* with the exception of names of ethnic/racial categories (i.e., Hutu instead of Bahutu, Tutsi instead of Batutsi, and Twa instead of Batwa) and of national designations (i.e., Rwandans instead of Banyarwanda). When using Hutu, Tutsi, or Twa as nouns, I do not anglicize them by adding an *s* in the plural. I hope that this practice reminds the reader that these words are primarily adjectives and undermines the notion that these labels apply to corporate collections of individuals.

Genocide Lives in Us

Introduction

In April 2000 I interviewed Donatia, a genocide survivor, about her work with a network of rural women's groups. As an unmarried Tutsi, she had faced several harrowing months hiding from killing squads during the genocide. She survived thanks to a network of friends who hid her in their homes. During the interview she recounted the anger and bitterness she felt in the months following the genocide:

> I wasn't really alive anymore; I was consumed with hate. I felt like God had renounced us. How else could such awful things have happened? My entire family was dead. I was the only one who survived. I didn't trust anyone, not even those who helped save me.
>
> Father Félicien saw me in my suffering. He came to me and listened to me. We prayed together. Little by little he helped me see outside of myself, my hate. I began to heal. Eventually, he suggested that I work with the widows in Musozi. Even though I didn't want to, I agreed.

> Working with the widows helped. Listening to their stories. They had
> lost their entire families, their homes, their livestock, their livelihoods; but
> they were even more miserable than I. They were farmers, uneducated, and
> many of them had children to feed. But it's impossible to farm alone. (Field
> notes, April 2000)

Donatia's story highlights the question at the heart of this book: How do
survivors rebuild their lives in the aftermath of genocide? This project grew
out of a curiosity about the ways noncombatants cope with warfare and
violent political conflict and how their experiences of violence shape them.
Understanding the strategies survivors deploy and the culturally appropriate
coping mechanisms they use to go on with their lives after the unimaginable
has happened can contribute to the creation of postconflict interventions in
war-torn societies.

This book is an ethnography of survival about women in the aftermath
of the 1994 Rwandan genocide. Between April 6 and July 4, 1994, approximately 800,000 Rwandans lost their lives in a genocide planned and perpetrated by state authorities.[1] Roughly three-quarters of the Tutsi population
in the country died along with thousands of Hutu who opposed the killings,
making it the swiftest genocide in history (Des Forges 1999). On the
evening of April 6, 1994, unknown assailants shot down President Juvénal
Habyarimana's plane as it prepared to land at the international airport on
the outskirts of Kigali as he was returning from peace talks in Arusha,
Tanzania. He died in the crash along with members of his inner circle of
advisors and the president of Burundi, Cyprien Ntaryamira. In the months
that followed, Interahamwe militiamen, Forces armées rwandaises (FAR)
soldiers, policemen, government authorities, and civilians recruited to killing
squads cordoned off the country to search for and kill *ibyitso* (accomplices),
inyenzi (cockroaches), and "enemies of Rwanda." While announcements on
the government-controlled Radio Rwanda or the extremist hate-radio Radio-
télévision des mille collines (RTLM) and commands given by local government officials used this coded language, the population understood that all
Tutsi—young or old, male or female, wealthy or poor, educated or illiterate—
were targets for elimination. For four months, individual fates were decided
at roadblocks throughout the country according to the ethnicity marked on
national identity cards. Tens of thousands of Tutsi sought refuge in churches,
hospitals, and government buildings, but they soon found death in massacres
organized by government officials and carried out by police, the military,
militias, and civilians enlisted to help. Others hid under beds, in cupboards,
in dropped ceilings, or in hastily dug holes awaiting death but hoping that
the Hutu and Twa who helped them hide would not turn them over to the
killing squads. In the forests and valleys, *ibitero* (killing squads) hunted

Tutsi, accomplices, and cockroaches and "flushed" them from hiding so that they could be killed.[2] The smell of roasting meat from thousands of slaughtered cattle—historical symbols of affinity, wealth, and friendship, now symbols of Tutsi oppression in the parlance of Hutu extremist hate media—emanated from cooking fires around the country where Interahamwe militias and civilian killing squads celebrated the success of their "work," as they called it.

The genocide ended when the Rwandan Patriotic Front (RPF), a rebel movement that had invaded Rwanda in 1990, seized the majority of the country's territory in early July 1994. The FAR, government officials from the national level to the grass roots, the Interahamwe militias, and over one million civilians fled the advancing RPF lines and crossed into Zaire (now Democratic Republic of the Congo). They took with them everything that could move, including trucks, cars, windows, doors, and even light switches, and intentionally destroyed infrastructure such as buildings, bridges, and government records as they withdrew. The RPF found itself charged with creating a state and restoring the rule of law without so much as a piece of paper or a pencil in local government offices. The approximately six million civilians who remained in Rwanda, including several thousand genocide survivors who were physically and psychologically traumatized, had to pick up the pieces of their lives with little assistance from international aid agencies, whose efforts focused on the humanitarian crisis emerging in refugee camps on Rwanda's borders in eastern Zaire and western Tanzania.

This book attempts to answer several interrelated questions about genocide survivorship, reconciliation, and peace building. What are the long-term effects of war and genocide on Rwandan women's daily lives? Why did so many women end up as heads of household after the genocide? How did survivorship and gender intersect? What effects did violence have on the social categories mobilized during genocide? How do ordinary people perceive ethnicity or race in the aftermath of genocide? How do survivors remember and restore the dignity of loved ones who died in ignominious ways? How do they rebuild society in the aftermath of genocide? Are justice and reconciliation possible when evil has destroyed trust among family, friends, and neighbors? How did women come to gain so many political positions in the postgenocide government? Why did women organize across ethnic lines? These questions fall into three general themes—coping mechanisms, the politics of memory, and reconciliation—that are at the heart of this book.

The first theme, coping mechanisms, is a foundational theme examined throughout this book. During the civil war from 1990 until 1994, most Rwandan women did their best to continue life as normal: sharing food and hospitality with family and friends, joining women's cooperatives, praying in church, and working the fields without much concern for ethnic distinctions. In this everyday pursuit of a normal life, women exercised agency and remade their social worlds. Yet racist anti-Tutsi propaganda and incidents of communal violence against Tutsi and Hutu opposed to the Habyarimana government gradually redefined normal. During the genocide, women were more likely to survive than men, but they often experienced sexual violence—rape, sexual torture, and sexual enslavement. After the genocide, many women found themselves as heads of household because their husbands were dead, had fled into exile, or were imprisoned on accusations of genocide. In the aftermath of the genocide, Rwandan women transformed society by breaking cultural taboos that defined the proper role of women. They broke these taboos not because they sought liberation from gender oppression but because they had no other choice—their male kin and neighbors were dead, imprisoned, or untrustworthy. The coping mechanisms used were individual, familial, community level, and national, but sometimes strategies deployed by women were at odds with those deployed by families, communities, and the national government. This tension leads to the second theme—the politics of memory.

While the 1994 genocide was a period of intense violence that targeted specific categories of people, violent conflict characterized the entire decade of the 1990s in Rwanda. Though not all Rwandan women were genocide survivors, they all lost loved ones in the genocide (April–July 1994), in the civil war (1990–94), in the refugee camps or rainforests of eastern Zaire (1994–97), or in the insurgency in northern and western Rwanda (1997–2001). All women—Tutsi, Hutu, and Twa—have violent pasts to remember. As research on the Holocaust has demonstrated, memory is a fundamental need of survivors. Memory is also important for humanity if we accept the call of "Never again!" and want to take action to prevent genocide in the future. The collective experience of violence and loss of loved ones has the potential to unite survivors, but in postgenocide Rwanda the politics of memory—who is publicly remembered and how—continued to divide the population.

Chapters 2, 3, and 4 explore the ways women remember the genocide, civil war, and other violent experiences, the tension between individual memory practices and those of the RPF-led government, and the ways social categories mobilized during the genocide affect daily life in postgenocide Rwanda. The final theme, reconciliation, is considered in chapters 5, 6, and 7. In particular, I delve into women's roles in postgenocide reconstruction and reconciliation. In reaction to diverse experiences of violent conflict, Rwandan women had varied explanations of the violent past and diverging views of the future—some toward forgiveness, reconciliation, or peace; others toward revenge, punitive justice, or renewed violent conflict. Women were leaders in the country's reconstruction and in reconciliation. Yet their leadership position in reconciliation was not predestined by biology or by an "innately nurturant, maternal" female essence (di Leonardo 1991). Rather, it was their position in Rwandan society as the primary social connection between nuclear family units and the community that made their roles possible. The various roles of women in postgenocide reconstruction in Rwanda are relevant to all postconflict societies because they suggest possible paths to build a peaceful society and to reconciliation and can contribute to developing preemptive interventions that can avoid genocide in the future.

In my research, the vast majority of research participants were Rwandan women from diverse educational, experiential, regional, and ethnic/racial backgrounds. Most of these women survived the 1994 genocide and coped with catastrophe in the genocide's aftermath. In the lexicon of postgenocide Rwanda, however, only Tutsi women can be called "genocide survivors." Hutu women who were targeted for killing or raped by Interahamwe militiamen or whose husbands and children were killed in the genocide are not called "survivors" in Rwanda today. To resist this erasure of survivor status from those who experienced the genocide as victims, I do not use the term "survivor" only for Tutsi women. In fact, during my research I was often unsure of the ethnicity of interviewees, since asking direct questions about it was forbidden in practice, and more recently by law, in Rwanda. While most of the voices in this text are female, many of my conclusions apply to men as well as women. Thus, when I discuss issues common to men and women, I write "Rwandans" or "citizens" without specifying gender.

The old caseload refugees, as the primarily Tutsi refugees who lived in exile and returned to Rwanda after the RPF victory in 1994 were called by the United Nations High Commission for Refugees (UNHCR), have predominated in the postgenocide government and economy.[3] Their voices appear less frequently in this text for several reasons. First of all, since my research focused on survivorship, I interviewed fewer Tutsi returnees because they were not in Rwanda at the time of the genocide. In my daily life living in Rwanda, I came to know many old caseload refugees, but few of them ever became formal research subjects who consented to be studied through an informed consent procedure. Second, in my rural field site there were very few old caseload refugees—a sector-level government official and an elderly man repatriated from the Congo by the UNHCR after he nearly starved to death in a prison in Lubumbashi during the Congo wars. Because the Tutsi returnees in my sample were so few, I cannot sufficiently disguise their stories to protect their anonymity. Thus, knowledge of their understandings of the New Rwanda informs my analysis, but their voices rarely appear in this text.

Beyond the lessons that Rwanda can teach us about processes of category making, survivorship, memory making, and reconciliation, understanding what happened in Rwanda can teach us about ourselves. As Alexander

Hinton writes, "To reflect on genocide . . . is not just to explore evil but also to gain greater insight into ourselves and the society in which we live" (2005, 5). While many observers of African atrocities tend to regard them as a "natural" effect of the "tribalism" endemic to the "Dark Continent," the social, economic, and political processes that create violent conflict in Africa are not inherently different from those elsewhere in the world. Global forces from outside Rwanda, including international development aid, international commodity price networks, Structural Adjustment Programs, and international arms trade, helped create the context that made genocide possible (D. Newbury 1998, 88–91). In other words, genocide is a crime that has "a deep and complex relationship" with modernity (Hinton 2005, 5). As David Newbury writes, "There is a danger in 'distancing' genocide to some remote, 'exotic' locale" (1998, 73). The challenges Rwandan women faced in the aftermath of the genocide connect to realities elsewhere in the world. By seeking to understand the empirical realities of Rwandan women's survival, we can uncover paths to recovery in other conflict zones in the world and suggest interventions that could prevent genocide before it occurs.

The Politics of Memory

The politics of memory in Rwanda today are intimately connected to questions of identity. To remember is to assert a claim about one's own being. For individuals in microlevel settings, remembering may be less problematic, as it can be separated from broader historical, cultural, and political narratives and discourses.[4] Individual and familial narratives do not necessitate the production and reproduction of categories, although in some cases they may.[5] Such memory, moreover, often reflects the inherent contradictions of experience, thus destabilizing simple notions of identity. Yet for Rwandans in public or semipublic settings, remembering is a political act that must take into account the powerful moral discourses concerning Rwandan society as well as collective "mythico-historical" narratives.[6] It is such discourses that produce and reproduce the language of social category, terms such as "Hutu," "Tutsi," "Twa," "Interahamwe," "killer," "survivor," "victim," that mold the ways Rwandans answer the question, "Who are we?" The "we" in this question is highly dependent on context, denoting in some instances the entire nation ("we Rwandans") or a subgroup of it ("we Tutsi," or "we Hutu," or "we survivors"). When remembering becomes a collective process, the structuring effect of hegemonic discourses overpowers the diversity of individual experience, erasing difference or disguising it in such a manner as to preserve the broad categories of social delineation, whether based on nationality, ethnicity, gender, or class.

The title of this book comes from a statement made by Donatia. We were discussing the effects of genocide memories on survivors and society more broadly. Starting in 1995, the RPF-led government dedicated the month of April to genocide commemoration with ceremonies taking place in communities throughout Rwanda. In 2000 Donatia and I discussed the preparations under way for the annual genocide memorial service in Musozi scheduled for April 21. She explained how throughout March the women's groups had helped search for the remains of victims in the makeshift graves that dotted the hills. During the slaughter, bodies had been thrown into pit toilets and irrigation ditches and then hastily buried. I asked her whether the work was difficult for the women. She explained that although it often brought back traumatic memories, it was important for the survivors to give "proper," "sacred" burials to the victims, especially for those who had discovered the remains of family members.

During our conversation, I commented that since I had begun my research I dreaded the month of April. Surprised, she asked, "Why?" I explained that I could feel the rising stress level in everyone around me as April 6 approached. To illustrate this, I recounted a few examples of research participants and friends whose everyday problems seemed to become amplified during the weeks leading up to April 6 or other individually important dates related to the genocide. I then explained how the first (and only) executions, in April 1998, of genocide perpetrators who had been sentenced to death by Rwandan courts had affected me, although I had been back in North Carolina at the time.

In the days leading up to the executions, I followed the news in Rwanda via the Internet and e-mail as well as the occasional coverage on National Public Radio (NPR). On the eve of the executions, however, I forgot about them, as I was busy with my graduate school work. During the night, I had difficulty sleeping. When I did sleep, I had nightmares. In the morning, as I lay in bed listening to NPR, I heard news coverage of the executions:

> A good three hours before the executions I went to see [Nyamirambo] in Kigali, people were already arriving at the stadium and, you know, crowds came and came as the day progressed.
>
> And by the end, I think we're talking about a figure of around 30,000 people there. . . .
>
> The mood was fairly celebratory, particularly when the bullets were finally fired. There was quite a long delay and people were getting quite restive, but certainly it was very much a case of push to the front and try and get the best position.
>
> I think it's—it—there may have been an element of voyeurism there. There may have been quite a few curiosity seekers there. But there were certainly also relatives of those who died in 1994 who had come to see justice done.

> And the mood at the end was a mixture of triumphalism—a lot of righteousness; a certain amount of elation. It was a very, very strange mood and one—as an outsider, one felt very much not a part of it. (Simpson 1998)

As I listened, I imagined what effects the executions might have had on friends in Rwanda. I wondered how genocide survivors felt about the executions. Were the survivors happy? "Triumphant"? Upset that some of those who had killed their family members were still unknown—still alive and free? I thought about the families I knew who lived near the Nyamirambo stadium in Kigali, where the executions had taken place. Many of these families had returned to Rwanda from exile in Zaire in early 1997 when the refugee camps were attacked by the Rwandan Patriotic Army (RPA). They had been back in Rwanda only a little over a year. Most of them were still unemployed and lived meagerly from the charity of friends or relatives. How did they feel? I wondered whether they were harassed by the crowds who had gone to see the executions. How did the families of the executed prisoners feel? As these thoughts wandered through my mind, it occurred to me that I had some kind of an explanation, no matter how illogical, for my night of insomnia and bad dreams. Somehow, the realization made me feel worse instead of better.

As I explained it to Donatia, it was as if my body remembered the executions even though my mind had forgotten them. I then recounted the story of Victorine, a genocide survivor. Since 1994 Victorine often had episodes when her heart raced inexplicably and her blood pressure rose to dangerous levels. After extensive testing at the National University of Rwanda Hospital in Butare, the doctors told her that her physical problems were due to "psychological trauma." They prescribed sedatives to help her sleep, a rigorous program of exercise to relieve stress, a diet that excluded foods or beverages known to be stimulants or to raise blood pressure, and blood pressure medication. Victorine told me that the doctors warned her that she should follow the regimen strictly or she risked suffering a stroke. Despite these precautions, Victorine continued to have episodes of dangerously high blood pressure followed by dangerously low blood pressure and exhaustion.

In response to the story, Donatia replied, "Yes, that's how it is for us. The genocide lives in us."[7] Her statement, combined with the sad, heavy tone of her voice, evoked an image of the palpable and ineluctable presence of the genocide in the bodies, minds, and spirits of survivors. In the course of my research, I came back to her words frequently as I interviewed Rwandans and witnessed the long-term effects of violent memories and psychosocial trauma in their daily lives. At first, I found her statement applicable only to genocide survivors; but the deeper I delved into Rwandans' diverse understandings of the 1994 genocide, the civil war from 1990 through 1994, the massacres in eastern Zaire in 1996 and 1997, and the insurgency in Rwanda from 1997 until 2001, the more her statement seemed to capture the essence of the societal experience of genocide and violent conflict. While Rwandan women employ diverse strategies—collective amnesia, memorializing, retribution, seeking justice, and forgiveness—in their struggle to survive, they cannot completely escape the violence they experienced. Donatia's phrase reflects the experiential nature of memory for survivors, perpetrators, witnesses, bystanders, and liberators. Because memories are so deeply embedded in their daily lives—in their bodies and minds as well as in the landscapes they inhabit—Rwandans cannot escape them. The 1994 genocide continues to haunt them regardless of ethnic identity and regardless of whether they live at home or in exile.

Given Rwanda's long history of strong, centralized state power, the ways that individuals make sense of the past are caught up in local and national politics, state building, and the (re)writing of Rwandan history. While cultural traditions of mourning may be impossible to practice in the wake of genocide, Rwandans improvised their own means to put aside their grief and go on living. By burying themselves in the minutiae of everyday life, they succeeded in cordoning off their memories of the genocide and the intense emotions attached to them. To protect themselves, Rwandans crafted a form of collective amnesia vis-à-vis the "events of 1994," as many Rwandans referred to them. Yet the unexpectedness of everyday life in the form of a sound, an object, an action, or a place broke through this amnesia and forced them to remember. Over time, some individuals and families recovered the remains of loved ones and buried them in consecrated graves. Yet these mourning practices were also shaped by government-sponsored genocide commemoration activities.

In the aftermath of the 1994 genocide, the Rwandan government faced the challenge of rebuilding the nation and promoting peace in a deeply divided society. To this end, the RPF regime adopted a policy of "national unity," abolished ethnicity as an official factor in bureaucratic life, and attempted to rebuild society around a unified national identity: "We are all Rwandan." Despite this official policy, state practices of national memory maintained an ethnic dichotomy (Hutu/Tutsi) by politicizing victimhood and emphasizing the distinction between victim and perpetrator in national ceremonies commemorating the genocide. As a result, Hutu who did not participate in the genocide as well as Rwandans in ethnically mixed marriages and families were erased from the national imagination. Nationalized mourning for the 1994 genocide and its victims limited the possibility of publicly mourning all victims of violence associated with the civil war (1990–94), genocide (April–July 1994), and insurgency (1997–99).

Women, Conflict, and Peace

Since the early 1990s, international policy makers and humanitarian workers have attempted to address the unique role of women in conflict and post-conflict situations. They tend to portray women in conflict zones in one of two ways. The first views women as disempowered victims of warfare and violence, lacking any ability to protest their situation or improve the world around them. The second represents women as innate peacemakers who are "fed up" with the male-dominated politics that brought war and conflict in the first place and who transform postconflict societies with their energy. Both tendencies rely on stereotypical images of women as inherently nurturing and kind (see di Leonardo 1991) and promote an idealized, "universal woman" (cf. Malkki 1995). While these portrayals are seductive—useful in mobilizing distant observers to action and intervention or inspiring donors to give money—they oversimplify the complex and contradictory roles women play in conflict and postconflict societies.

This book examines the agency and subjectivity of Rwandan women in the aftermath of the 1994 genocide, the attempt by the Rwandan state to forge a unified national memory of the genocide, and women's reactions to the hegemonic power of the state to create a unified memory. The central argument is that Rwandan women played diverse, often conflicting, roles in the civil war and genocide and that they have varied explanations of the violent past and visions of the future—some favoring forgiveness, reconciliation, and peace, others leaning toward revenge, legal retribution, and a renewal of violent conflict. Attempts by the RPF regime to codify collective memories of the genocide and civil war into a single, uncontested history have not unified Rwandan women. Government-sanctioned commemorations of the genocide perpetuate generalizations of Tutsi as the innocent victims and Hutu as the bloodstained perpetrators. Rather than actively resist this monolithic history, many women choose to remain silent, preserving the singularity of their experiences in private.

During the civil war from 1990 through 1994, most women were noncombatants. Yet even as noncombatants women were not always pacific. Some mothers encouraged their sons to join Hutu extremist militias; others dutifully sent their sons to fight for the Tutsi-dominated RPF. Some wives exhorted their husbands to join opposition political parties in the hopes of gaining access to patrimonial wealth and influence; others begged them not to get involved. A few women assumed prominent public roles in the conflict. President Habyarimana's wife was the primary social connection among members of the elite inner circle (Akazu) who planned the genocide, although her role in the planning itself is as yet unclear. On the other side, Rose Kabuye, the highest-ranking woman in the armed wing of the RPF who served in several important administrative positions after the genocide, and Aloisea Inyumba, an important woman in the political wing of the RPF who was appointed as the first Minister of Family, Gender, and Social Affairs after the genocide, played significant roles in the struggle of the RPF rebels.

To a certain extent, women transformed Rwandan society. Out of necessity, women broke traditional taboos in the aftermath of the genocide. As the primary social mediators between households, kin group, and community, Rwandan wives and mothers had the opportunity to promote reconciliation and build peace if they chose. Women at all rungs of the socioeconomic hierarchy, urban elites and subsistence farmers alike, facing similar challenges, joined cooperatives and other organizations for mutual support. In these forums they found emotional and economic sustenance with which to rebuild their lives. They used their voices to call for change and succeeded in ensuring that the new Constitution of 2003 recognized the equality of women and reserved a minimum of one-third of the positions in all government decision-making bodies for women. While many women came to enjoy these newfound freedoms, they continued to long for the lives lost to war and genocide. These women were clearly not passive victims, but neither were they intentional gender revolutionaries.

At first glance, women in postgenocide Rwanda appear to be an idyllic success story—the classic example of women as innate peacemakers. Yet a closer look reveals how difficult their struggle has been. Organizations that brought together women of different ethnicities faced stiff opposition from government administrators and outright hostility—sometimes even violence—in the communities in which they were based. On a number of occasions, their leaders were brought in for questioning by the police or local government officials. Some were given explicit warnings to give the "correct image" of Rwandan society to foreigners, including to American anthropologists such as myself. Within the organizations themselves conflicts arose that mirrored the broader divisions of Rwandan society. As a result, some organizations foundered. In others, however, members who had known and worked with each other since before the genocide took conscious steps to oppose divisive rhetoric or actions. Outside factors, such as support from international donors or the RPF's policies to promote women, helped advance their agenda, but in the end, their success rested on the shoulders of a few courageous women who actively pursued reconciliation, justice, and peace.

Rwandan Politics and the Meanings of Hutu, Tutsi, and Twa

When discussing Rwanda in writing, in a formal presentation, or in idle conversation, I often find my interlocutors—whether academics, students, or others—insistent upon asking such questions as the following: "Who were the killers again? The Hutsi or the Tutus?" (an eminent scholar at a reception); "So, I don't understand. Is she a Hutu or a Tutsi?" (a colleague offering feedback on an article); "Was he on the side of the killers or the victims?" (an American friend asking about a Rwandan friend); "I just want assurances that she wasn't on the side of the hackers" (a US asylum judge). This seemingly obsessive need to delineate "Hutu" and "Tutsi," "killer" and "victim," "hackers" and "hacked" ignores the complexity of ethnic/racial categories in Rwanda and obscures the reality of ethnicity/race as, in the words of Lee Ann Fujii (2009, 19), a "social interaction." In other words, identities are not innate essential traits, nor are they static external social constructions. Rather, identities consist simultaneously of structure—a set of categories—and agency—the actions through which those categories and the boundaries they signify are created. Building on Bowker and Star's (1999) methodology in tracing the production and reproduction of race categories in South Africa, I approach ethnicity/race in Rwanda as simultaneously an externally constructed set of social categories with a history and a range of possible actions or reactions in applying (or not applying) those categories. From this perspective, identity groups only exist as long as they are made and remade in the act of distinguishing between categories.[8]

Virtually any glyph of Rwandan society states that the population is comprised of three ethnic groups: Tutsi at 15 percent of the population, Hutu at 84 percent, and Twa at less than 1 percent.[9] Yet the origin of these widely cited statistics is unclear. They themselves form part of the "mythico-histories" that structure reality. The terms "Hutu," "Tutsi," and "Twa" are quite old in Rwandan social discourse, predating the colonial era, but their meanings and importance have changed dramatically over time and varied by region (C. Newbury 1988). Since the late 1960s most scholars have described these social categories as "ethnicity," but they are not marked by differences in language, culture, religion, or territory in recorded history. Historical linguistic and archaeological evidence indicates that the people who populated what today is Rwanda have shared similar ways of life, language, and culture since approximately 500 BCE (Schoenbrun 1998, 155). This shared cultural heritage was what made them Rwandans. Nonetheless, we should not be seduced by idyllic depictions of a precolonial Rwanda where social harmony and ethnic equality were predominant features. The politicization of the categories "Hutu," "Tutsi," and "Twa" began in the mid to late nineteenth century under the reign of Mwami Rwabugiri (Kimonyo 2001, 88). These classifications were further politicized during the colonial encounter. Belgian colonizers brought their own nineteenth-century ideas about race and experiences of ethnic difference and mapped them on to the indigenous categories "Hutu," "Tutsi," and "Twa."

Ethnicity alone is an incomplete explanation of the complex social, political, and economic processes at play in Rwandan history (see D. Newbury and C. Newbury 2000; C. Newbury 1988). Regionalism, kinship, and educational background have also played significant roles in Rwandan history and the episodes of ethnic violence that punctuated the end of colonialism. Rwandan political processes gave ethnic categories new meaning and an agency of their own. Under Belgian colonial administration, the Rwandan monarchy's oppression of the rural population increased with a disproportionate burden borne by Hutu peasants, while Tutsi peasants were spared some of the most exploitative corvée labor requirements (C. Newbury 1988). By the 1950s colonial demands for labor and taxes along with the abuses of many chiefs "had created bitter resentments and a lively political consciousness among rural dwellers" (C. Newbury 1992, 196). A social reform movement emerged in central Rwanda among a Hutu counterelite, most of whom had been educated in the Catholic seminaries (Lemarchand 1970, 112; Reyntjens 1985, 229–313). This movement called for transformation of the oppressive political and economic system before independence.

In November 1959 proindependence demonstrations shifted into attacks against Tutsi political elites and their families: a few hundred were killed, a few thousand homes were burned, and approximately ten thousand (predominantly Tutsi) refugees left the country (Reyntjens 1985, 261). Realizing that the end of its colonial rule was near, Belgium developed a hasty decolonization plan. The plan called for a transition to a participatory democracy with multiple political parties. Although a few political parties attempted to appeal to voters across ethnic lines, the largest parties mobilized along ethnic lines. The 1961 legislative elections confirmed the ethnic cleavage, with "Hutu" parties winning the majority of seats (Reyntjens 1994, 22). By the end of the transition in 1963, Rwanda had a democratically elected Hutu president, Grégoire Kayibanda.

By the end of 1963, between 130,000 and 300,000 (mostly Tutsi) Rwandans had fled the country, becoming refugees in Uganda, Burundi, Zaire, and Europe.[10] In late 1963 and early 1964, a series of pogroms against Tutsi resulted in 10,000 to 14,000 deaths (Lemarchand 1970, 225; Reyntjens 1985, 467). These massacres sent another wave of (mostly Tutsi) refugees into exile. Following these massacres, ethnicity largely faded into the background of daily social interactions between average Rwandans until 1972, when President Kayibanda's regime redirected growing regional opposition from northern Hutu into ethnic conflict. In early 1973 Tutsi students were forced to leave secondary schools around the country and at the National University and National Pedagogical Institute in Butare. In the private and public sectors, Tutsi were fired, and blacklists were posted in offices to intimidate them. In rural areas, Tutsi were "asked" to leave, and their houses were burned. A few hundred Tutsi were killed (Reyntjens 1985, 503). The political situation in the country continued to devolve into chaos until July 1973, when Juvénal Habyarimana, a Hutu from Ruhengeri prefecture and a general in the army, took power in a coup d'état.

President Habyarimana quickly restored peace and quelled fears on both sides of the growing ethnic divide. Habyarimana instituted strict, single-party rule with the outward appearances of a benevolent dictatorship. The ethnic question again fell largely into the background of daily interactions among people inside the country. Yet ethnic categories continued to be redefined in response to contemporary conditions and became further entrenched in the government bureaucracy and state power.[11] President Habyarimana instituted a policy of "ethnic equilibrium" that allocated positions in educational institutions and in the state apparatus on a quota system to correct the favoritism toward Tutsi in the Belgian colonial system. Although intended to ensure ethnic "equity," Habyarimana's quota system virtually excluded Tutsi from lucrative posts in the government and civil service (C. Newbury 1992).[12] In the 1980s, Rwanda was the darling of international development programs in Africa because of its well-organized state apparatus and relative lack of corruption.[13] President Habyarimana's government appeared to be well ensconced in power until 1989, when plummeting coffee prices damaged the Rwandan economy and international development circles began tying aid to democratization efforts.

Then, on October 1, 1990, the RPF attacked with the intention of liberating the country from President Habyarimana's dictatorship. This civil war continued throughout the early 1990s and shaped the emerging rhetoric of ethnic hatred of Hutu extremists who controlled the reins of power. The Habyarimana regime was eventually forced into peace negotiations with the RPF from which emerged a power-sharing agreement between the Habyarimana regime, opposition political parties, and the RPF, known as the Arusha Peace Accords. Between 1990 and early 1994, the Rwandan state under the Habyarimana regime as well as the FAR, the Rwandan military, targeted Tutsi as well as opposition politicians, human rights activists, and journalists who were critical of the regime.[14]

In April 1994 Hutu extremists opposed to the power-sharing agreement seized power following the assassination of President Habyarimana. They immediately began to execute their genocidal plan, a final solution to eliminate "Tutsi" opposition to Hutu rule. Between April and July 1994, all Tutsi were targeted for killing, while Hutu members of opposition parties, human rights activists, and anyone opposed to the genocide were also targeted for elimination. In 1994 there were at least three different types of violence, each with a different motive: (1) killings, rape, torture, and other acts of violence perpetrated against Tutsi and moderate Hutu civilians by the Interahamwe militias, the FAR, and civilian-based death squads; (2) intentional killings of soldiers and accidental killing of civilians in the course of combat between the RPF and the FAR; and (3) killings perpetrated by the RPF against militiamen and civilians. In my interviews I also encountered numerous cases of the "settling" of personal "scores" and other murders motivated by theft that were made possible by the chaos. Research by Straus (2006) and Fujii (2009) has established that low-level civilian genocide perpetrators were often not motivated by atavistic ethnic or racial hatred. Rather, they made minute-by-minute, calculated decisions in a complex and rapidly changing situation about the course of action that would incur the least risk or bring the most gain. Others, however, accepted the genocide government's logic that "the enemy" (understood as "Tutsi" and their "Hutu accomplices") had to be rooted out and defeated to ensure national security.

The genocide ended when the RPF took military control of the majority of the territory, driving the Hutu-extremist government into exile along with over a million civilians. The RPF has remained in control of the government since 1994, first under a "consensual dictatorship" (1994–2003) and then under a nominal democracy following presidential and parliamentary elections in 2003.[15] While members of the RPF have frequently been portrayed as saviors and peacemakers, their rule has not been a universally positive experience for Rwandans regardless of their ethnicity. In 1994 and 1995 the RPF's military wing was responsible for killing unknown numbers of civilians, including Hutu and Tutsi (author interviews, 1999, 2000, 2001, 2003, 2004, 2006; Degni-Segui 1996; Des Forges 1999, 705–14; HRW 1996b; Médecins sans frontières 1995; Pottier 2002; Reyntjens 2004).[16] In 1996 the RPF forced the repatriation of nearly a million refugees living in eastern Zaire and organized the massacres of hundreds of thousands more under the guise of a "Banyamulenge rebellion" in eastern Zaire. Between 1997 and 1999, Rwandans inside the country found themselves caught between RPF soldiers and an insurgency comprised primarily of former Interahamwe militiamen and FAR soldiers along with recruits from the refugee camps.[17] Both sides were responsible for brutalities against the population that included killings, rapes, and torture. In 1999 the RPF changed its counterinsurgency tactics by relocating the civilian population in northwestern Rwanda so as to physically separate them from the insurgents. The RPF then succeeded in pushing the insurgency into eastern Democratic Republic of the Congo by early 2001.

After the RPF came to power in July 1994, Rwandans opposed to the genocide (of all ethnic groups), whether inside or outside the country, were hopeful that the RPF would lead the effort to create a unified Rwandan state where ethnic identity played an inconsequential role in political and economic life. The RPF regime undertook a nation-building project, referred to by some as the New Rwanda (e.g., de Lame 2005b; Jefremovas 2000, 2002; Pottier 2002). This nation-building project was intended to unify the divisions between Hutu and Tutsi that were rendered violently material in the 1994 genocide. Yet it also had to cope with differences generated by waves of migration that were tied to Rwanda's violent political history.

Since its formation in the late 1980s, the RPF promoted an ideology of ethnic inclusion, which it called "national unity." The RPF emphasized unifying aspects of Rwandan history and culture (i.e., shared language, culture, religious practices) and blamed the country's "ethnic problems" on colonialism, arguing that the divisions within Rwandan society were created and perpetuated by the colonialists (Pottier 2002, 109–29). When the RPF took power in 1994, it created the Government of National Unity, which purported to follow the power-sharing agreements outlined in the Arusha Peace Accords. The RPF promised that after a transitional period of five years, national elections would choose a new government.[18] Based on these initial actions, the RPF appeared to be committed to its ideology of national unity, and Rwandans inside the country (whether Hutu or Tutsi) remained hopeful that the genocide would be the end of political dictatorship and ethnic discrimination.

Despite the postgenocide government's policy of national unity and reconciliation, ethnic differences (or at least the perceptions of ethnic difference) have continued to shape Rwandan social interactions. Although communal violence largely ceased, Rwandans could not pretend that ethnicity made no difference in their daily social lives. Individuals and families constructed narratives about their experiences of marginalization and violence in the past to explain the power of ethnic distinctions in the present. These mythico-histories drew on master narratives of collective marginalization, contained elements of truth, and were based on lived experiences, so they had great power to explain the present. Nonetheless, ethnic identity rarely operated as the sole determining factor in interactions and perceptions at either the individual or the societal level. Ethnicity was interconnected with other forms of identity (lineage, clan, gender, region, profession, politics, etc.) and tied to personal experience and the perception of one's place in the world.

Despite ethnic divisions, numerous other aspects of identity and subjectivity served as points of connection, or at least of understanding, among Rwandans of diverse backgrounds. Since women and girls share similar experiences of inequality, inhabiting a world structured by the same cultural repertoire of ideas, images, and symbols, gender has the potential to act as a bridge spanning ethnic and other divisions. Although Rwandan women and girls continue to be divided by ethnicity, class, education, age, generation, region, degree of urbanization, religion, economic condition, and personal history, they share similar experiences as women faced with inequality. Their experiences of marginalization can serve as a basis for mutual understanding, one of the steps in the process of reconciliation. With the profemale policies of the RPF government, women and girls have all benefited from increased access to education, preferential hiring practices, and statutory guarantees of representation in government structures at all levels.

Defining Genocide

In the 1948 Convention on the Prevention and Punishment of the Crime of Genocide, the crime of genocide is defined as the "intent to destroy, in whole or in part, a national, ethnical, racial or religious group" (United Nations 1948). One difficulty with the legal definition of genocide is that it is a crime distinguishable by motive (Destexhe 1994). This aspect of the definition makes prosecuting cases of genocide somewhat tricky: not only must the actions of the accused be proved, but his or her motives must be proved as well.

Thus, when I talk about events in Rwanda, I employ "genocide" to denote only the killings, rape, torture, and other acts of violence perpetrated against Tutsi, Hutu who were married to Tutsi, and Hutu opposed to the genocide by the Interahamwe militias, FAR soldiers, and civilians recruited to killing squads between April 6 and July 14, 1994. Including in the genocide the tens of thousands of Hutu who died alongside Tutsi is important because they died in the same circumstances yet have been excluded by the RPF-led government's policies and official history (Vidal 2001, 7). My use of the term "genocide" diverges from that of some scholars, such as Harff and Gurr (1998), who adhere to the strict legal definition of genocide in the 1948 UN Convention on Genocide and classify violence against Hutu during the genocide as "ancillary" to the genocide and call it "politicide." Yet my usage is in line with that of others, such as Helen Fein (1990) and Alexander Hinton (2005), who adopt a more open definition that includes social or political groups as potential victims. As Hinton notes, the preliminary resolution passed in 1946 included "political and other groups" among the protected categories (2002, 3). In the end, however, this language was removed from the final draft on account of objections raised by the Soviet Union and other countries that such groups did not fit the "etymology of genocide, were mutable categories, and lacked the distinguishing characteristics necessary for definition" (Hinton 2002, 3, citing Kuper 1981).

In the Rwandan case, defining genocide to include the elimination of political groups is appropriate because it mirrors Rwandan experience. Hutu members of moderate political parties, Hutu journalists critical of

members of the extremist Hutu Power movement, who organized the genocide, and Hutu human rights activists were among the first to be killed as
the genocide plan was implemented (Des Forges 1999; Prunier 1997).[19]
Furthermore, the Hutu Power propaganda before and during the genocide
encouraged the population to seek out "enemies of Rwanda," "accomplices"
of the RPF, "cockroaches," and "infiltrators," including Tutsi who had
changed their ethnic identification to Hutu (Des Forges 1999, 15, 75, 202–3;
Prunier 1997, 171). While these labels became increasingly identified with
the Tutsi as the genocide progressed, in the initial days of the killing they
encompassed prominent Hutu likely to oppose the genocide (Des Forges
1999, 202–3). In addition, under the Hutu Power propaganda, Hutu who
showed "too great a tolerance for Tutsi" or a "lack of commitment to Hutu
solidarity" were presumed to be Tutsi who had successfully disguised themselves (Des Forges 1999, 75). This broader usage of the term "genocide" is in
line with that of many regional specialists, including Des Forges (1999,
199–205), Catharine Newbury (1995, 1998), David Newbury (1997, 1998),
Pottier (1996, 2002), Vidal (1998, 2001), Straus (2006), and Fujii (2009),
among others.

     Nonetheless, my usage of the term runs somewhat counter to that
of the Rwandan state. Until 2008 the genocide was called *itsembabwoko
n'itsembatsemba* (genocide and massacres) in most official state discourse.
Johan Pottier explains: "Official discourse on the 1994 genocide maintains
in practice the ethnic division which the RPF-led government denounces in
theory: only Tutsi are victims of genocide; moderate Hutus are victims of
politicide who died in massacres. . . . The distinction has an implied moral
hierarchy" (Pottier 2002, 126). Although this language imposed a moral
hierarchy, it acknowledged the tens of thousands of Hutu who died in the
genocide, victims who were later erased by new official terminology imposed
by a constitutional amendment in 2008.

     During my fieldwork between 1997 and 2001, however, I found that
ordinary Rwandans usually referred to the genocide as *amarorerwa yo muri
94/les événements de '94* (the events of '94), *itsembabwoko/le génocide* (the
genocide), *intambara/la guerre* (the war), or simply *muri '94/en '94* (in '94).
The two most frequently used expressions were "the events of '94" and "in
'94." When I asked interviewees why they chose this terminology, they
explained that saying "the events of '94" covered everything that happened
in 1994 and not just the genocide. Since I first began conducting fieldwork
in Rwanda in 1997, I have observed a gradual shift in the language used by
ordinary Rwandans: use of the word "genocide" in all three languages became
increasingly frequent. This shift was already well advanced when, in a 2008
constitutional amendment, the government officially adopted new and
more exclusive terminology: *jenoside yakorewe abatutsi* (genocide against

Tutsi) in Kinyarwanda and "Tutsi genocide" in English. In this formulation, the government replaced the indigenous term *itsembabwoko*, a neologism created in 1994 from two root words, *gutsemba* (to kill) and *bwoko* (ethnicity), with a borrowed word, *jenoside* (genocide).

Conducting Research in a Postconflict Zone

Conducting research in a conflict or postconflict zone brings numerous physical, psychological, and ethical risks. When I first went to Rwanda in 1997, I was ill prepared to deal with most of these risks. Although I had read everything I could find about the situation on the ground, I had no idea how to make decisions about where it was safe to go or whom it was safe to interview, and I had little capacity to handle the emotional stress of living in difficult conditions and of interviewing women about their experiences during the genocide. As a foreigner in Rwanda without a vehicle at my disposition and trying to live on fifteen dollars per day, I was an anomaly. I quickly learned that expatriates working for NGOs or the UN had little useful information about public transportation or inexpensive places to eat. I became accustomed to relying on Rwandans for advice and camaraderie.

I first arrived in Rwanda in May 1997 on the twice-weekly Sabena flight from Brussels. As the plane approached Rwanda and night fell, my anxiety began to grow. I had spent the past several months convincing faculty advisors, grant committees, and my parents and friends that it was safe for me to go to Rwanda to conduct predissertation research. I had spent months preparing for the trip: meeting with people who had recently lived or worked in Rwanda, buying supplies, and tracking down the friend of a friend of a friend who lived in Rwanda and who had agreed to find me a place to stay in exchange for a few tubes of toothpaste and a bottle of Bailey's Irish Cream.

Outside the airplane window, a brilliant array of stars lit the night sky. Below there was impenetrable darkness broken only by the occasional wavering light from a fire. As the plane descended through the darkness, I finally admitted to myself that I was scared. Only two months earlier, the stakes had gone up in Rwanda. Two Spanish doctors volunteering for Médecins du monde (Doctors of the World) had been killed in their house in northwestern Rwanda in an attack blamed on insurgents. Three Belgian UN workers had died when their car was ambushed on a national highway while they were traveling through the Nyungwe Forest. The Rwandan government had also blamed this attack on insurgents. Up until that point, foreigners had been largely immune to the postgenocide violence—or at least so it seemed in the international news coverage.

Suddenly, a hilly landscape, outlined by dots of electric lights, emerged from the darkness only one hundred or so feet below the plane. The plane landed and taxied down the runway. When I emerged with my carry-on luggage, I saw the dark terminal building of the Grégoire Kayibanda International Airport, named after Rwanda's first elected president.[20] The majority of the plate glass windows were broken, lasting signs of the battle for control of the airport during the 1994 genocide. I gripped my bags more tightly, swallowed the lump in my throat, and proceeded down the stairs and across the tarmac toward the terminal doors with the other passengers. After finishing immigration procedures, I went down the stairs to baggage claim. The windows inside the terminal were also broken, and the place was only dimly lit by a few working lights.

I waited impatiently for my bags until eventually I was the only person left. It seemed that my luggage was lost. I wandered out into the lobby looking for Dave, the friend of a friend of a friend, but I only found a few airport employees. Instead of sobbing like I wanted to do, I tried to find someone who could file a claim for my lost luggage. Eventually, I found a tired-looking Rwandan woman in a uniform who said she could help.

As I sat in a cramped office, piled high with unclaimed (lost?) luggage, the agent filled out the paperwork by hand; I was convinced that I would never see my luggage again. Then a white man and an Asian woman entered the office and asked me in English whether I was Jennie. "Yes!" I exclaimed, relieved that someone had come for me. Henri and Janet explained that Dave had sent them to pick me up because he was out of town. They apologized for being late.

After the agent completed the paperwork for my luggage, Henri and Janet drove me through Kigali in their beat-up Range Rover emblazoned with NGO placards. I would have felt conspicuous except that the streets were completely deserted. We only encountered two other vehicles and not a single pedestrian during the fifteen-minute drive. Later in my research, I learned to read deserted streets as a sign of insecurity. The streets were completely dark, lined with broken street lamps, and heavily pitted with potholes; Henri periodically jerked the steering wheel or slammed on the brakes to avoid them. After several miles we turned off the paved road onto a dirt one. We bumped along for another ten minutes until we turned in the entrance of a small compound marked with a Médecins du monde emblem.

We went inside, and I met my hosts. They were about to go out to a bar for a few drinks. I was hungry and tired, so I declined their invitation to join them and went directly to bed, since there wasn't any food in the house. A few hours later, I heard everyone return home and lock the doors. An hour or so later, I awoke to the sound of a blaring siren. I was unsure whether the noise was coming from our compound or a neighbor's. I then heard people running past my window, and two male voices whispered to each other only a few feet away through the open but barred window. Surprisingly, no one in the house moved. Eventually, the voices outside fell silent, and the siren stopped. I lay awake in bed most of the night certain that I might be killed at any moment.

In the morning I learned that several men had come over the compound wall and made a half-hearted attempt to break into the house. They had run off when the guard sounded the alarm. I was the only one in the house who had heard anything. It seemed the others were too tired or drunk to have noticed. Since Médecins du monde had recently lost their Spanish colleagues, the robbery attempt on their headquarters in Kigali inspired a series of stringent security measures to prevent further incidents.

Much of my first trip to Rwanda was punctuated by security concerns. A series of attacks on foreigners' houses took place during my four-month stay in Rwanda. It was unclear whether the attackers were active-duty soldiers or had been recently demobilized, but they wore military uniforms, were well armed, and planned their attacks in advance. In the majority of cases, they carted everything in the house away with them after tying up all the foreigners. In a few cases, they raped the women. Because the attacks generally occurred when all the residents were home, some foreigners suggested in quiet whispers that the attacks might be organized by the army or government in an attempt to terrorize "undesirable" foreigners.

Although often referred to as a postconflict society, Rwanda in 1997 was still embroiled in the aftermath of the 1994 genocide and civil war. The recent forced repatriation of over 1.5 million refugees from eastern Zaire and Tanzania had led to increased instability and insecurity. Since at least the end of 1989, when the country entered an economic crisis, Rwanda had endured a series of internal conflicts stemming from ethnic, economic, and regional discord. Sometimes these tensions broke out into open violence; at other times they simmered quietly.

Given the length and degree of conflict in Rwanda, my research on the difficulties and contradictions of daily life in the postgenocide period was bound to touch upon areas of great sensitivity. Initially, I had hoped to examine what happened during the genocide and how these events affected reconciliation. However, I found during my dissertation research that few Rwandans were willing to discuss the genocide in detail. For many, questions about the genocide remained too painful because of the memories they provoked or too dangerous because of the risks interviewees ran of implicating themselves or their family members as perpetrators. Unlike some other anthropologists of war and conflict (Aretxaga 1997; Feldman 1991; Nordstrom 1997) who found people more willing to talk about the past than the present, Rwandans felt more comfortable discussing their current circumstances than the past. As a result, the complexity of daily politics in postgenocide Rwanda became clear to me early in my research. Although the majority of women spoke without hesitation, they shared their stories on condition of anonymity. Out of respect for their wishes, I do not refer to specific communities in this book, and I disguise individual identities by changing personal details in their stories that might be used to identify them. At the same time, I attempt to maintain the structural integrity of life histories and individual stories. I do not combine the words of different people. For various reasons, I was unable to make audio recordings of my interviews. Thus, when I present Rwandans' words as direct quotations, these are in fact taken from "transcripts" reconstructed immediately after the interviews by myself and my research assistants from handwritten notes. Interviews were conducted primarily in French or Kinyarwanda. For most interviews in Kinyarwanda, I relied on translators for assistance. In the early years of my research (1997–99), I could exercise little control over transla-tion. In later years (2000–2011) as my Kinyarwanda proficiency improved, I exercised tight control over translation and understood the majority of interviewee responses without translation. During this period, I relied on my translators to help me ask questions politely and to assist me in under-standing proverbs, coded language, and poetic phrasing.

In order to reflect the diversity, complexity, and multiplicity of Rwandans' narratives and experiences, I have extended the geographic scope of my investigation as widely as possible. My conclusions are based on more than three years of ethnographic fieldwork in nine of the twelve prefectures of Rwanda (Kigali Town, Kigali Ngali, Gitarama, Butare, Gikongoro, Cyangugu, Kibuye, Gisenyi, and Ruhengeri) (fig. 1).[21] My research included surveys of women's organizations and cooperative networks and focus groups, interviews of individuals and groups, and participation in daily life in two communities. In the course of this research, I interviewed over five hundred people, including leaders of women's organizations, NGO workers, com-munity leaders, and government officials as well as ordinary Rwandans. Intensive participant observation was conducted in two communities, one a middle-class neighborhood in the capital, Kigali, and the other a rural community in southern Rwanda.

Writing a detailed account of the tight-knit webs of power relations in these communities would be dangerous for people there, so I have inter-spersed accounts from these two communities with stories and ethno-graphic data from others. Even without the legacy of the genocide, Rwanda is a very reserved society where people hide their emotions and motivations. In addition, there is strong pressure to conform to community standards. As one person told me, "Everyone goes to church on Sunday because they know their neighbors are watching." Rwandans tend to observe each other

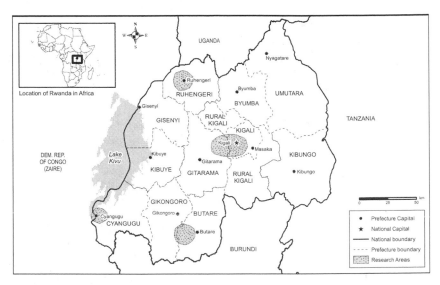

Figure 1. Map of Rwanda, administrative boundaries (1996–2001). Created by Jacob Noel and Carie Ernst.

closely, a practice I often found disturbing. For instance, more than once a distant acquaintance or even someone I had just been introduced to would remark that he had seen me the previous week walking downtown. Government officials also kept close tabs on my activities. In virtually every instance, government officials met me with open arms and encouraged my research. Yet, based on the experiences of other researchers and on cautionary statements from Rwandans themselves, I assumed that my movements and actions were under the close watch of military intelligence. I made an effort to conduct my research out in the open so as not to draw unnecessary suspicions.

I came to reside in a middle-class neighborhood of Kigali largely by chance. A Rwandan friend offered me a room in her house when she heard that I was coming to Rwanda to stay. Upon arrival, I found the neighborhood well suited to the type of research I wanted to do. It was a middle-class neighborhood by Rwandan standards, but almost anywhere else in the world it would be called a shantytown. Twenty years ago this hill of the capital city had been covered with banana plantations and agricultural fields. One long-term resident, Jeanne, explained that she and her husband had built their house there twenty years ago because "land was cheap" (it was basically free, if it had not already been claimed), yet it was within walking distance of the downtown area where they worked. Jeanne complained frequently that the population of the neighborhood had changed since the war. Many thousands had been killed in the genocide, including Jeanne's husband, while many others had fled into exile. On one occasion Jeanne laughingly told me how in the days just after the RPF victory, the returning old caseload refugees would come to her house and ask where the "wealthy people" had lived so that they could go and loot their belongings or claim the houses as their own. These returning refugees took over much of the neighborhood and treated those who had lived there before the genocide with disdain. In 2011 Jeanne told me why she moved out of the neighborhood. Beginning in 2003, she and her children would awake to find human feces inside the gate. They complained to local authorities and tried to find the culprits, but they did not succeed. Eventually, tired of the harassment, Jeanne rented out her house and moved to another neighborhood. By 2011 virtually all the women I had known in the neighborhood in 2000 had left. Several had left the country for the United States, Europe, or West Africa, while others, like Jeanne, had moved to other neighborhoods in the capital city.

The neighborhood was a mix of wealthy, middle-class, and poor families. In the area where I lived, the houses crowded in on each other around footpaths and makeshift gutters into which households illegally dumped raw sewage. Nonetheless, several neatly laid out roads cut across the neighborhood and divided it into blocks. Up the hill and across the central artery (a dusty main road that carried most of the traffic into and out of the neighborhood) were the large houses of the wealthy laid out on orderly avenues. Many belonged (at least legally) to former statesmen of the Habyarimana era. In more recent years, a few important statesmen of the postgenocide government had purchased large tracts in the area in order to construct sprawling mansions or more modest housing for sale or rent to middle-class families.

After my departure in 2001, the community underwent a dramatic transformation. The two thoroughfares that cut through the houses leading up to the summit, formerly dirt roads, were paved with asphalt. An impressive roundabout with a modern gas station sprang up in the immense, dusty field in front of a Roman Catholic church where five roads came together at odd angles. The neighborhood market closed, and residents were forced to travel to the large Nyabugogo market on the other side of Kigali to buy food and other necessities or to purchase them at much greater expense at a "modern" supermarket. Residents with titled parcels saw the value of their homes double or even triple thanks to these infrastructure improvements, but for middle-class and poor families the closing of the neighborhood market was a hardship. Some of the nontitled homes have been slated for expropriation and demolition to make way for modern buildings.

My arrival in my other field site was far less happenstance. I spent more than six months selecting a rural community based on survey research in Gisenyi, Ruhengeri, Kibuye, Cyangugu, Gitarama, and Butare prefectures. In choosing my site, I took several factors into consideration, including how well the genocide had been documented in the community, whether it had been considered "secure" for a significant amount of time, whether there were active women's groups or cooperatives present, and whether I felt welcomed by the population and local officials. I eventually found a community in Butare prefecture (now South province) not far from Butare town (now Huye) down a dirt road whose condition varied radically between the dry and wet seasons. Although it was within a half day's walk of town, the community was rather isolated because commercial taxi buses did not serve it and the public bus only passed by twice a week. The only other means of transportation into or out of the community was by foot, bicycle, motorcycle taxi, or private car.

In one important sense, the commune was almost unique. According to census data from 1983, the ethnic makeup of the commune was about 57 percent Hutu, 42 percent Tutsi, and 1 percent Twa, very different from the widely accepted national averages of 85 percent Hutu, 14 percent Tutsi, and 1 percent Twa. The unusually large number of Tutsi is explained by the pastoral character of the region: historically it was known for cattle and milk production. In 2000 the commune's former ethnic makeup was most evident in absence and silence. Entire hills in the commune lay deserted, covered with the destroyed remains of houses, normally a surprising sight in this densely populated country. Although the Tutsi population had been decimated during the genocide, the commune was home to a large number of genocide survivors, especially widows. Their presence was an important consideration in my choice of the commune as a site for my research.

The commune's poverty increased its isolation. Other than a tea factory in a neighboring commune and the production of charcoal, there was little economic activity. The soil in the region was infertile, and farming was futile without access to manure to fertilize the crops. Although the area was once known for its pastures, the cattle population had been annihilated by looting and slaughter during the genocide. In addition, the Habyarimana regime's reforestation and wetland reclamation projects had resulted in the region's best pastures (formerly on the highest mountains or in the valleys) being turned into eucalyptus forests managed by commune officials. In addition to the lack of fertilizer, agriculture suffered from an acute shortage of labor. Many genocide survivor households were comprised only of women and young children, their husbands, fathers, brothers, and cousins having been killed during the genocide. Other families likewise suffered from a shortage of labor, as their fathers, husbands, brothers, and cousins were in prison accused of genocide, had died returning from refugee or internally displaced persons camps, or had remained in exile because they feared or opposed the RPF government.

Although the genocide did not break out in this community until several weeks after it had begun in other regions, it was nevertheless extensive. Tens of thousands of Tutsi had sought shelter at the parish church and commune office in 1994. The genocide commenced when the local burgomaster, who had been protecting the Tutsi, "switched" his support to the Hutu extremists after the Butare prefect, a Tutsi who had actively resisted genocide directives coming from Kigali, was replaced. On the site surrounding the church and commune office, over ten thousand Tutsi lost their lives once the massacres started on April 21, 1994. Others fled en masse toward the border with Burundi but were hunted down and killed on the way. Still others were trapped and killed at the border by bands of Interahamwe militiamen and FAR soldiers waiting for them.

Upon a return visit to this rural community in 2007, I was shocked at its decline. In the administrative reorganization of 2001 the local government seat had been moved to a neighboring commune and then in 2006 to Huye town (fig. 2). While the community did boast a new church built by the Roman Catholic diocese, the dirt road to Huye had fallen into utter disrepair. Although I visited during the dry season, I found the road difficult to traverse with the Toyota RAV4 I had rented. When potholes made avoiding them impossible, large protruding rocks scraped the bottom of the vehicle. The road leading up from the valley to the plateau where the village center stood had been washed out almost completely, the narrowest portions being preserved only by tree limbs stuck into the crumbling earth along the edge. I recognized many of the faces of my former neighbors despite their gaunt appearance after several years of unpredictable rainfall, poor crop yields, and loss of cattle and other livestock to illness and malnutrition. It appeared to me as if my former neighbors had been forgotten or abandoned by the district authorities in Huye.

In my most recent visit in 2011 I was relieved to find the community in much better shape. The main road was in excellent condition, and the side road from the valley had been repaired. The population no longer looked malnourished and reported that adequate rainfall had resulted in high crop yields. The valley below the village center had been improved with government funds and contained a fish hatchery project and potato crops farmed by an agricultural collective. The government's policy of free and mandatory primary school education for all children meant that all children on the hill attended school for at least a half day.

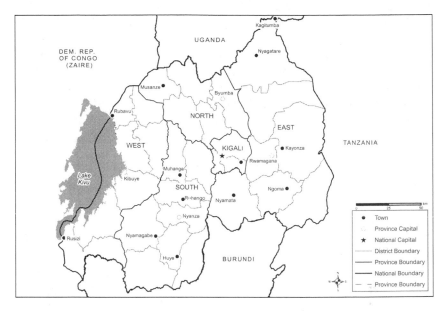

Figure 2. Map of Rwanda, administrative boundaries (2006–present). Created by Jacob Noel and Carie Ernst.

Over the course of my research, I met with some resistance from potential research participants and especially some Rwandan women's organizations. The major source of their reluctance to participate in my research project stemmed from previous experiences with foreign researchers and journalists who showed up to collect data, then disappeared never to return to share the results of their research. I had especial difficulty during my predissertation research, when I was trying to make initial contacts. Many of the women's organizations I contacted declined to meet with me, and those that agreed did so on condition that I work as an intern with their organizations and help with some applications for funding. During a return visit to a local widows-of-the-genocide association, the executive director and general secretary met me with hostility. They accused me of having published articles about their organization without consulting them first and without providing them with copies. I explained to them that I had not yet published anything about their organization or any other organization and that it must have been another researcher. I reassured them that I would provide them with copies of any and all publications resulting from my research.

Other Rwandans were reluctant to participate in my research because they worried about my "real" purpose. In my long-term research sites, more than one community member accused me of being a spy. In my search for a rural research site, I found some local government officials suspicious of my true intentions. I opted not to select these communities in order to avoid provoking trouble for myself or others.

On a brief visit to my rural research site in 2002, some of the women who worked with me asked how the *igitabo kinini* (big book, i.e., my dissertation) was coming. When I told them I was still writing, they chastised me for not finishing more quickly. Yet at the same time, they seemed relieved. They went on to encourage me to tell their stories "in America," but they entreated me not to say too much: "We know you are a wise girl. You've become Rwandan like us. You know it's not wise to say everything." I understood their request cum warning as an expression of fear over the potential repercussions of the publication of my research for them and their lives. Indeed, shortly after I had moved out of the community at the end of my field research in 2001, several women who had visited me frequently and other neighbors had been called in for questioning by the local *officier de la police judiciaire* (police investigator). Whether the timing of their summons was a coincidence, had been merely delayed until my departure, or was a deliberate attempt to terrorize or punish people close to me was unclear, but the message received was "Be careful what you say!"

Toward an Anthropology of Postconflict Rwanda

Hundreds of books, dissertations, and master's theses have been written about the Rwandan genocide, its causes, and its repercussions. These works vary greatly in their scope, perspective, and quality. The nearly unimaginable magnitude of killing, the swiftness of it, and the widespread popular participation that characterized it have drawn a great deal of attention. Many foreigners' impressions of Rwanda have been heavily colored by stereotypes of Africa's supposedly endemic problems: tribalism, poverty, underdevelopment, poor governance, corruption, and so on. Furthermore, the Rwandan state before, during, and after the genocide has manipulated foreign interventions in the country in order to further its own agenda (see Pottier 2002).

As a result, the Rwandan genocide signifies different things to different people. For some of the young Americans I encounter in university courses, Rwanda is the "heart of darkness" where people wake up one day and decide to kill their neighbors with machetes. These students' images of Africa have been powerfully shaped by Hollywood's neocolonial depiction of courageous (mostly white) American soldiers trying to save black Africans from their own savagery (e.g., *Tears of the Sun* and *Blackhawk Down*). For certain journalists, Rwanda was the latest "hot spot" between 1994 and 1997. Many journalists arrived in the country knowing little or nothing about it and its history, and yet they were expected to produce viable news stories on short deadlines for media in the age of satellites and the Internet. Frequently, they accepted at face value the versions of Rwandan history and current events proffered by government officials. As a result, much of the reporting on the genocide, on postgenocide Rwanda, and on the Congo Wars tended to fall into a moral discourse that demonized "Hutu" as the perpetrators and sympathized with "Tutsi" as the victims. For certain conservative academics and foreign policy makers, the Rwandan genocide represents the unleashing of the primordial "tribalism" they believe to be characteristic of the African continent (see, e.g., Kaplan 1992, 1994). For human rights advocates, Rwanda signifies the failure of the international community to intervene in a situation of crisis and has inspired calls to action in subsequent intrastate conflicts (e.g., Kosovo). For some UN bureaucrats and NGO workers in the mid-1990s, Rwanda was a place where one could advance one's career (service in Rwanda looks attractive on a résumé) and make a great deal of money.

For many academics, the dynamics of the Rwandan genocide resemble other processes of transformation elsewhere in the world. Rather than an aberration, the ethnicization of political conflict to these scholars is a frequent characteristic of globalization. Others have seen Rwanda as a case of "democratization gone awry" (C. Newbury and D. Newbury 1999, 305). Yet among academics, the quality of scholarship on the Great Lakes region has varied widely. One problem in common with many journalists is a lack of critical perspective. Another is the failure to take into account the rich pregenocide scholarship on the region. Much of this literature is in French, and many Anglophone scholars relied on the limited offerings in English. The most widely available and compact of these was the 1961 translation of Jacques Maquet's *Le système des relations sociales dans le Ruanda ancien* (1954), titled *The Premise of Inequality in Rwanda*, which painted Rwanda as a timeless feudal society, stratified into castelike ethnic groups. Although Maquet's functionalist representation of Rwandan society was heavily critiqued and thoroughly refuted in both French and English by a new school of scholarship beginning in the 1960s, many scholars new to the region in the 1990s were unaware of this criticism and accepted Maquet's vision of precolonial Rwanda without reservation, basing their own work upon it (Pottier 2002).[22]

Nonetheless, many specialists on the Great Lakes region and Rwanda have written and reported much of value on the genocide. Although criticized by some for its uncritical stance toward the RPF, Gérard Prunier's 1995 book, *The Rwanda Crisis*, was seminal as one of the first explanatory histories of the genocide and rich in empirical detail. In the second edition

(1997), Prunier added an additional chapter that takes a more critical view of the RPF, its policies, and its invasion of Zaire and forcible closing of the refugee camps in 1996. The first comprehensive human rights report on the genocide, *Death, Despair, and Defiance* (African Rights 1995a), collected harrowing but valuable firsthand testimonies from its victims but did not delve into the historical and sociological causes.[23] Catharine and David Newbury, in their numerous articles and books, have placed Rwandan ethnic categorization in its historical context (C. Newbury 1988, 1992, 1995, 1998; D. Newbury 1991, 1997, 1998, 2001), examined the influence of competing visions of Rwandan history on the conflict (Chubaka and Newbury 1980; C. Newbury 1998; D. Newbury 1997; C. Newbury and D. Newbury 1999), and brought to light the contested views of the genocide in Rwanda today (C. Newbury 2004; C. Newbury and D. Newbury 1999; D. Newbury 2004). Alison Des Forges's (1999) definitive historical examination of the genocide traces the penetration of the ideology of genocide from an inner circle of political elites in Kigali to local government officials and extremists in the hills. It is by far the most complete and thoroughly researched work on the genocide and, in its study of the Butare and Gikongoro prefectures, begins to remedy the lack of detailed empirical research at the local rural level. In his book on the role of Christianity in the genocide, Timothy Longman (2009) documents the variation in the methods and motives for killing in rural communities. His long-term experience in Rwanda before and after the genocide yields a nuanced understanding of rural communities. Scott Straus (2006) and Lee Ann Fujii (2009) investigate the reasons ordinary citizens perpetrated the genocide and the power dynamics at work in rural areas to discipline the population into complying with the genocide orders.

The work of anthropologists on the subject has been somewhat limited and tends to be based either on long-term fieldwork conducted before the genocide or on short-term field visits following it. Danielle de Lame's *Une colline entre mille* (1996), revised and translated into English as *A Hill among a Thousand* (2005a), is by far the most detailed look at rural life in Rwanda ever published. Based on six years of fieldwork conducted in the 1980s in a rural community in Kibuye prefecture, de Lame's book captures the complex and interwoven social, political, and economic relations among rural families. The final chapter examines the effects of the genocide on the community based on interviews with refugees living in Zaire. Christopher Taylor's *Sacrifice as Terror* (1999) presents a highly theoretical analysis of the symbolic systems at work in ethnicity and killing during the 1994 genocide. Villia Jefremovas (2002) documents the transformation of the Rwandan political economy and gendered aspects of labor, production, and control of capital through a case study of the handmade brick industry in Rwanda in the 1980s.

It is understandable that anthropologists have yet to publish work based on long-term ethnographic research in postgenocide Rwanda, as ethnographic research can be very lengthy. My own attempt at such an undertaking has continued more than fifteen years. Yet given the unique perspective offered by anthropology, the commitment of time is a worthwhile investment. An ethnographic view of genocide and war reveals the complexity and contradictions of ethnic identity, individual experience, mythico-histories, familial and communal conflict, and master narratives of race and nationality and their articulation with national and international politics. For each individual in every community, there are multiple levels of both victimhood and perpetratorhood going back many generations. Ethnographic methodology makes it possible to bring together the seemingly irreconcilable points of view of victims, survivors, perpetrators, bystanders, and witnesses of genocide, war, and other sorts of violence. Their points of view are only irreconcilable insofar as they are incomplete, grounded in particular historical experience rather than a broader view of Rwandan society and history. A family who lived under what they perceived as the "dual colonialism" of Belgian and "Tutsi" rule will have a very different perspective from a family who fled killing squads in Rwanda in 1963 to live in a refugee camp in Uganda. They in turn will have a different perspective from a family who lived in Burundi.

Most importantly, an anthropological approach to the Rwandan genocide goes beyond the mere observation and description of journalism. First, it situates observation in the broader historical context of the precolonial, colonial, and postcolonial periods. Second, it regards the voices and thoughts of the individual actors involved as an essential starting point for analysis. Rather than merely reporting what Rwandans say, as journalists do, the anthropologist attempts to understand why Rwandans say what they say. Finally, an anthropology of postconflict Rwanda attempts to situate its analysis within a broader conceptual framework of social theory.

Listening to Silence

Anthropology's core methodology, participant observation, relies on a "dialectic of experience and interpretation" (Clifford 1988, 38) that requires the anthropologist to establish competence in the language and culture of her subject matter as well as to develop an empathy with research participants that facilitates a profounder understanding. Ruth Behar (1996) has developed the notion of the anthropologist as "vulnerable observer" and advocates a deep empathy with research subjects. In an application of this concept, Behar retells the memoir of a single woman, Esperanza, and frames her story together with Behar's own. Esperanza's story takes place in rural

Mexico. While Behar's technique makes it possible for the anthropologist and reader to relate at a personal level to Esperanza's tragic life and struggle to change her own world, we are left wondering about other points of view. In my own fieldwork, I applied Behar's technique of deep empathy as much as possible with my interviewees, yet I have attempted to avoid partiality by including multiple perspectives. One way I cultivated empathy with my subjects, moreover, was by respecting their silence.

As well as respecting silence, I also learned to "listen" to it. Listening to silence means paying attention to what people avoid saying as well as noting the occasions when they fall silent. Because I found that the majority of genocide survivors did not want to relate their experiences of genocide to me in formal, linear narratives, I waited for their stories to emerge in the course of daily life: a minor detail of quotidian experience might suddenly bring to the fore a memory, and they would narrate a fragment of their story. For one genocide survivor, a particular place evoked the memory of sending her children off into the care and protection of a stranger in the hope that they might survive. For another, the smell of beef cooking brought back the fear she experienced while hiding in her own home as her neighbors cooked and ate the cattle of murdered Tutsi. As Elaine Lawless found in her collection of life stories of women survivors of domestic abuse, I became convinced that "we must hear and 'read' these stories as they have been delivered to us, as they come to us, interrupted and broken by gaps and ruptures" (2000, 68). The atrocities of Rwanda in the 1990s were unspeakable, language failing to describe "that which cannot be de-scribed; that which is in-scribed already on flesh and bod[ies] cannot be spoken" (Lawless 2000, 71). By respecting and listening to Rwandans' silences, I found that when and where they chose to speak revealed the nature of their memories and experiences.

Beyond the methodological advantages of "deep empathy," using this technique in postgenocide Rwanda forced me to develop in myself separate, compartmentalized personas, one to empathize with each of the very different subject positions of the Rwandans who shared their stories. At times using this technique proved nearly impossible, for example, when a group of acquaintances (mostly Tutsi who had grown up in exile in Burundi) began maligning a friend, one man calling him "that northerner," "that mountain dweller," "that peasant" (all coded synonyms for "Hutu" in their usage).[24] On another occasion, I interviewed a Rwandan man living in exile in the United States, and he denied that the "events of 1994" were a genocide. He said in an angry tone, "It's simple. It was a civil war. They were killing us, so we had to defend ourselves." It was extremely hard for me to suppress my natural reaction against statements of this sort, but I tried to turn such moments into an opportunity to probe interviewees' opinions and knowledge. When I managed to maintain an empathetic stance, these moments often yielded breakthroughs in my research, as I finally gained access to people's deeply held convictions about who (or what) they felt they were, about the nature of ethnicity in Rwanda, and about Rwanda's history.

Another facet of ethnography and participant observation is its reliance on intersubjectivity, that is, the dialogue and interactions between the anthropologist, her research topic, and her research participants as well as between the conflicting points of view of her research participants. Ethnographers arrive at an intersubjective perception through three different means: self-reflection, interactions with research participants, and the juxtaposition of different voices and points of view in their analysis. Ethnographers engage in self-reflection in the sense that participant observation is a reflexive practice that requires the anthropologist to reflect on her own subject position(s) in her relationship not only with research participants but also with her discipline, her field of inquiry, and her research questions. As the anthropologist acquires new experiences through fieldwork, she interprets them based on prior experiences. To achieve scientific results and escape the trap of subjectivity, she must interpret new experiences in light of prior experience in the field and in her life "back home." Pierre Bourdieu (2003) refers to this sort of deep reflexivity as "participant objectivation." According to Bourdieu (2003, 283), the researcher must analyze her own "social origins, her position and trajectory in the social space, her social and religious positions and beliefs" with the same detached, "objective" eye that she turns on her subjects. This parallel examination allows the researcher to escape ethnocentrism and the biases of older anthropological work.

Through interactions with participants the anthropologist builds up, over time, a "common, meaningful world, drawing on intuitive styles of feeling, perception, and guesswork" (Clifford 1988, 36), while at the same time she is drawn into the local webs of power relations of her host community. The scientific validity of ethnography relies on long-term fieldwork because it is only through the accumulation of experience and interpretation along with involvement in local webs of power that the anthropologist is able to see past her own subjective interpretations and those of her interviewees. Long-term participant observation begins with a thorough immersion in a language and culture, which, once proficiency has been achieved, makes possible the accumulation of direct experiential knowledge. For example, the central conclusions of my own research changed almost completely over the course of my second year of fieldwork. It was not until I became more aware of my position in the local webs of power, my beliefs about human nature, and my exposure to the dominant discourses about nationality and the genocide that I realized how these factors had shaped my perspectives and conclusions about Rwandan ethnicity and gender identities. Although I expected there would be some difference between Rwandans' public and private selves, the success with which many friends, acquaintances, and interviewees hid their most strongly held convictions was surprising to me. The complexities of conflict and reconciliation in postgenocide Rwanda did not become intelligible to me until Rwandan families invited me into their homes and lives.

Rwandan culture makes very strong demarcations between the public and the private, and Rwandans do not readily invite strangers into their homes. Numerous Americans working in Rwanda voiced their frustration that their Rwandan coworkers had never invited them over. I felt this same frustration during my first stay in Rwanda in 1997. When I returned to Rwanda in 1998 and stayed with a Rwandan family, I gained instant access to Rwandan social life because I had a ready-made social identity—I became the daughter of the family I stayed with and was adopted into their social networks. The busy schedule of social visits soon became tiring and, at times, difficult to manage. Once I had gained access to Rwandan social life and learned some of the social conventions, I began to establish relationships on my own without direct connections to my original host family. This process raised some conflicts with my original host family, as they were suspicious of Rwandans they did not know. At that point I began to experience the divisions within Rwandan society that at the macrolevel correspond roughly to ethnic and regional differences but that at the microlevel are much more complex and personal, involving issues of class, education, family history, and gender.

Once I had established myself within a diverse set of Rwandan social networks, it still took me years to begin to understand Rwandan emotions. Rwandan culture admires people who master their emotions and who always show a calm exterior. Coming from the United States, where emotive excess is promoted as contributing to mental health, for a long time I found Rwandan emotions inscrutable. When I interviewed genocide survivors, they would recount their horrific stories without shedding a tear. Gradually, however, I learned to perceive the muted signs of emotion on interviewees' and friends' faces. Eventually, even my own body language began to conform to Rwandan patterns. I came to know through my own experience the degree to which Rwandans in their public life and interactions conform to socially and politically acceptable ideologies, while in their private life and interactions their true feelings and convictions are revealed.

The third means through which the anthropologist achieves an intersubjective approach—the juxtaposition of the diverse and often contradictory voices and points of view of research participants—relies on her ability to make herself a vulnerable observer in relation to a wide variety of people. Through empathetic listening to diverse points of view, the anthropologist can begin to perceive the complexity of social relations, discourses, and mythico-histories and their inherent contradictions both within an individual's own perceptions and narratives and between those of different people. The juxtaposition of these different voices and points of view allows the anthropologist to arrive at an intersubjective objectivity that Donna Haraway calls "situated knowledge" (1991, 183–201). The objectivity of situated knowledge arises from the "contestation, deconstruction, passionate construction, webbed connections, and hope for transformation of systems of knowledge and ways of seeing" (Haraway 1991, 191–92). It is by analyzing the validity of contradictory points of view and revealing their partial and complementary truths that the ethnographer is able to arrive at a deeper objectivity than that obtained, in a more conventional approach, through reliance upon a single (albeit scientifically controlled) point of view. In short, the ethnographer extracts the tension of multiple truths from a "situated" and yet constantly shifting intersubjective position.

After the Genocide

In the eighteen years since the genocide ended, Rwanda has undergone remarkable change, emerging from the holocaust of genocide. The population in the capital city, Kigali, has more than tripled from around 258,000 in 1994 to over 908,000 in 2009. Shining new skyscrapers are emerging on the skyline of downtown Kigali. Enormous billboards with Western-style commercial messages selling cell phones, soft drinks, and beer or promoting public service messages adorn the major intersections. Asphalted main roads lined with neat sidewalks and side roads paved in cobblestones traverse the city. The city is decorated with manicured landscaping in medians and statues in the roundabouts at major intersections. Each morning teams of women sweep the main streets and sidewalks with hand brooms, while men water the flowers or cut the grass. An astounding number of new sport utility vehicles, used cars, Toyota minibuses, and "taximotos" flood the roads between 6:30 and 7:00 a.m. as the city's professional workforce heads to their jobs. Most physical traces of the 1994 genocide on the cityscape have been erased.

The country has boasted remarkable economic growth in every year since 1994, when the gross domestic product was only $753 million with an annual growth rate of negative 50 percent.[25] By 2009 the gross domestic product was over $5 trillion, and the annual growth rate was a respectable 4.1 percent in the midst of a global economic downturn. According to a 2010 progress report, Rwanda made "impressive" progress toward many of the Millennium Development Goals (United Nations Development Program

2010). Rwanda has already met its targets for gender equality in primary and secondary education and in seats held by females in parliament (ibid., 11). In fact, Rwanda boasts the highest percentage of women in a national legislature (56 percent) in the world. Data on percentage of the population living in poverty or suffering from nutritional deficits have shown improvement, but Rwanda is unlikely to meet these targets by the deadline (ibid., 26). In particular, the rural poor seem to be left out of Rwanda's economic progress (Ansoms 2008, 2010; Ansoms and McKay 2010; Ingelaere 2010). Nonetheless, Rwanda is seen as a leader on the continent for promoting economic growth, maintaining political stability, fighting corruption, creating a business-friendly environment, and establishing a rational taxation policy. Furthermore, Rwanda has emerged as a leader on gender equality not only for Africa but for the world. Rwandan women have been part of the nation-building project of the New Rwanda. They have not remained passive victims. As the pages that follow demonstrate, Rwandan women exercised their agency in strategic ways that allowed them to make sense of their lives in ways that sometimes fall afoul of official government narratives of the genocide and war of 1994.

Structure of the Book

In chapter 1, I examine the evolution of two systems of social classification in Rwanda—gender and ethnicity—and the effects of the dual influences of state power and violence on their changing structure. As early as the precolonial period, centralized state power privileged certain social categories ("the nobility," "Tutsi," "Banyanduga") and marginalized others ("the peasants," "Hutu," and "Bakiga"). Under first German and then Belgian colonialism, the state continued to transform the structure and meanings of social categories. In particular, European notions of the gendered division of labor and of the association of women with the private, domestic world transformed the social world in which Rwandan women lived and undermined their autonomy and customary bases of power. Discerning the roles of state power and violence in shaping the evolution of gender and ethnicity is fundamental to interpreting the ways Rwandan women coped with violence in the 1990s.

In chapters 2, 3, and 4, I explore the politics of memory in postgenocide Rwanda, the multiple forms of silence, and the ways ordinary women contested state-imposed discourses about national history, the civil war, and the genocide. Chapter 2 examines the ways women coped with the social crisis created by the abundance of female-headed households and the ways ordinary women tried to maintain control over their memories of violence.

Among the many strategies women deployed—including collective amnesia, memorializing, retribution, seeking justice, and forgiveness—silence played a central role. Chapter 3 analyzes the amplified silence generated by state-sponsored memory practices, specifically, the month of national mourning and the creation of genocide memorial sites. In chapter 4, I delve into the ways women resisted the dominant social classification systems that were constructed around the politicized categories of "victim/survivor" and "perpetrator."

In chapters 5, 6, and 7, I examine women's engagement in several inter-related social processes that fall under the umbrella term "reconciliation." In chapter 5, I discuss the many ways that reconciliation has been defined by ordinary Rwandans, by the RPF-led government, and by the international community. These multiple definitions competed with each other in the postgenocide period, but national reconciliation practices had greater influence because of the government's greater power. As a result, national reconciliation practices circumscribed Rwandan women's agency and grass-roots reconciliation efforts. Chapter 6 describes several examples of the paths toward reconciliation taken by ordinary Rwandan women as well as those led by women's civil society organizations. In chapter 6, I conclude that pregenocide experiences of social relationships with people from different ethnic groups made reconciliation efforts more likely to succeed. Thus old caseload refugees who did not have these positive experiences were less likely to build close relationships across ethnic lines than were genocide survivors. Chapter 7 provides ordinary women's perspectives on the Rwandan government's largest reconciliation initiative to date—the use of reinvented, traditional conflict resolution mechanisms called *gacaca* to try over one million cases of genocide crimes in local-level courts on hills throughout the country. During the *gacaca* process, which spanned a period of approximately eight years, women faced particular challenges as a result of their unique social position in kin groups and communities.

In the conclusion, I synthesize the primary factors that led to women's leading role in Rwanda's apparent postgenocide renaissance. First, women were forced to take on new roles in the family, community, and broader society in the aftermath of the genocide. Life conditions required ordinary women to break cultural taboos and to advocate for women's rights for their own survival and not necessarily feminist intention. Second, Rwandan women's civil society organizations played a key role in advocating a place for women in rebuilding the country. Third, the RPF's conscious strategy to mainstream women within its own organs as well as the transitional govern-ment transformed ordinary Rwandan women's lives in positive ways, giving them greater economic autonomy, guaranteeing them equal access to edu-cation, and carving out new career paths for them. Finally, international funding for programs targeting women also played a significant role in supporting these transformations.

The challenges ordinary women faced in the aftermath of the genocide and war in Rwanda can help indicate paths to recovery in other conflict zones in the world and suggest interventions that could prevent genocide before it occurs. In the following pages, you will encounter many heartbreaking stories that may undermine your faith in humanity. Instead, I ask you to focus on the surprising resilience of women who faced terrible tragedy and hardship.

1

Social Classification, State Power, and Violence

During the years leading up to the genocide (1990–94) and those after the genocide (1994–2001), violence, war, and terror formed the backdrop of daily life in Rwanda. Understanding women's experiences of violence during each of these periods is central to explaining women's roles in postgenocide reconstruction. Gender is but one aspect of a whole network of interconnected social categories, including lineage, clan, ethnicity, economic class, political affiliation, and education level, in which Rwandan women are enmeshed. The ways women make sense of the past and explain the present are caught up in local and national politics, state building, the ways elites write history to suit their political agendas, and the ways the state's official history conflicts with individual lived histories and experiences of violence. I begin this chapter by examining the evolution of social categories, specifically, gender and ethnicity, from the precolonial period until the 1990s. I then analyze four constellations of state power and violent conflict from 1990 to 2001 that shaped the treacherous terrains that Rwandan

41

women navigated throughout the 1990s. Though not all Rwandan women are genocide survivors, they all found themselves the targets of state-led violence or oppression at some point during the 1990s.

Rwandan Gender Cosmology

Rwandan conceptions of gender diverge from the dominant binary system of male/female typical in Europe and North America. Rwandan gender categories are embedded in one's role in the kin group and in the community, and age and reproductive status serve as structural elements of gender. Table 1 represents the Rwandan gender cosmology. Male and female babies (*uruhinja*) and children (*abana*) under the age of four years are generally treated the same by their parents, relatives, and community members. In the recent past, there were no gender differences in dress for infants. Since the 1970s, the used clothing industry and preference for Western dress have changed this practice. Urban and rural families with the financial means to do so dress infants in gender-appropriate colors—blue for boys and pink for girls—following the Western idiom. Distinctions between sons (*abahungu*) and daughters (*abakobwa*) begin around four years of age when they take on household chores. Girls are more likely to be sent to fetch water, help with the preparation of food, and sweep out the family compound, while boys are more likely to be sent to watch over livestock. Yet life status or age distinctions are just as important and are directly linked to land rights. Daughters have roles in the family and society that are different from those of wives (*abagore* or *abategarugori*).

In the more distant past, young, unmarried women or maidens (*abari*) ranged in age from about fifteen to twenty years of age. "Maidens" is my translation of the Kinyarwanda word *abari*, which means roughly "girls ripe for marriage" and has no exact equivalent in standard American English. The word "maidens," with its connotation of virginity, is a close match. The word *abari* has a more positive connotation than *abakobwa* because it explicitly refers to a young woman's physical readiness to bear children and become a wife and mother. Maidens were integral to the family unit, performing important chores around the home such as cooking, cleaning, and fetching water and cultivating food crops alongside their mothers and other siblings. Once married, a maiden left her father's home and became part of her husband's patrilineage, where she relied on her husband, brothers-in-law, and sons for access to land. A wife (*umugore*) was and still is the economic as well as spiritual and moral center of the house (*urugo*, "compound," referring to the conjugal household comprised of husband, wife, and children). Motherhood is the best light in which females can be seen in

Table 1. Rwandan gender cosmology

Male	Female
uruhinja (newborn)	
umwana (child)	
umuhungu (son, boy)	*umukobwa* (daughter, girl)
umusore (bachelor)	*umwari* (maiden)
umugabo (husband, man)	*umugore* (wife, woman)
	umutegarugori (wearer of the *urugori*, wife-mother)
umupfakazi (widower, widow)	
umusaza (old man)	*umukecuru* (old woman)
[no male analogue]	*indushyi* (vulnerable [people], rejected wife)

Rwandan society (Schoenbrun 1998, 151–54), and a maiden (*umwari*) only truly became a wife (*umutegarugori*, "wearer of the *rugori*," a headband made of sorghum) upon bearing a son (*umuhungu*) to continue her husband's (*umugabo*, pl. *abagabo*) lineage. Wives were responsible for cultivating all food for the household on land belonging to her husband or his lineage, while husbands focused on the production of cash crops, managed the livestock, or migrated in search of paid labor (Jefremovas 2002, 87).

A single term, *umupfakazi*, applies to widowers and widows, although widowers rarely retained this status for long. Widowers quickly remarried, as any self-respecting man has a wife at home. Men, unlike women, are not limited by biology—they can procreate at any age. In the Rwandan worldview, the principal purpose of marriage is to have children, so women past their reproductive years have little hope of remarrying. Upon loss of her husband, a widow who had produced a son or sons for her husband's lineage retained the right to cultivate her deceased husband's landholdings, managing it for her sons until they were old enough to receive their inheritance and become heads of their own households. A widow who had not produced a son for her husband's lineage, on the other hand, was labeled *indushyi* (vulnerable or rejected) and returned to her father's family.[1] Her deceased husband's landholdings reverted to his patrilineage. The *indushyi*'s patrilineage was expected to provide a portion of land for her to cultivate until she remarried and left to join a new husband's lineage.

Under Rwanda's system of patrilineal kinship, widows, married women, and unmarried girls derived their social identities from the men to whom they were related. A Rwandan proverb states, "Abagore ntibafite ubwoko" (Wives have no identity), meaning that as a daughter, a woman or girl had the same identity as her father or brothers, but as a wife, she took on the identity of her husband and his patrilineage.[2] Precolonial and colonial naming practices illustrate another symbolic erasure of a woman's personhood. After her marriage, a woman would often be called a name derived from her husband's name, for example, Mukamanzi (wife of Manzi), or other anonymous kinship terms such as *umufashe* (helper, meaning wife) or *mama, nyoko,* or *nyina* (my mother, your mother, his or her mother), and the name she was given at birth would rarely, if ever, be used.

Each of these life stages is distinct and is associated with a specific body of knowledge. Certain types of knowledge, such as the details of sexual intercourse, childbirth, and the challenges of being a wife and mother, were kept secret from those who had not yet attained the status of husband or wife. The rigidity of the distinction between maiden and woman became clear to me after a failed interview with a women's group in a rural community in southern Rwanda. During our conversation, the women became visibly agitated. They suddenly and simultaneously announced that they needed to get back home. The group leader asked us to visit her at home later in the week. During our visit, she explained that the women had become upset because we were asking them personal questions about women's problems (*ibibazo by'abagore*). The women had not wanted to expose maidens—my research assistant and me—to the problems of women.[3] She said that the women were still upset. I explained to her that in the United States I was already considered a woman and that I knew about women's problems because I had been living independently for several years, even though I was not yet married. She recommended that I share this information with women before interviewing them so that they would be comfortable speaking with me about the harsh realities of their lives. In subsequent interviews, I followed her advice and found that women spoke much more openly about their lives. Many women expressed pity for me, being unable to imagine how my parents could allow their daughter to "live as an orphan." This fieldwork breakthrough enhanced my ability to interview women. The group leader's advice transformed my interviews from interrogations, during which I asked questions that women begrudgingly answered, to engaging conversations about gender roles and cultural expectations.

While age and life status structure Rwandan gender distinctions, gender stereotypes play on a dialectic of male/female distinctions (Herzfeld 1991). Women are viewed positively when they are reserved, submissive, modest, silent, and maternal, when they maintain a "respectable" household, and when they raise "wise" children. They are viewed negatively when they gossip, are loud and overly emotional, or have a dirty house or rude children. By contrast, men should be self-assured, dominant, logical, brave, and physically strong. The positive qualities associated with maleness are so strong that when a woman displays competence it can be a compliment to say, "Ni umugabo" (She's a man), although this usage is rare. The more commonly used phrase, "Ni igishegabo" (She's a big man-woman), is an insult used to describe a woman who displays characteristics desirable in a man, such as outspokenness and aggression, but objectionable in a woman.

When I began my fieldwork in rural Rwanda in the late 1990s, gender conceptions between urban and rural Rwandans were different. While most urban Rwandans advocated for gender equality, the basic premises of gender equality seemed ludicrous to most rural people. When I asked about gender equality, they responded, "Equal in what? Everyone [or at least every Rwandan] knows that husbands are superior to wives," both in body and in mind. As a woman from a rural community in the south explained,

> We wives, we're weak compared to husbands. In the first place, it's the maiden who goes to the bachelor's [*umusore*] home and not the opposite. Then, during intercourse it's the girl who loses and not the husband; they make love and the girl is torn and it hurts, while the husband enjoys himself from the beginning to the end. And after all that you maidens [*speaking directly to my research assistant and me*] chant, "We're equal to men." What equality? Girls who have studied a lot . . . I wonder sometimes whether you're normal in your heads because you're the ones chanting this equality of the sexes.
>
> A few months after the wedding, the wife is pregnant. She begins to vomit. She becomes picky about what she'll eat and what she won't. Then afterward she gets thin, her body weakens, she begins to hurt all over and in all her joints. In short, her body becomes like a ripe banana. And that for nine months, all the while her husband is there, next to her, waiting for his baby. Where is the equality between [the two of] you?
>
> The birth is something else. If they want, they cut you apart no matter where [*she gestures with a slash of her hand toward her abdomen*]. The pain is indescribable. After the birth, the wife becomes like a skeleton for a certain time. And even when her body returns to normal, she'll never be as strong as when she was still a girl. I tell you, before singing equality, you should first find a way for husbands to give birth. Until you've done that, forget talking about equality of the sexes. (Field notes, March 2001)

Notably, this woman repeatedly plays on the "losses" women experience in their interactions with men, first through the act of intercourse, then through childbirth, when the woman loses control of her body, and finally through the permanent loss of strength in comparison to the woman's previous state as a girl. In general, she focuses on the physical weakness of women and especially on the weakness caused by reproduction and childbirth. In my research, rural Rwandans often invoked childbirth as physically depleting for women and as a justification for the inferior position of women in the family and society. From their point of view, women are weak and vulnerable, and they need to be protected by men. In rural areas where birth control was unavailable in the late 1990s and early 2000s and where knowledge of customary birth-spacing methods had been lost, women often had between ten and eighteen pregnancies by the end of their reproductive years.[4] Constant pregnancy combined with poverty and cyclical famine are indeed physically depleting, and the risks of childbirth where medical care is difficult to access are great.

Thus, for many rural people gender equality ignores the differences between men and women that are visibly apparent in their bodies and actions. While rural women rejected gender equality as a laudable goal, they did not advocate for total male dominance or patriarchy. Instead, they frequently invoked the idea of complementarities (*kuzuzanye*) between men and women. In other words, husbands and wives have complementary, culturally defined roles in the family, extended kin group, and community. From this perspective, women are not powerless. When a husband does not uphold his duties, the wife is in theory free to leave and return to her father's home. Unfortunately, this theoretical liberty is circumscribed in practice by economic realities and land scarcity. During my fieldwork in the late 1990s and early 2000s, few women in unhappy marriages found the economic means or social support to leave their husbands. As I describe later in this chapter, tensions between wives and their mothers- or sisters-in-law often intersected with other social categories, including ethnicity and regionalism.

Ethnicity, Race, Gender, and the Colonial Encounter

The historiography of Rwanda has been shaped by images and stereotypes in the minds of observers. For many, "Rwanda holds the allure . . . of the 'paradigmatic' pre-colonial African state: centralized, stratified, ethnicized, and 'feudal'" (D. Newbury and C. Newbury 2000, 833). These persistent images have had dire consequences for the country, especially in the construction of the genocidal state of the 1990s.[5] The writing of state history was shaped by the colonial encounter.[6] Not only did this history hide political and economic processes; it cloaked Rwandan women in obscurity. Other than references to the queen mother and the power of her family at the *mwami*'s court, women were virtually excluded from Rwandan history until recently.[7]

A photograph from early in the colonial period represents the three so-called races of Rwanda as captured by the German explorer Adolf Friedrich zu Mecklenburg (fig. 3). This photograph was probably taken during his

Figure 3. Tutsi, Hutu, and Twa as captured on film by Adolf Friedrich zu Mecklen-burg's expedition in central Africa in 1907 and 1908. Courtesy of Archives and Museum Foundation of the United Evangelical Mission.

expedition to Rwanda and Burundi in 1907 and 1908. The photograph represents the races with their stereotypical attributes as understood through European theories of race at the time and the Hamitic hypothesis (discussed in the next section). The Tutsi is tall and thin, with aquiline features and a light complexion. The Hutu is shorter and more muscular with a broad nose and dark skin. The Twa is shorter still with a furrowed face and ribs showing.

Yet ethnicity in Rwanda, or anywhere else in the world, is not nearly that simple. Although the terms "Hutu," "Tutsi," and "Twa" are quite old in Rwandan social discourse and predate the colonial era, their meanings and importance have changed dramatically over time and varied by region.[8] While many anthropologists (myself included) view "tribes" in Africa as a modern phenomenon created through European colonialism (see, e.g., Southall 1970), "Hutu," "Tutsi," and "Twa" never fit the characteristics of micronations usually attributed to tribes (Prunier 1997, 5). What foreign observers have called ethnicity in Rwanda has not been marked by differences in language, culture, religion, or territory in recorded history and evidence indicates that the people who populated what today is Rwanda have shared similar ways of life, language, and culture since approximately 500 BCE (Schoenbrun 1998, 155). These categories acquired their social meaning and political importance through successive waves of state building.

The term for ethnicity in Kinyarwanda, *ubwoko*, means "sort" or "type" and can be applied to trees or cattle as well as humans. Before the colonial period and up until the 1960s, "when you asked a man what was his *ubwoko* he could answer, according to the context, with *muhutu* (Hutu), *mugoyi* (resident of the Bugoyi region), *musinga* (member of the Basinga clan), or give his profession. . . . Applied to humans, the *bwoko* was social identity, being Hutu, Tutsi or Twa was not fundamental" (Franche 1997, 18). Thus, to be "Hutu," "Tutsi," or "Twa" was but one aspect of a complex social identity that included clan, lineage, profession, ethnicity, region of birth, region of residence, economic class, and so on.

In the precolonial period, especially in regions peripheral to central Rwanda, the categories "Hutu," "Tutsi," and "Twa" were often quite flexible and largely contingent on the local context.[9] Clan and lineage affiliations were the most relevant social categories in daily interactions among ordinary Rwandans. Some scholars have argued that the distinctions between Hutu, Tutsi, and Twa were distinctions of caste or economic class (see, e.g., Codere 1973; d'Hertefelt, Trouwbourst, and Scherer 1962; d'Hertefelt 1964, 1971; Maquet 1954, 1961). While it is true that the majority of ruling elite were Tutsi, Hutu chiefs held important positions at court and ruled northwestern Rwanda with autonomy until the late nineteenth century.

In the latter half of the nineteenth century, the distinctions between Hutu, Tutsi, and Twa rigidified under the reign of Kigeri Rwabugiri (Kimonyo 2001; Pottier 2002, 120). Rwabugiri introduced new institutions, including new forms of corvée labor (*uburetwa*), land tenure (*igikingi*), and cattle clientage (*ubuhake*) that politicized the categories Hutu and Tutsi among ordinary Rwandans for the first time (C. Newbury 1988, 82; Pottier 2002, 13).[10] These new controls over the means of production and labor intensified the Tutsi nobility's potential exploitation of ordinary Rwandans (whether Hutu, Tutsi, or Twa) and accentuated the distinctions between the nobility and the rest of the population.

Europeans "brought their own kind of racism" to the Great Lakes region (Des Forges 1995, 44). Since roughly the seventeenth century, the Hamitic hypothesis shaped European thinking about the people who lived in the rest of the world. The Hamitic hypothesis stated that "everything of value ever found in Africa was brought there by the Hamites, allegedly a branch of the Caucasian race" (Sanders 1969, 521). British explorer John Hanning Speke brought the nineteenth-century version of the Hamitic hypothesis to the Great Lakes region of Africa. When Speke encountered the Bugandan kingdom (in what today is Uganda), he "attributed its 'barbaric civilization' to a nomadic pastoralist race," the Hima (Sanders 1969, 528). Speke's conclusion, drawn without any evidence, was eventually expanded to include the Hima and Tutsi of Rwanda and Burundi, who phenotypically resembled the Ugandan Hima and who reigned over similarly complex sociopolitical systems (Kimonyo 2001, 65). Eventually, the Hima, the Tutsi, and the Maasai came to be lumped together under the term "Nilo-Hamitic" or "Semi-Hamitic" because their phenotypes were deemed "less Caucasoid" than the Copts, Berbers, or Abyssinians (Kimonyo 2001, 65) but presumably "less Negroid" than the Hutu or other "Bantus."

The Hamitic hypothesis had been thoroughly disproved by the 1940s, but the history written and promoted by the postcolonial Rwandan state continued to disseminate the Hamitic hypothesis's major points. As a result, many Rwandans believe that Rwanda was populated by the migration of Hutu into the region and their subsequent conquest by invading Tutsi. Narratives of a "lost tribe of Israel" bringing civilization to sub-Saharan Africa are very appealing to some foreign audiences, including white supremacists and Zionists. Even today, some websites continue to portray Tutsi as a lost tribe of Israel, recapitulating the Hamitic hypothesis in new language with new political intentions.[11]

Some European colonialists projected their racist ideas onto Rwandan society and "ascribed stereotyped intellectual and moral qualities to the people of each category," with Tutsi at the top of the hierarchy and Twa at the bottom (Des Forges 1995, 44). They often paid little attention to distinctions among the clans, which were very important among the ruling (Tutsi) elite and among peasants, both Hutu and Tutsi, from different regions.[12] Under Belgian colonialism, the now exclusively Tutsi monarchy's oppression of the rural population increased, with a disproportionate burden borne by Hutu peasants, while Tutsi peasants were spared some of the most exploitative corvée labor requirements.[13]

European colonialism transformed Rwandan economic relations and undermined women's economic autonomy and sources of social power. The colonial taxation system and agricultural development projects pushed men into the cash economy, while their wives became solely responsible for cultivating food for the household on land belonging to their husband's lineages (Jefremovas 2002, 87). The banking and commerce laws created by the colonial state only applied to Europeans, other foreigners, and Rwandans who qualified as "civilized." This situation disadvantaged all Rwandan colonial subjects in terms of land and other property rights, but it especially marginalized women. The "tribal courts" that adjudicated cases involving customary law were run by local chiefs, who were all men. Tribal court rulings were often biased against women, who had less direct power in local communities, where their social ties were usually mediated by their husband's patrilineage. Increasing land scarcity made it more difficult for women to leave unsatisfactory marriages because their brothers were reluctant to share land with them (Jefremovas 2002). These changes during the colonial period virtually excluded women from the cash economy (Jefremovas 1991, 2002) and undermined women's sources of power in marriage and kin groups, thus subordinating women to men in new ways.

Gender and Ethnicity in Postcolonial Rwanda

Belgian colonialism in Rwanda did not end peacefully. Along with independence movements across the continent, Rwandans began to demand an end to Belgian rule. In November 1959 proindependence demonstrations shifted into attacks against Tutsi political elites and their families: a few hundred people were killed, a few thousand homes were burned, and approximately ten thousand (predominantly Tutsi) refugees left the country (Reyntjens 1985, 261). Realizing that the end of its colonial rule was near, Belgium developed a hasty exit strategy. By the end of the transition in 1963, Rwanda had a democratically elected Hutu president, Grégoire Kayibanda, but the electoral process and communal violence had confirmed the cleavages between "Hutu" and "Tutsi."

Under Kayibanda, the new government attempted to correct many decades of discrimination against Hutu. The president promoted Hutu to prominent positions in his cabinet and government, but he preferred Hutu from southern and central Rwanda over those from other regions. Ongoing violence targeting Tutsi elite in 1963 and 1964 caused waves of (mostly Tutsi) refugees to flee. These Rwandan refugees later proved important in the emergence of the Rwandan Patriotic Front (RPF) and the evolution of the civil war from 1990 through 1994.

Under the First Republic, government services targeted women directly for the first time. While several hundred young women were trained as midwives during the 1950s, ordinary Rwandan women remained illiterate. The new government created social centers (*foyers sociaux*) for women in each prefecture (province). These centers focused on public health education and literacy for rural women, and they provided leadership opportunities for the educated women who staffed them. These centers laid the foundation for the Rwandan women's movement that would emerge in the 1980s.

By 1972 President Kayibanda's regime faced growing opposition from northern Hutu who felt marginalized by the state. President Kayibanda redirected this opposition into ethnic violence targeting Tutsi. This violence produced memories of ethnic violence that altered the population's behavior and influenced their understandings of the political situation during the civil war in the 1990s and the 1994 genocide. In 2000 I visited the rural birthplace in central Rwanda of Josephine, a genocide widow in her forties. We parked my truck at the end of a dirt track and walked down a footpath. As we walked, Josephine, whose parents were Tutsi, pointed out her paternal uncles' homes. In front of one enclosure she stopped and pointed to a line of trees on the other side of the path. "My father's house used to be there. Can you see the remains?" I nodded and asked what happened to it.

> They came and burned it in the seventies. My father always had a big mouth [*she laughed*], so there were some people around here who didn't like him. When the whole thing [referring to the demonstrations and associated attacks against Tutsi in 1973] started, he knew he was in trouble. He had friends at the *gendarmerie* [police], so he went there and stayed for something like two weeks. When the mobs came, they couldn't find my father, so they burned down the house instead. After things calmed down a bit, my father came back, escorted by his friends [the police]. When he saw the house, he decided to rebuild farther from the main road. [*She pointed to the highway visible on the next hill.*] He said, "They won't bother to burn it down if they can't see it from the road."

I asked Josephine if her father had been correct. She looked puzzled and asked what I meant. I replied, "Well, did they burn the house in 1994?" She laughed and said, "No, I guess they didn't. They stole absolutely everything from it, including the roof, but the house was still standing." This brief exchange illustrates the profound and long-term structuring of present experience by the past. The persistent memory of the family's displacement in the form of the remains of the old house, the location of the new house, and the family's oral history shaped both their strategies of survival at future moments of ethnic or communal conflict (e.g., in 1994) and their understanding of these events.

Women who were in their forties when I interviewed them between 1998 and 2002 remembered incidents in 1972 and 1973 when Tutsi students were sent home from school. Isabelle, whose mother was "Tutsi" and whose father was "Hutu," explained: "In my family, the subject never came up. We were Banyarwanda. My mother and father never talked about Tutsi this or Hutu that. We [the children] didn't even know what we were, and we didn't care. We were simply the children of a love [whose political implications] had nothing to do with us" (author interview, 1999). Isabelle's mother and father were both living in Zaire (now Democratic Republic of the Congo) when they met. Isabelle and her siblings were born and grew up in Zaire. In that context, the most relevant factor was that they were Banyarwanda— Rwandans, as opposed to Congolese. As a result, Isabelle did not learn about

Hutu–Tutsi distinctions until she went to live with her uncle in Rwanda to attend secondary school. Although Isabelle's official bureaucratic category was "Hutu," since her father was "Hutu," she encountered problems because she "looked Tutsi." In 1973, during her fourth year of secondary school, the headmaster expelled her; he insisted that she had lied about her ethnicity. Isabelle returned to her uncle's home. When he returned from work and found her there, he immediately took her back to school and explained to the headmaster that she was his niece and that she was indeed Hutu. Because her uncle held a position in the prefectural government, the headmaster immediately readmitted Isabelle to the school and apologized for his mistake.

Violence targeting Tutsi came to an end when Gen. Juvénal Habyarimana, a professional soldier, seized power in a coup d'état in July 1973. Under Habyarimana ethnic categories became further entrenched in the government bureaucracy. Thus, Rwandans who grew up under Habyarimana learned what they were when they went to school, obtained their national identity cards (around the age of sixteen), or applied for jobs. Young women who were in school in the 1980s learned their ethnicity when the time came for national exams: teachers asked them what their ethnicity was. On some occasions teachers would ask children in the classroom to stand up according to their ethnic category (author interviews, 1999, 2000, 2011). In other instances (Tutsi) girls learned what their ethnic category was when they did not receive an enrollment in secondary school or in the National University even though other (Hutu) students with lower exam scores did (author interviews, 1997, 1998, 2000).

Under the Second Republic, a Rwandan women's movement emerged despite the tight control the Habyarimana regime maintained over civil society. Rwanda sent several delegates to the United Nations' Third World Conference on Women, held in Nairobi in 1985 (Kanakuze 2004). These women brought back many ideas about how to involve educated women in improving all women's lives. Several national women's organizations were founded in the late 1980s, including Duterimbere, a women's banking and microlending cooperative modeled on the Grameen Bank; Haguruka, an advocacy group for women's and children's legal rights; and Réseau des femmes œuvrant pour le développement rural, an organization that provided technical assistance to rural women's organizations. Following pressure from the nascent women's movement, the Habyarimana government in 1992 created the Ministry for the Promotion of Women and the Family, whose primary mandate was to promote economic development to improve the status of women and children (ibid.). The first woman prime minister in Rwanda, Agathe Uwilingimana, a member of the Mouvement démocratique républicain (MDR), the opposition party, was appointed in 1993.

Constellations of State Power and
Violence in the 1990s

The state's impact on social categories escalated in the 1990s as the state's monopoly on the legitimate use of force was challenged through armed conflict and multiparty politics destabilized Habyarimana's hold on power. Changing political contexts and different regimes created a situation where state-sponsored violence targeted different categories of people. At times, state-sponsored violence primarily targeted Tutsi, while at others it targeted Hutu. The armed groups fighting for control of the state also targeted different social categories. Thus not all the violence fit the Hutu/Tutsi dyad associated with the 1994 genocide. Rwandans from all social categories felt targeted by violence at some time, although many of them are not publicly recognized as victims in postgenocide Rwanda. Throughout the 1990s, Rwandan women of all social categories faced an increased threat of sexual violence.

The following life history narrative illustrates the complex interactions between social categories and constellations of state power and violence. Antoinette's life story emerged in bits and pieces over the many years that I knew her. In her birthplace in Gitarama prefecture, Antoinette's family was categorized as Hutu, yet many Rwandans assumed that Antoinette was Tutsi based on her appearance. Antoinette was very beautiful, with "cow's eyes," straight teeth, a shapely physique, and a demure grace, all stereotypical markers of "Tutsiness" for women.[14] Antoinette had grown up in a rural area where her father bought land for a large farm near where he had grown up. Like most families from central or southern Rwanda, Antoinette's family had a history of intermarriage with Tutsi. Antoinette's paternal grandmother had been Tutsi, and her paternal grandfather was a wealthy Hutu farmer with lots of land.

Antoinette's father, Celestin, was one of the few Hutu men educated by Belgian priests late in the colonial period. Celestin was an avid supporter of the social revolution represented by the independence movement, although he did not embrace the ethnic aspects of the Parti du mouvement de l'émancipation hutu (PARMEHUTU) political party's platform. Antoinette's father found the polemical denunciations of Tutsi hegemony to be incompatible with his own experience. Instead, Celestin viewed the 1959 revolution as the rural population's rejection of the monarchy's exploitation and of the Belgian colonial presence simultaneously.

Under Kayibanda, Celestin held positions in the regional government and was sent to Belgium for advanced studies. Following the coup d'état in 1973, President Habyarimana removed Kayibanda supporters, PARMEHUTU members, and Banyanduga (literally, "people from Nduga," meaning anyone from southern or central Rwanda) from their positions and replaced them with kinsmen and other trusted people from his natal region (i.e., Bakiga, northerners, people of Rukiga). At this time Celestin spent a few years in prison, but he was eventually released instead of starving to death like many of Kayibanda's associates (Reyntjens 1985, 508–9). Celestin became a regional administrator near where he was born in a remote part of what is today West province.

As the child of educated members of the elite, Antoinette went to secondary school, an opportunity offered to very few girls in the 1980s, and eventually graduated with a teaching degree. She moved back home and became a schoolteacher. She married an engineer who worked in a state-run business near her father's home. Her husband, Dismas, was from northern Rwanda (i.e., a Mukiga, singular of Bakiga). Antoinette's parents supported the marriage and did not seem concerned that regional tensions between northerners (Bakiga) and southerners (Banyanduga) would affect the marriage. Antoinette's mother had come from an area far south and east of Celestin's natal region, and they had not had problems. In addition, they had known and observed Dismas for a few years before the couple married. Although Dismas did not actively hold prejudices against southerners, his mother and sisters did. For much of her married life, Antoinette listened to insults from her mother-in-law and sisters-in-law, who referred to her as "uriya Mututsikazi" (that Tutsi woman) and "uriya Munyandugakazi" (that southern woman). Antoinette explained that although her father-in-law, who had been educated in the United States, loved and defended her, her mother-in-law and sisters-in-law, who were uneducated peasant women, constantly persecuted her and tried to persuade Dismas to leave her. Although these women's insults focused on Antoinette's appearance and regional origin, their sentiments were likely fueled by the normal Rwandan tension between female in-laws. In the more distant past, a bride arrived in her husband's family and lived like the indentured servant of her mother-in-law and sisters-in-law until she gave birth to a son. Since Antoinette was educated and worked outside the home and because she and Dismas did not live near Dismas's family after their wedding, Antoinette escaped this hardship. In addition, since Antoinette continued to work as a schoolteacher, she had a servant at home who helped with cooking, cleaning, and taking care of the children. Thus, her mother-in-law's and sisters-in-law's hatred toward her was likely provoked by jealousy over her elevated standard of living as much as by her regional origin and appearance.

In 1990, a few weeks after the RPF invasion, several hundred Tutsi were massacred in the region where Antoinette's father lived. Celestin publicly opposed the killings and protected Tutsi in his home. Like many Rwandans from central Rwanda, Celestin joined the MDR political party during the multiparty politics of the early 1990s. When the MDR split between the Hutu

Power movement, loyal to the Hutu extremist elements of the Mouvement révolutionnaire national pour le développement (MRND) and Coalition pour la défense de la république (CDR) parties, and the moderates led by Faustin Twagiramungu, Celestin followed the moderates. Unbeknownst to Antoinette or her mother and siblings, he also became a secret member of the RPF. During the genocide, the Interahamwe militia repeatedly came to Celestin's house to kill him. Because he was perceived as an opponent of Hutu Power he was suspected of being an RPF accomplice (*umuyitso*) and was thus targeted for killing. Celestin fled to another region where anonymity, his "Hutu" looks, "Hutu" identity card, and friends protected him. When the genocide ended, Celestin returned home and became a local government official under the RPF-led regime.

Antoinette and Dismas and their children first directly experienced the chaos of war in 1992. At that time they were living and working in a rural area of Byumba prefecture. Unexpectedly, the RPF suddenly advanced into the region where they lived, and they were forced to flee with their children with bullets flying around them. They spent the next two years living a somewhat marginal existence as internally displaced persons in Kigali. Although the government provided them with temporary jobs and continued to pay them, the family was forced to live with Dismas's brother's family in cramped quarters. The civil war had displaced several hundred thousand Rwandans and provoked a housing crisis in Kigali, so affordable rental property was unavailable.

On another occasion, Antoinette explained how her appearance had caused problems during the genocide. When the genocide began, she and Dismas were living in the capital city, Kigali, with their children. As the RPF advanced on the city, they took the advice of Dismas's brother, a FAR soldier, and decided to flee. When they attempted to cross the city to join Dismas's brother, they were stopped at a roadblock. The Interahamwe militiamen refused to believe that Antoinette was Hutu, even though her identity card was marked "Hutu" and Dismas was there to vouch for her. Dismas tried to convince the militiamen that they should not kill Antoinette because his brother, the FAR officer, would be very angry. The Interahamwe allowed Dismas to go and find this brother while Antoinette waited with the children at the roadblock. Antoinette described the tense hours that she and the children spent at the roadblock waiting for Dismas's return. On several occasions the drunken Interahamwe threatened to kill them. After two hours Dismas returned with his brother, who escorted the family on the rest of their journey using his military credentials and rank to pass through the remaining barricades.

After the genocide, in 1996, Antoinette's father, Celestin, was promoted to a national-level government position. Suddenly, he was accused of genocide and imprisoned. He spent four years in prison and was eventually released in 2000. During the entire time he was imprisoned, Tutsi genocide survivors from his birthplace repeatedly lobbied the government for his release. They testified that he had protected Tutsi in 1990 and that he had tried to protect them during the genocide and himself became a target of the Interahamwe militias.

As for Antoinette and Dismas, they spent two years in the refugee camps in Zaire after the genocide. After the initial period of chaos, they lived a fairly good existence in the camps, thanks to their employment with international NGOs, until rumors spread that Antoinette's father was a member of the RPF and a local government official back in Rwanda. The family then faced threats from the Interahamwe militia, who retained control over the camps. Despite the threats, Antoinette and Dismas remained in the camps until they were attacked in 1996. As Antoinette explained, her husband's brother, the FAR officer, continued to influence her husband, convincing him that it was too dangerous to return to Rwanda.

Fortunately for the family, their camp was not among the first to be forcibly dismantled by the Alliance des forces démocratiques pour la libération du Congo-Zaïre (AFDL) and their allies, the RPA and the Ugandan army. As a result, the family fled in advance of the AFDL, along with Dismas's brother and the remaining FAR in the camp. Antoinette described to me their time in the rainforests following the forced closing of the camps:

> ANTOINETTE: After the camps were attacked I kept begging Dismas to come back home [to Rwanda], but his brother kept saying, "Stay with us. We'll win the war soon. You'll see." We would listen to the radio, announcements of where UNHCR [United Nations High Commissioner for Refugees] trucks were meeting refugees to transport them. But he kept telling Dismas that it was just a trick.[15]
> JENNIE BURNET: Were you in the forests the entire time?
> ANTOINETTE: For a long time.
> JENNIE: What did you eat?
> ANTOINETTE: The men would go and get things for us. At first they bought things. Then, when the money ran out, they would sell or trade our things for food. That's how I lost my wedding band. In the end we were starving. We went to a village and farmed for a family in exchange for food and a place to sleep. Me, Dismas, and the children . . . farmers in rags, with our hair a mess and our skin ashy! Finally, Dismas relented. He listened to me, and we came back here. We preferred to die at home where we could breathe rather than die choking in the forests of Congo.

Antoinette's final statement was echoed by many refugees who had been in the camps in Zaire. When describing their experiences in exile to me, they often said that the air in Zaire made them "choke" or described it as "bad," "heavy," or "unclean." In contrast, they would describe the air in Rwanda as "fresh," "clean," or "sweet," or they said that they could "breathe freely" in Rwanda. Many said that although they were scared out of their wits when returning to Rwanda, they enjoyed breathing the clean air of their home country. At first, I thought these descriptions reflected the poor air quality in the refugee camps or were a metaphor of exile. Yet as this genre of statements continued, even from refugees who had lived in towns rather than in refugee camps, I came to understand the statements as an embodiment of refugees' exile. Their bodies rejected their exile status and yearned for the sweet, fresh air of home.

Antoinette and Dismas managed to return to Rwanda with their nuclear family intact despite all the upheaval. Upon their return, they struggled to find a place to live, to find work, and to reestablish their lives. When Dismas and Antoinette returned from the refugee camps in Zaire, they were forced to live with Dismas's family in a rural zone in the North. During this period, Antoinette faced the relentless insults and persecution of her mother-in-law and sisters-in-law.

> ANTOINETTE: The worst was when we lived with them [during the insurgency in 1997 and 1999]. I had to listen to their insults morning, noon, and night. I couldn't say anything. My sisters-in-laws were even worse than they had been before. Perhaps they were jealous, since Dismas was still there.
> JENNIE BURNET: What do you mean? Were their husbands gone?
> ANTOINETTE: Yes. One husband was in prison. [Now] she doesn't know where he is. He escaped or died when the infiltrators [abacengezi] attacked the prison in 1998. The other one was a soldier before the war [genocide], so he never came back from Congo.

When I first met Antoinette in 1999, she and her husband were still unemployed, although they both had spent time at a reeducation camp (ingando) to qualify themselves to return to work.[16]

Antoinette's experiences highlight the complexity of identity and subjectivity in Rwanda. Although "Hutu," Antoinette at times suffered discrimination because of her "Tutsi" looks or because of her family's ties to the RPF. Although not recognized as a genocide survivor, Antoinette faced the threat of death at the hands of the Interahamwe's machetes. As a result, Antoinette understood in a limited sense the lasting psychological trauma of Tutsi genocide survivors. Nonetheless, she retained a belief that Hutu had been persecuted and discriminated against during the colonial period. Furthermore, she rejected the version of Rwandan history put forward by the postgenocide government. She refused the portrayal of the "social revolution" of

Hutu intellectuals in the late 1950s and early 1960s as a "bloody revolution" and straightforward oppression of Tutsi.

Civil War
(October 1, 1990–July 4, 1994)

The civil war began on October 1, 1990, when the RPF invaded from Uganda (Prunier 1997, 94). The RPF's origins lay in the hundreds of thousands of Rwandans living in exile in Uganda, Kenya, Tanzania, Burundi, and Zaire. Comprised primarily of Tutsi, the majority of refugees lived in Uganda (Reyntjens 1994, 25). The diaspora maintained social ties through cultural associations (Prunier 1997, 66). These refugees played a vital role in recruiting fighters, financing the armed struggle, and lobbying for political support.

With assistance from Zaire, France, and Belgium, the FAR pushed the RPF back to Akagera National Park in the far northeast of the country. The RPF suffered heavy losses and changed tactics to low-intensity guerrilla warfare. Thus began a prolonged civil war between the RPF rebels and the Rwandan military and Habyarimana's government. By 1993 the RPF occupied the northern third of the country. Hundreds of thousands of displaced civilians lived in crowded internally displaced persons camps or with relatives.

From the beginning of the war through the start of the genocide in April 1994, ordinary Rwandans faced violence at the hands of state authorities, civilian militias, and the RPF rebels. Civilians risked being caught in the crossfire of advancing battle lines, and women faced increased risks of sexual violence. The state under Habyarimana targeted Tutsi in general as well as opposition politicians, human rights activists, and journalists who were critical of the regime.[17] The Rwandan government regularly reported RPF killings of civilians, but these reports were exaggerated. Human Rights Watch confirmed some small-scale killings by the RPF in 1993, but most evidence indicates that the RPF was fairly restrained in its treatment of civilians, although they did execute known members of the Interahamwe and extremist Hutu political parties (HRW 1993, 23). The war created an atmosphere of insecurity among ordinary Rwandans and provided material for the emerging racist anti-Tutsi rhetoric of Hutu extremists.

The war gave President Habyarimana "the chance to exploit the invasion to consolidate [his] power base, which had been slipping" (Des Forges 1995, 45). A few days after the 1990 invasion, Habyarimana staged an attack on the capital, Kigali. Then the government jailed thousands of Tutsi and opposition politicians of all ethnic categories for "collaborating" with the RPF (Reyntjens 1994). The RPF provided the Habyarimana regime with a common enemy that was simultaneously external (RPF combatants and the

Rwandan exiles who supported them) and internal (embedded RPF rebels, Tutsi inside Rwanda whom Hutu extremists presumed to be RPF accomplices or sympathizers, and Hutu members of the political opposition). The enemy, embodied in the RPF and their "accomplices," meaning Tutsi civilians and Habyarimana political opponents, aided Hutu extremists in rallying segments of the population behind their anti-Tutsi program.

While the seeds of genocide existed in the population in the form of ethnic categories, ordinary Rwandan men and women had to be convinced that their Tutsi neighbors were the enemy. Hutu extremist media were key to spreading the ideology of genocide to the broader public. Private media outlets quickly multiplied with the advent of multiparty politics in 1991. While the independent media struggled to provide an alternative to the government, hate media outlets quickly emerged and nurtured a culture of fear, suspicion, and terror among the Rwandan population. They were backed by wealthy businessmen who had a vested interest in keeping Habyarimana in power and opposing any concessions with the RPF. The Hutu extremist media trumpeted overt hate speech against Tutsi with such persistence that it became the norm.

State actions to normalize violence established a culture and vocabulary of war and genocide. Rwandan citizens learned that state-sanctioned violence against "enemies," defined as all Tutsi, political opponents, human rights activists, and journalists, was normal. Fear inspired by the violence that was perpetrated by the FAR and the RPF and paranoia caused by the state's stranglehold on the media and flow of information terrorized the population. In this context, many everyday words and practices took on new meanings.

Many Rwandans came to equate "democracy" (*demokarasi*), meaning multiparty politics, with war, assassinations, communal violence, and eventually genocide.[18] Another term redefined in the Rwandans' vernacular was *umuganda* (communal labor), a monthly civic duty organized nationally and performed locally that included community development projects such as road maintenance, building school or government buildings, or cultivating crops for indigent community members. During the civil war, *umuganda* became a tool for mobilizing the population to "clear the bush," meaning to hunt down and kill RPF rebels or their "accomplices."

Another cultural change wrought by the war was directly related to the gendered aspects of the violence. In the past, Rwandan women did not wear undergarments. From the 1960s onward, educated women or women married to educated men began wearing European-style undergarments. Rwandan men, on the other hand, usually wore two undergarments: a tight-fitting pair of briefs with nylon sports shorts or boxer shorts (*umugondo*) on top. With the advent of the civil war in 1990, the general state of security in the country declined, and sexual assaults on women increased.

In response, government officials began to encourage women to wear *umugondo* as added "protection" against rape. These undergarments became so normalized for women that it is still common to find old women in the countryside digging under their skirts for money hidden in the pockets of their *umugondo*.

Genocide
(April 6–July 4, 1994)

The genocide began on the night of April 6, 1994, when the presidential plane, carrying President Habyarimana and President Cyprien Ntaryamira of Burundi, was shot down as it prepared to land at Grégoire Kayibanda International Airport near Kigali.[19] Within a few hours, elite military units known as the Presidential Guard began killing moderate Hutu members of the transitional government and prominent Tutsi whose names appeared on the preestablished lists that had been circulating for months (Des Forges 1999, 208; Straus 2006, 46–48).[20] Soldiers went from house to house executing whole families and searching for those trying to hide with friends or neighbors. In provincial capitals and rural communities where Hutu extremist political parties dominated, the slaughter began on April 7. Civilians not caught up in these initial waves of executions sat at home and waited to find out what was happening by listening to their radios. Along major roads in the capital city and provinces, the Interahamwe and the Impuzamugambi militias set up roadblocks. By April 8 Hutu Power elements had maneuvered a coup d'état and taken control of the interim government (Straus 2006, 46–47). They issued formal orders to kill all Tutsi and enemies of the state. Genocide became official government policy.

The strategies used to carry out the genocide shaped the violent terrain that Rwandans of all social categories negotiated. Beyond the operations to locate and eliminate preestablished targets described above, state authorities used several other strategies to perpetrate genocide, including large-scale massacres, roadblocks, communal labor, *ibitero* (killing squads), and sexual violence.

In previous episodes of ethnic violence, Tutsi had found safe haven in churches, hospitals, government offices, and schools. Once again, Tutsi, along with others who feared being targeted, made their way to these sites. Government officials encouraged them and promised to protect them. FAR soldiers, police, and militiamen organized attacks on the thousands of Tutsi gathered at these sites and enlisted local civilians to help in the killing (Des Forges 1999, 209). Large-scale massacres continued throughout the month of April. The attackers did not distinguish between Hutu and Tutsi at these sites; the victims' presence made them targets for elimination.

At the roadblocks throughout the country, Interahamwe militiamen along with men recruited from the community checked people's identity cards. People with "Tutsi" marked on their identity cards were executed immediately. The men at the barriers carefully scrutinized cards to make sure that they had not been altered. They examined people's faces and bodies in order to "expose" Tutsi who were trying to pass as Hutu (Des Forges 1999, 213). In cases where militia members suspected people had altered their identity cards, the militiamen interrogated them in order to determine whether they were Hutu or Tutsi. A Tutsi genocide survivor whose identity card was marked "Hutu" explained:

> They would look at my identity card and then start insulting me. "You Tutsi whore, you think you can fool us?!? Look at you! That nose! You may be dressed in rags and your hair may be nappy, but we can see you're too beautiful to be Hutu." I answered them, "Heh! You insult your sister like that! You think Hutu women can't be beautiful? Can't you see I live in Gikondo [a neighborhood infamous for the strength of the Hutu Power movement]! Do you think I could have gotten all the way here without someone killing me if I were Tutsi? Go ahead, kill me, but you'll be sorry when my family hears that my brothers killed me."
>
> That's how I did it. All the way to Gitarama. Sometimes they would beat me [with a stick] on the tops of my feet [in an attempt to make her confess that she was lying], or they would take my clothes. I was quite a sight. I arrived with only my underwear. (Author interview, 2000)

In another case, two sisters, Jolie and Carinne, born of a Hutu father and a Tutsi mother, were fleeing Kigali for Goma, Zaire. At the roadblocks they had trouble because the men would let Jolie pass, but they accused Carinne of lying about her ethnicity. Jolie screamed: "'But she's my sister, she's my sister!' But they wouldn't believe me. They said, 'You don't look alike! You with your Hutu nose, but her. She looks Tutsi. You can't be sisters!' We would stand there for hours trying to convince them that we were sisters. I would be crying and crying, begging for my sister's life. That's how it was." The roadblocks were an effective means of controlling the population's movement and catching Tutsi who were trying to hide.

In local communities, *ibitero* were organized by local officials who called the population to meetings or special *umuganda* (communal labor). As with regular *umuganda*, every household was expected to contribute one man. The *ibitero* searched for Tutsi trying to escape under cover of darkness and rooted out those hiding in banana plantations, forests, or underbrush. Many perpetrators reported that their first participation in the genocide was by hunting for Tutsi who were hiding (Mironko 2004). They later escalated their involvement and participated in killing.

Sexual violence and rape were significant strategies of genocide. While men and boys were executed immediately, soldiers and militiamen would sometimes spare women and girls. Both Tutsi and Hutu women became victims of sexual violence during the genocide, but Tutsi were targeted in a systematic fashion. Rape became a weapon of genocide used to destroy the Tutsi ethnic group as well as "to terrorize the community and warn all people of the futility of resistance—those targeted as victims as well as those who might wish to protect the intended targets" (Turshen 2001, 59). Interahamwe militiamen often raped or sexually tortured Tutsi women before killing them (HRW 1996a).

Beyond the physical brutality, sexual violence during the genocide became symbolic and psychosocial violence as well. Perpetrators some-times mutilated women during the rapes or before killing them by cutting off their breasts, puncturing the vagina with sharp objects, or disfiguring body parts such as long fingers or thin noses that looked "Tutsi" (Des Forges 1999, 215). Perpetrators targeted the normally privileged role of Rwandan women as mothers. Pregnant women were disemboweled, and their fetuses were cut out of their wombs. In other cases, Tutsi women were sexually enslaved by or "married" to Interahamwe militiamen in exchange for having their lives saved (Des Forges 1999; HRW 1996a). Some women who were gang-raped were told that bullets shouldn't be "wasted" on them because they would "die of AIDS," presumably contracted during the rapes (author interviews, 1999, 2000, 2002). Extremist rhetoric also targeted Tutsi beauty and desirability—militiamen were promised the opportunity for sexual intercourse with Tutsi women as a reward for their "work." Survivors frequently reported that perpetrators said that they wanted "to see if Tutsi women were like Hutu women" (HRW 1996a, 42). Many perpetrators insulted Tutsi women for "their supposed arrogance" while they were being raped, as Tutsi women were "said to scorn Hutu men" (Des Forges 1999, 215). Beauty as a marker of Tutsiness was so strong in the popular imagination that female Hutu who were "beautiful" risked being mistaken for Tutsi and raped, sexually tortured, or even killed (author interviews, 1998, 2000, 2002, 2009).[21]

A third aspect of rape as a strategy of genocide was the political economy of rape. During the genocide the Rwandan state sought to eliminate the Tutsi ethnic group through the systematic stripping of assets as well as through physical destruction. Tutsi homes and businesses were looted and burned; soldiers, militiamen, and civilian perpetrators were "rewarded" for their work with property taken from Tutsis. Within this context, Tutsi women and girls were often treated as property (Turshen 2001, 60). At a nursing school, Rwandan soldiers ordered the school director to give them women students as *umusanzu* (a contribution to the war effort) (Des Forges

1999, 216). At a Roman Catholic seminary soldiers took some young female employees as *umusanzu* and raped them (ibid., 494). Rape came to be known as *kubohoza* (to be liberated) during the genocide.[22] When used as a euphemism for rape during the genocide, it meant the liberation of Tutsi women from their Tutsiness.

The genocide planners recognized "the importance of women's productive and reproductive capacities" and shaped their strategies accordingly (Turshen 2001, 61). In some communities, local authorities worked to keep the Tutsi wives of Hutu men alive because "depriving a man of the productive and reproductive capacities of his wife harmed his interests" and could diminish these men's willingness to support the genocide (Des Forges 1999, 296). Women's land rights were sometimes part of the "reward" for militiamen. One survivor recounted how the head of the local militia gave her and her sisters to militiamen as "wives," and their father's land was split among the girls' "husbands" (HRW 1996a, 59–60). Finally, the genocide planners and perpetrators sought to destroy Tutsi women's reproductive labor by making them unacceptable to their community through rape or by physically destroying their capacity to bear children through mutilation (HRW 1996a, 54; Turshen 2001, 62).

As the genocide unfolded, the constellations of state power and violence evolved as local, national, and international constituencies reacted to the changing context. The genocide began immediately in communities where local administrators either "took public leadership of the killing campaign" or "collaborated reluctantly, from fear of losing their posts or their lives" (Des Forges 1999, 592). In others, where the local administrators opposed attacks against Tutsi, the genocide began more slowly. Administrators who opposed the genocide faced the threat of losing their own lives or of having their family members killed. Under this pressure many began to support genocide, while others were removed from office or killed. By the end of April, Des Forges (1999) estimates, perhaps half of the Tutsi population in Rwanda had been killed. When UN diplomats began to use the word "genocide" to describe what was happening in Rwanda, the interim government shifted from large-scale massacres to a smaller-scale approach of eliminating Tutsi more "discreetly" (ibid., 283).

As the FAR lost territory to the RPF in May and June, the interim government extended the campaign of killing to Tutsi women married to Hutu men and to their children and resumed large-scale massacres at the few sites where large groups of Tutsi remained (Des Forges 1999). In mid-June FAR soldiers and militiamen bussed in from neighboring regions renewed attacks against the tens of thousands of Tutsi who had taken refuge in the mountainous forest of Bisesero in Kibuye province. The interim government issued an order that the operation be finished by June 20, the date when

French soldiers were expected to arrive in the region (ibid., 219). Although these Tutsi had survived and fended off attacks since April, most of them died during these few days in June. When the French troops finally arrived on June 30, they found only eight hundred Tutsi who had survived (ibid., 681).

In most places in the country, the genocide stopped when RPA troops took control. As the RPF advanced, thousands of Rwandans fled in front of them, in part because of the Hutu Power government's propaganda against the RPF. These refugees were predominantly but not exclusively Hutu, as they included many Tutsi wives and mixed children and others who had successfully hidden their identities. Many others fled when ordered to by local officials or under threat from the militias. Over a million Rwandans fled the advancing RPA and crossed the border into eastern Zaire (present-day Congo) or western Tanzania (Prunier 1997, 297). Hundreds of thousands remained in Rwanda in the Zone turquoise, a "protected zone" for civilians in southwestern Rwanda set up by French troops who were sent in June 1994 (ibid., 290). Although Opération turquoise saved thousands of lives, many scholars and critics have criticized the mission because the French government refused to arrest the genocidal leaders who began to flood into the Zone turquoise as the Rwandan forces (FAR) continued to lose territory to the RPF (Des Forges 1999, 686). The vast majority of genocide planners and leaders from the national down to the commune level eventually fled the country into Zaire either through the Zone turquoise or through the northern route of FAR withdrawal via Gisenyi and Goma (Des Forges 1999; Prunier 1997).

The Government of National Unity
(1994–96)

The genocide ended when the RPF seized Kigali on July 4, 1994. Following its victory, the RPF swore in a new government it called the Government of National Unity on July 19 (Prunier 1997, 299). The new government followed many of the power-sharing provisions agreed upon in the Arusha Peace Accords except that the RPF took the posts formerly held by members of the MRND or CDR parties who had carried out the genocide. The RPF created the position of vice president, filled by RPF leader Paul Kagame (ibid., 300). Initially, it appeared that the RPF wanted to establish a government that would appear legitimate in the eyes of the population. Many observers, Rwandan and foreign alike, hoped that the RPF would fulfill its promises of national unity. While members of the RPF have frequently been portrayed as saviors and peacemakers, their rule has not been a universally positive experience for Rwandans regardless of their ethnicity.

The new government faced nearly insurmountable obstacles. As the FAR fled, soldiers, militiamen, and civilians looted anything of value from government offices, schools, health centers, and businesses and then destroyed what could not be removed. The leaders of the fleeing government had taken foreign currency and large amounts of Rwandan cash from the Rwandan National Bank (Prunier 1997, 306). In the cities there was no running water or electricity. In the countryside crops rotted in the fields because there was no one to harvest them. The majority of the population still inside the country was displaced. Although the new government was in place, it had little effective power, as officials lacked phones, vehicles, offices, and even pens and paper. The RPA was the real authority in the country (Prunier 1997).

Beyond the physical destruction, the Rwandan social fabric had been destroyed by the genocide. The basic familial and social relationships that normally form a cushion for individuals had been put under enormous strain or shattered by the genocide. Husbands had killed wives. Mothers had poisoned children. Brothers had denounced brothers-in-law. Godparents had abandoned godchildren. Neighbors had massacred neighbors. According to a report by the Emergency Project for Orphans' Care, 66 percent of Rwandan children had witnessed the violent death of their parents, and 88 percent of children had witnessed the death of someone they knew (quoted in Degni-Segui 1996, 11). An international human rights observer explained to me that the psychological trauma to children was obvious in the months after the genocide. When she drove down rural roads, the children who usually ran toward her car exuberantly yelling "Muzungu! Muzungu!" (Foreigner! Foreigner!) lay despondently on the side of the road barely looking as the vehicle passed.

The genocide brought about a dramatic demographic shift in the composition of Rwandan society. In 1995 Human Rights Watch (1996a) estimated that 70 percent of the population inside Rwanda was female. As internally displaced persons and refugees returned home, this demographic shift slowly began to return to normal. A demographic survey conducted in late 1996 and early 1997 established that the overall sex ratio (number of males per one hundred females) for the Rwandan population was eighty-six, meaning that women constituted 53.7 percent of the adult population, an abrupt shift from the estimate only one or two years earlier (ONAPO 1998, 18). While the 2002 Rwandan National Census reported the overall sex ratio as 91.25 (meaning that 52.2 percent of the total population was female, compared with 51.2 percent in 1991), the sex ratio for people seventeen years or older was 87.07 nationwide, a notably larger gap (Republic of Rwanda 2003, 17, 39). Although these overall figures may not sound very dramatic, in specific age brackets in specific communities the absence of men was noticeable. In my own census of a rural community in Butare prefecture in 2001, adult women comprised 55.6 percent of the adult population. Yet in the forty- to fifty-year age bracket, women were 65.4 percent.[23] The 2002 Rwandan National Census reported the lowest sex ratio (77.94) for those seventeen years of age or older in Kibuye prefecture (ibid., 39).

Beyond these dramatic demographic changes, the harsh material realities of postgenocide Rwanda created an entirely new context for kin and social relations. The civil war and genocide produced over two million refugees along with hundreds of thousands more internally displaced persons. The economic and physical infrastructure had been destroyed at every level. Many survivors had nothing left—no clothes to wear or food to cook, much less a pot in which to prepare it. Survivors, particularly women, found that "traditional" ways of life and modes of being were no longer possible. Many women found themselves as heads of household because their husbands were dead, in exile, in prison, or in military service with the RPF. Women took on new roles in the domestic and public spheres that Rwandan society had previously not ascribed to them, including everyday tasks customarily taboo for women like putting roofs on houses, constructing enclosures around houses, and milking cows, and roles in society, such as government administrator. Prior to the genocide, Rwandan law forbade women to engage in commercial activities, enter into contracts, or seek paid employment without authorization from their husbands (HRW 1996a, 22). In practice, many husbands (and even most husbands in the cities) allowed and even encouraged their wives to work because it benefited the whole family, but husbands often controlled their wives' salaries or revenue. Women-owned businesses were vulnerable, in practice and by law, to plunder by their husbands (whether to support the husbands' own businesses, their drinking, or even their mistresses) or to complete takeover (Jefremovas 2002, 97–108).

With the disruption in gender relations, some women found the freedom to pursue careers or commercial activities without these risks. Yet this opportunity to challenge customary notions of womanhood and women's roles in the family and community should not be portrayed too rosily, as some journalists and feminist policy analysts have tended to do. For peasant women in rural areas, the absence of husbands increased the burden of crushing poverty as well as social isolation. Farming without their husbands' labor resulted in a heavier workload and lower yields, and it reduced women's social status in the community, where no one had the time to hear about or assist with "widows' problems," as more than one widow told me. The lack of income from husbands' labor in the cash economy left widows and prisoners' families destitute, without the necessary cash to pay for health care or school fees.

For middle-class and elite women, their newfound "freedom" was bitter-sweet. Even the most successful businesswomen lamented the heavy burden of bearing sole financial responsibility for themselves and their children—not to mention the social, emotional, and psychological consequences of widowhood or single motherhood. As time went on, the most difficult burden for many was solitude. Many female genocide survivors reported that perpetrators who spared them said, "You will die from solitude" (Aghion 2002). In 2007 a genocide widow whose two surviving children were studying abroad wrote me, "I'm becoming old, and I'm bored a lot here [in the town where she lives]. I'm beginning to feel bad being alone." The understatement of her phrasing only emphasized her suffering. Another widow, who had had a series of intermittent, clandestine relationships with married men and even a Roman Catholic priest, stated her physical needs to me in a surprisingly straightforward declaration: "I burn for a man." Her expression of physical solitude in a Western idiom sounded like a direct challenge to Rwandan ideals of chastity and emotional reserve for women. The possibility that she could imagine stating her desires so matter-of-factly, in a way so antithetical to Rwandan cultural ideals of femininity, points to a transformation in subjectivity.

As soon as the RPF took Kigali on July 4, 1994, thousands of old caseload refugees who had been living in exile began returning to the country.[24] These returnees were composed primarily of Tutsi who had been exiled in several waves between 1959 and 1973. Among them was a second generation of refugees, many of whom had never lived inside the country. By 1993 an estimated six hundred thousand old caseload refugees lived in Uganda alone (Prunier 1997; Reyntjens 1994), with tens of thousands more in Burundi, Zaire, and Tanzania (Kumar et al. 1996, 91). The desire to return to Rwanda was a common feature among the old caseload refugees due to varying degrees of marginalization in their countries of asylum as well as fond memories of life "back home" (ibid.). By the end of 1997 approximately eight hundred thousand old caseload refugees had returned home, according to government sources (HRW 2001b, 65; Kumar et al. 1996, 91). After their arrival, old caseload refugees filled positions in the government as the RPA turned control over local areas to civilian authorities. Many genocide survivors, whether Tutsi or Hutu, were still too physically and emotionally traumatized to function on the job, and the majority of educated Hutu had fled into exile. Thus old caseload refugees were better qualified than other Rwandans who applied for government jobs. Old caseload refugees quickly became overrepresented in the government administration and on the staffs of international NGOs.

After the RPF victory, as genocide survivors and others who had fled in search of safety during the genocide returned to Rwanda, they found their homes destroyed or occupied by soldiers and old caseload refugees (Degni-Segui 1996; Prunier 1997). When owners returned, they encountered great difficulties in repossessing their property. In some cases, they met with threats, accusations of genocide, imprisonment, and even death instigated by the individuals who did not want to give up the property (African Rights 1996; Degni-Segui 1996, 28).

Insecurity reigned for months, and no one was spared. Genocide survivors faced attacks by genocide perpetrators who wanted to eliminate potential witnesses. Anyone (Tutsi or Hutu) involved in bringing genocide perpetrators to justice or perceived as supportive of genocide survivors, including local authorities, remained vulnerable to similar attacks. Survivors felt threatened by old caseload refugees or RPA soldiers who assumed that survivors must have been complicit in the genocide to survive. Old caseload refugees were vulnerable to killings perpetrated by genocide perpetrators or to incursions from the refugee camps across the border in Zaire or Tanzania (African Rights 1996; UNHRFOR 1997b). Hutu faced the burden of being presumed to be genocide perpetrators by virtue of their ethnic identity. The weak state infrastructure and severely handicapped justice system contributed to this globalization of guilt. In some communities, genocide survivors exacted revenge on Hutu by destroying their homes, taking their livestock, throwing stones at them, beating them with clubs, or killing them. Hutu who attempted to reclaim property risked being accused of genocide and being imprisoned in life-threatening conditions with little hope of a trial. Everyone risked falling victim to banditry, rape, or murder due to the general insecurity.

The population also faced human rights violations perpetrated by the RPA. After combat ended, RPA troops killed groups of unarmed civilians in eastern, central, and southern Rwanda (Des Forges 1999, 705). Human Rights Watch documented many such cases that occurred in 1994, as did a mission from the UN Human Rights Commission (Degni-Segui 1996; Des Forges 1999). Another common phenomenon was the arbitrary execution of people associated with the previous government, army, militias, or other groups perceived to be hostile to the RPF (Des Forges 1999, 709). The RPF authorities attributed these killings to aggrieved RPF soldiers who acted in isolated cases of revenge; however, a survivor of one massacre argued that it had been a methodical attack (ibid., 714). One genocide survivor who was sent by the RPA to an internally displaced persons camp in Byumba explained that the RPA soldiers killed groups of Hutu every day (author interview, 2005). She said that she did her best not to see or to know what was happening because she was afraid of being targeted herself (ibid.).

As incidents of human rights abuses by the RPA escalated, prominent members of the new government protested. Throughout 1995 prominent

Hutu members of the transitional government resigned and fled the country (*Dialogue* 1995a, 1995c, 1995f). The human rights situation continued to deteriorate. From October through December 1995 the number of arrests increased dramatically following the incursions of infiltrators (*abacengezi*) from the camps on Rwanda's borders. Targeted in these waves of arrests were local government administrators, teachers, NGO workers, former FAR soldiers, and Hutu businessmen (Degni-Segui 1996). Most of those arrested were not informed of the reasons for their arrest, nor were they formally charged. They languished in jail for years and eventually faced charges of genocide crimes.

Forced Closing of the Refugee Camps (October 1996–May 1997)

The mass exodus of refugees from Rwanda in 1994 instigated a humanitarian crisis, easily understandable to the international community. Whereas from April to July 1994 the UN, NGOs, and diplomatic community had been unable to agree how to intervene and stop the genocide, the sight of millions of men, women, and children huddled hungry, sick, or dying on lava rock in eastern Zaire elicited an almost singular and overwhelming response: "We must provide relief." Thus the vast majority of international aid in the aftermath of the genocide flowed into the refugee camps in Zaire and Tanzania instead of into Rwanda. The UNHCR and humanitarian agencies organized the camps according to geographic regions in Rwanda and used the former administrative structure to distribute relief. This policy had the unintended effect of reinforcing the authority of the former government, military, militia, and community leaders responsible for the genocide (Kumar et al. 1996, 92). Although human rights organizations, humanitarian agencies, the UNHCR, and the Rwandan government repeatedly demanded international intervention in the camps to separate armed elements or genocide perpetrators from unarmed or innocent civilians, the international community failed to act (HRW 1997, 7).

The deteriorating situation in Rwanda made it difficult for the 1.5 million refugees in eastern Zaire and western Tanzania to return home, as the violence legitimated their fears (Pottier 1996). Refugees who wanted to return home were threatened and coerced by camp leaders, who sought to maintain a large refugee population in order to prepare for an invasion of Rwanda (Kumar et al. 1996). In 1995 the Hutu extremists in the camps launched several attacks into Rwanda, killing hundreds of survivors and old caseload returnees (UNHRFOR 1997b, 1997c). As Hutu extremists gained an increasingly effective control over the camps and as the flow of arms into the camps increased (Kumar et al. 1996), the Rwandan government increased the urgency of its calls to close the camps in eastern Zaire and Tanzania.[25] Despite repeated warnings, the international community failed to take decisive action to end the stalemate so that the refugees could return home (Reyntjens 2009, 45–47).

The refugees in eastern Zaire increased instability in a region that had already experienced ethnic tensions for many years. North and South Kivu provinces were home to many Banyarwanda (ethnic Rwandans who were Zaire citizens) before the influx of refugees in 1994 (HRW 1997, 8).[26] Banyarwanda had been present in the region before the drawing of colonial boundaries, while others had migrated there during the twentieth century for economic or political reasons. The majority were considered to be "Hutu" (ibid.). In the early 1990s, civilian militias in Zaire, known as the Mai-Mai and Bangilima, had attacked Hutu and Tutsi Banyarwanda in the Kivus (ibid., 9). The influx of Rwandan refugees in 1994 exacerbated tensions between indigenous Banyarwanda and other Zaireans. The Hutu Power elements in the camps encouraged attacks on Tutsi in the Kivus.

In 1995 the RPA began recruiting Zairean Tutsi men and training them in combat (Reyntjens 2009, 48). In October 1996 a "Banyamulenge uprising" supported by the RPA began seizing territory in south Kivu (ibid., 50–52). At the time, the Rwandan government insisted that it did not have troops in Zaire and that the Banyamulenge were operating independently. The Banyamulenge and other Zairean Tutsi, joined by other armed opposition groups in Zaire, eventually formed a coalition known as the Alliance des forces démocratiques pour la libération du Congo-Zaïre (AFDL) (HRW 1997, 10). Under the cover of the "Banyamulenge uprising," the RPA undertook operations to eliminate the security threat posed by the camps. These operations involved direct shelling of the camps to force the refugees out (Reyntjens 2009, 51). Eyewitness reports indicate that the majority of these attacks seemed to be intended to forcibly disperse the refugees in the camps, presumably to "encourage" them to return home (HRW 1997, 10). A flood of over six hundred thousand refugees began crossing the border back into Rwanda almost immediately (UNHCHR 1997b, 13).

Yet hundreds of thousands of refugees fled in the opposite direction, into the rainforests of Zaire. AFDL soldiers killed thousands of civilian refugees who fled into the rainforests following the attacks on the camps (Reyntjens 2009, 93–99; Stearns and Borello 2011; UNHCHR 1997b, 12; 2010, 510–22). According to the 2010 "Report of the Mapping Exercise" by the United Nations High Commissioner for Human Rights, the victims numbered in the tens of thousands (2010, 31). Other tens of thousands of refugees died from exhaustion, starvation, malaria, cholera, or dysentery as a result of the AFDL's systematic blocking of international humanitarian assistance to the refugees (UNHCHR 1997b, 13; 2010, 510–22).

In the chaos of the refugees' initial return to Rwanda, UNHCR procedures for processing the refugees were abandoned. The continuous flood of humanity trudged back to their home communes under the direction of RPA soldiers. Upon arrival, they were held in temporary camps while the local authorities registered them. Authorities arrested thousands of returnees on genocide charges and sent them directly to prison to await trial. Other refugees returned to their homes but found them destroyed or occupied by genocide survivors or old caseload returnees. Local authorities arrested thousands more returnees in the months that followed as new accusations of genocide surfaced. While many of these accusations were based on truth, people made false accusations against some returnees to prevent them from reclaiming their homes.

The Insurgency in the Northwest
(1997–99)

From 1997 through 1999, the Rwandan population was caught between two sides of an insurgency: the infiltrators (*abacengezi*), comprised of former FAR soldiers, Interahamwe militia, and other people opposed to the Rwandan government, on the one side; and the Rwandan Patriotic Army, on the other. Many of these insurgents had been living in (and controlling) the refugee camps prior to the forcible closing of the camps. The insurgency eventually evolved into a coordinated effort to overthrow the Rwandan government. The *abacengezi* set up a command structure and operated out of bases in eastern Democratic Republic of Congo (Zaire's new name as of May 1997). In the northwestern prefectures of Gisenyi, Ruhengeri, Kibuye, and portions of Byumba, "disappearances," extrajudicial executions, and killings of unarmed civilians by the RPA and infiltrators devastated the population. By 1998 local civilian authorities had withdrawn from large zones in Gisenyi prefectures because they could not be assured of their own personal safety due to insurgent attacks. As a result, insurgency forces moved in and took control "to the extent that they [were] alleged to be running markets and distributing their own newsletters" (Amnesty International 1998, 14).

The civilian population was frequently caught in the crossfire between RPA and insurgency forces. The conflict also had a dramatic effect on Rwandans' livelihood. While thousands of Rwandans in the Bugesera region of southern rural Kigali prefecture faced starvation due to prolonged drought, many families in the northwest were prevented from planting, tending, or harvesting their crops by the fighting. Few vehicles were willing to take the risk of transporting goods from the northwest, and sacks of potatoes bound for market rotted on the sides of the national highway. In some cases, RPA soldiers ordered civilians to cut down their banana plantations to prevent the *abacengezi* from hiding in them (Amnesty International 1998).

Eventually, the RPA's counterinsurgency operations began to succeed. RPA troops fighting in the Congo (formerly Zaire) disrupted the infiltrators' ability to maneuver and receive supplies. Inside Rwanda, the government began moving the population into displacement camps to protect them from the insurgents and, more importantly, to keep civilians from supporting them (HRW 2001b, 17). In addition, the central government replaced some of the civilian authorities in the region with people better able to convince the population to side with the government. Finally, the RPA curbed its abusive treatment of the population in its counterinsurgency activities (Prendergast and Smock 1999). By mid-1998 government forces again controlled most of the country (HRW 2001b). The population in the north-western provinces began to feel as if they could live without constant fear of being attacked or killed.

In other regions, Rwandans lived in fear of the war "coming to them" (author interviews, 1998, 1999, 2000). Many Rwandans from the northwest relocated to Kigali or to other prefectures to escape the insurgency and counterinsurgency operations, but they met with constant suspicion and discrimination by local officials and residents. At identity checkpoints on main roads, young men of "fighting age" from the northwest were regularly detained and sometimes arrested or disappeared (Amnesty International 1998, 5). The "infiltrator problem" provided justification for the Rwandan government's continued control of information about and access to the northwest and for its strict security policies, which frequently resulted in serious human rights violations.

Conclusion

These successive waves of violence affected Rwandan women living every-where in the Great Lakes region in the 1990s. The civil war between October 1, 1990, and July 4, 1994, polarized ethnic categories and recalled previous episodes of violence targeting certain social categories—whether Tutsi generally, the nobility specifically, or members of certain political parties—and mythico-histories of marginalization of other social categories—whether Hutu generally or Banyanduga or Bakiga specifically—by the state. The changing constellations of state power during the 1990s and earlier structured the ways women experienced violence. At times certain categories of women were targeted by state authorities, at others by an armed and organized opposition, and at others by armed mobs of civilians—their neighbors and kin. Throughout the 1990s women of all ethnicities had to discern the political terrain of the moment so that they could navigate their way through the violence to survival. Rwandan women's apprehension of violence in the present and the entities who used it to achieve political ends was structured by women's interpretations of the past, both their personal experiences and the country's political history, and structured the ways they remembered violence in the future. Chapters 2, 3, and 4 examine the ways women remember the past, the relationships between memory and silence, and women's contestation of state-sponsored memory practices.

2

Remembering Genocide

Lived Memory and National Mourning

It is difficult to overestimate the physical, social, emotional, and psychological devastation of the 1994 genocide in Rwanda. Rwandan women found themselves in a horrifying situation: the hills, fields, and churches were full of corpses; husbands, children, brothers, sisters, parents, cousins, and neighbors had been hunted like quarry and slaughtered; women had lost all their material possessions—their homes, clothing, farming implements, and cooking pots; government buildings had been looted and destroyed. The harsh material realities of postgenocide Rwanda created an entirely new context for kin and social relations. The approximately six million civilians who remained in Rwanda, including several thousand genocide survivors who were physically and psychologically traumatized, had to pick up the pieces of their lives with little assistance from international aid agencies. Initially, the population was in a state of shock as a result of the devastation. Many survivors were utterly incapacitated by their mental and emotional states. A Catholic priest, himself a genocide survivor, described his arrival at a rural parish in southern Rwanda: "The bishop sent me here in November 1994 to give Mass. When I arrived the church was full of survivors—women and children. They were staying here. When I spoke to them, they didn't even look up. They were empty—physically and spiritually. They had nothing to eat, no soap to wash with, nowhere to live. I realized they could not receive Mass, not in the state they were in. They weren't even human anymore."

While cultural traditions of mourning may be impossible to practice in the wake of genocide, Rwandans have improvised their own means to put aside their grief and go on living. Some have moved to live in a new place to avoid remembering. Others remarried or gave birth to new children. By burying themselves in the minutiae of everyday life, a life that slowly regained normalcy with the passage of time, they succeeded at least partially in keeping their memories and the negative emotions attached to them—sadness, anger, guilt, and hatred—at bay. In a sense, Rwandan women have crafted a form of collective amnesia vis-à-vis the "events of 1994," as many Rwandans refer to them.[1] Yet sometimes the unexpectedness of everyday life (the recognition of a moment in time, a place, a sound, an object, an action, or a confluence of these and other factors) breaks through this amnesia and transports someone back to the genocide, to a place of violence, fear, and terror. These remembrances are embedded in everyday life and thus impossible to control completely.[2]

One ethnographic example illustrates the intrusion of lived memories into everyday life and how individual mourning becomes political. Immaculée lost her husband the same day the genocide started in their community in southern Rwanda on April 21, 1994. Immaculée hid with her children for several weeks at a neighbor's house until she decided to try to escape to the Zone turquoise, a humanitarian zone controlled by French soldiers. A friend found them identity cards marked "Hutu," so Immaculée and the children attempted to travel by taxi-bus, hoping to blend in and avoid drawing attention to themselves. When the taxi-bus arrived at a roadblock near her husband's birthplace, the Interahamwe stopped the bus to check the passengers' identity cards. One of the men recognized Immaculée's sons, who greatly resembled their father, and forced the family to get off the bus. Immaculée pleaded for their lives for a long time. The negotiations ended when her oldest son said, "Mom, let them kill us so that you [Immaculée and her daughters] may live." The Interahamwe butchered her sons with machetes and forced Immaculée and her daughters to watch. The Interahamwe then told them to leave, saying, "Let the others finish you off. We've worked enough."

After the genocide, Immaculée rebuilt her life "from less than nothing," as she put it. She opened a shop in a provincial town as she and her husband had planned before the genocide. Over many years, she built it into a successful business. Like many survivors, Immaculée refused to join a survivors' organization because she disliked their political agenda. Immaculée preferred to share her grief privately with her daughters because "we know what we have suffered. We survived it together." Immaculée once explained her refusal to give me an interview about her experiences during the genocide in similar terms. She said that she only discussed "those things" with her daughters because they understood what they had survived together. On another occasion she commented on my description of a friend who categorically refused to talk about the "events of 1994." She said, "Many of us don't like to talk about those times. If I think about that, I fear that I might go crazy for good. Someday, they'll find me up on the roof, naked, screaming hysterically. The girls and I share those things between us because we don't need to explain [it to each other]. We know what happened."

Immaculée's burden was further exacerbated by public and private accusations that she must have a secret lover who was the "real" force behind her business success. Although women have been successful in business since before the genocide, their success was presumed to be predicated on men, usually husbands, fathers, or brothers.[3] Women's economic lives were circumscribed by contemporary interpretations of patrilineal inheritance systems whereby women remained economically harnessed to economic units controlled by male relatives. The increasing monetization of the Rwandan economy under the colonial state further concentrated economic decision making in the hands of men and relegated women to the vital (yet disrespected) domain of overseeing the household economy by cultivating foods (Jefremovas 1991, 2002). In the postcolonial era, Rwandan law codified male economic control by requiring women to seek permission from their husbands (or fathers) to take paid employment, to open a bank account, to take out a loan, or to open a business.

The dramatic demographic shift, discussed in the previous chapter, magnified the impact of these constraints as wives, widows, and daughters found themselves without the protection of husbands, fathers, and brothers, who assured women's rights under the customary land-tenure system (Burnet and RISD 2003). In this context, the gendered constraints on access and control of the means of production gave rise to a social crisis. Genocide widows, in particular, were burdened with securing economic security (or at least a livelihood) for themselves and their children, yet they did not have men on whom they could rely for protection because their fathers, husbands, and brothers were dead. Before the genocide, gendered social discourses kept businesswomen "in line" by equating economic power with loose sexual morality (Jefremovas 1991, 2002). These discourses continued to operate after the genocide, placing widows, particularly genocide widows, in a double bind: they could live on their own and endure salacious rumors of their illicit affairs, or they could have illicit affairs and endure the same rumors. Because the primary purpose of marriage in the Rwandan social imagination is to have children, marriage was not possible for widows beyond their reproductive years. If a widow sought a companion, she could choose from married men, Catholic priests, or gigolos (*uwinjira*, a man who enters the home of a widow and fulfills the role of a husband), who lived off the widow's property and income.[4]

In Immaculée's case, rumors stated that she had a powerful lover who assured the success of her business. Immaculée was well aware of the rumors, and she joked about them with her regular customers. Certain clients would facetiously ask how "*monsieur*" was doing, and Immaculée would respond laughingly, "Very well, thank you." It was when I overheard one such exchange that I became aware of the situation. As Immaculée explained, "It's the ones [men] I've refused who believe in him [her imaginary lover] the most. They don't understand how I can live like this [all alone and self-sufficient]. They can't understand that I live for my daughters now." The rumors persisted despite the fact that Immaculée was careful about when and where she paid social visits and whom she received in her home. Furthermore, Immaculée rarely found the time to be away from her shop, and thus she could have had little opportunity to see her "lover" anyway.

In 2001 Immaculée proudly gave me a tour of her new house that she had built after seven years of sacrifice and saving. In each room she stopped to explain the purpose and rationale behind the design of the room. When we arrived in her bedroom, she motioned at the single bed and said, laughing softly instead of crying:

> Jennie, you may think I'm crazy; many people do. Since I moved from my tiny house [she had been living in a small annex that used to be a storage shed], people think that I should buy a double [bed]. The truth is I can't sleep in a double. (*She shook her head.*)
> When I went to Kampala last, they gave me a hotel room with a double bed. I didn't sleep at all that night. You know I have trouble sleeping anyways—I only sleep when I fall in bed exhausted. But that night in the double bed, I thought my heart would explode and suffocate me. No, me . . . I choose to sleep in a single bed so that I don't remember.

It was clear to me that the empty bed brought back memories of her dead husband and, by proxy, her dead children. By filling her everyday life with other things (her business, her daughters, her house) and by limiting the size of her bed, she could forget things too painful to remember. Yet it was clear to me from what she said and what she left unsaid that a half-empty bed embodied far more than the absence of her husband. This space evoked all her burdens (emotional, financial, and physical) and provoked vivid memories of her husband's and sons' murders as well as her and her daughters' fear and anguish. Further, her empty bed was the focus of other people's criticism on a daily basis. For Immaculée, the simple act of getting in bed, something we do every day, became a political act problematizing her survivor status and her ambivalent success as a businesswoman. To understand the intensity of memory evoked in Rwandans like Immaculée by everyday objects requires some examination of the relationship between time, place, objects, and memory.

Taussig describes the everyday as a "knowledge that lies as much in the objects and spaces of observation as in the body and mind of the observer" (1992, 141). Thus, memories do not reside only in the minds of survivors; they inhabit the landscape, objects, habits, and practices that constitute everyday life. According to Taussig, the power of the everyday lies in the interplay between "tactility" and distraction. It is when we really feel everyday objects (their texture, their weight), which normally we touch with the distraction of habit, that they can become dynamic evocations of the past. The Rwandan spatiotemporal landscape consists of a piling up of memories in places, objects, and bodies. At any moment, a simulacrum between past and present can transport a person back in time. Memories live in the landscape as much as they live in people's minds.

Thus Rwandans cling to a normalized reality, where the genocide and war do not exist. In an effort to return to the routine of everyday life, an amnesiac veneer has covered over the metaphysical remains of genocide much in the same way that the physical signs of the genocide have largely been covered over through the necessary repairing of roads, buildings, and other infrastructure. While survivors exhibited visible signs of suffering in the months following the genocide, through the return to the routines of everyday life and the avoidance of reminders, little by little and with great effort they have placed boundaries around and cordoned off "the genocide" from their everyday lives. Understandably, constantly remembering the machetes, screams, blood, bodies, bombs, and other material realities of genocide would incapacitate them; there are those who have never been able to forget these things or return to the normalcy of everyday life. These survivors lead a marginal life, labeled "insane," "addled," or "traumatized."

Encounters between everyday practices and the tactility of remembrances constitute a living memory of the genocide embodied in survivors as well as in the physical and spatiotemporal landscapes they inhabit. While these individual remembrances are intensely personal, they are inherently political because they articulate with multiple discourses about the individual, about the genocide, and about national history. The RPF-led government has a vested interest in controlling how the genocide is remembered.[5] As discussed later in this chapter, the government attempts to control the remembrance of the genocide through nationalized mourning and genocide memorial sites.

Resisting the Narrative Form: Time and Memory

During my multiple field trips between 1997 and 2011, I found that Rwandans' willingness to talk about and remember the genocide changed. As the genocide receded further into the past, fewer survivors were willing (or able) to recount their stories as detailed narratives. On my first trip in 1997, I found several genocide survivors willing to talk openly about their experiences during the genocide. In particular, members of genocide widows' associations seemed compelled to give testimony about what they had survived. Yet some genocide survivors were unwilling or unable to speak at length or in narrative form about their experiences.

Understanding the reluctance of some Rwandan women to recount their experiences during the genocide in narrative form should take into account the political context in 1997. Between November 1996 and May 1997 over a million Rwandans returned from exile in Zaire and Tanzania. Their return was not voluntary; it occurred in the midst of military operations by the RPA in eastern Zaire that included bombardments of refugee camps. The atmosphere during my first trip to Rwanda in 1997 was one of tension, animosity, and fear bordering on paranoia. Genocide survivors feared additional massacres at the hands of the returnees, and the new returnees feared reprisals by genocide survivors and RPA soldiers. As a result, few people dared speak frankly in my interviews. The refugees who had recently returned from exile were reluctant to be interviewed at all. Most Hutu members of a rural women's development association answered my questions with one-word responses.

The survivors who gave lengthy testimony in 1997 seemed to be severely traumatized by their experiences and had not yet been able to go on with their lives. As one of the leaders of a genocide survivor association explained to me, "These women don't have anything; they lost everything. They don't know what to do. They don't know how to live." At the time, I was conducting a survey on the economic impact of the genocide with a Rwandan women's development organization. With the translation assistance of a Rwandan university student, I administered a questionnaire with open-ended questions. Most interviews lasted twenty minutes, but one old woman spoke for more than two hours when I asked what had happened in 1994. Once her narrative about her experiences started, it did not stop. As she spoke, she sometimes hid her face in her shawl or wiped her tears on its hem. As she continued, the assistant translated less and less, until she eventually stopped translating altogether. I became increasingly frustrated because I could not, at that point, understand a word of what the woman was saying. When the old woman finished, she said, "Thank you for caring enough to listen to me."

After the interview, I asked my assistant why she had stopped translating. Her answer angered me: "Everything she was saying wasn't important. She wasn't answering any of the questions [on the survey]." While on one level her response reflected her narrow view of research and how it should be conducted, on another level I suspect she was hiding her real motivation. In retrospect, I believe that she may have found the old woman's harrowing story overwhelming and could not find the words to translate it. Or perhaps as the daughter of a local government official who was Hutu, she feared the woman's testimony could implicate her father directly or indirectly.

When I returned to Rwanda in 1998, I found even fewer genocide survivors willing to talk in depth about the genocide. Instead, I waited for their stories to emerge in the course of everyday life or when they made the conscious decision to relate them to me. During a visit to a family in Kigali in 1997, I noticed a picture of their four sons in a prominent place in the living room. The father, Fidele, explained to me: "It is the only picture we still have. I had it in my pocket while I was hiding. After [the genocide], I asked a foreigner who works at [an international NGO] to enlarge it for us. I put it there so that we can always see them and get used to the idea that they aren't with us anymore [i.e., that they are dead]." In 1997 I had learned the basic outlines of Fidele's survival story. When the genocide began, he worked as a cook for the foreign members of an international NGO in Kigali. His wife and children lived on the hill where he was born and where he had a farm next to his parents' and brothers' homesteads. When Belgian paratroopers evacuated his employers in the first week of the genocide, they left him with food, money, a small radio, and batteries. He spent the next four months hiding in the roof of his employers' house, in the yard, and wherever necessary to avoid the Interahamwe and soldiers who were hunting Tutsi. When he thought it was safe, he listened to the radio, alternating between the state-run Radio Rwanda, which was broadcasting messages supported by the interim government responsible for the genocide, the privately owned Radio-télévision des mille collines (RTLM), which was the mouthpiece of Hutu extremism and helped coordinate killings during the genocide, and the "voice of the RPF," Radio Muhabura, which broadcast information about the RPF's progress in the civil war so that Tutsi survivors knew where to flee.[6] Fidele attempted to interpret information from the three partisan sources to figure out what was happening. Even though he had food, most of the time he could not eat because he was too anxious— worried about his family, afraid of being discovered, or terrorized by the announcements on Radio Rwanda and RTLM calling for the deaths of Tutsi in coded language.

The family did not share the story of how their sons had died until I returned in 1999. By that time, it seemed that the family was convinced that I was genuinely committed to trying to understand survivors' experiences. They had seen me leave and return twice and maintain contact during my absences through letters and faxes. Fidele, who knew that my research focused on women, arranged for me to interview his wife, Oliva, at their home on a Saturday afternoon. Since I was still learning Kinyarwanda, he offered to translate. Oliva recounted how she had survived the genocide.

In April 1994 Oliva was living in her husband's birthplace next to her in-laws. She cultivated the fields that belonged to her husband and took care of their six children. At the time, she was nine months pregnant. On April 7 she began to feel the early pains of labor. When it became clear that she and the children needed to flee for their own safety on April 9, she was in full labor. A Hutu neighbor took Oliva and hid her at her house. The neighbor helped deliver the baby, a boy, during the early-morning hours of April 10. The children were dispersed among neighbors so as not to attract attention. During the daytime on April 10, Oliva's friend heard rumors that Oliva's in-laws had been killed near their home by a group of local men enlisted through communal labor (*umuganda*). The next day, the same men began a house-to-house search. The friend hid Oliva and the baby in a tiny stock-room behind large granary baskets filled with beans and maize. After a week, it became too dangerous for Oliva and the children to remain in the region, as local residents participating in *umuganda* knew that Oliva and the children had not yet been killed.

Oliva left with the baby, her four sons, and her two daughters. They managed to travel on foot to her home commune in Butare. At each road-block she explained to the Interahamwe that she had lost her identity card and that she was headed home to Butare. Once they arrived in Butare, Oliva discovered that the genocide had not yet started there. She and the children stayed with her parents and hoped that the insanity would end soon. As they had always had good relations with their neighbors, Oliva's parents could not believe that the massacres occurring around the country would ever come home to their community.

Tragically, they were wrong. On April 21, the day after the central government replaced the Butare prefect, who had refused to implement the genocide, with a Hutu Power loyalist, all residents in Oliva's parents' commune were called to a meeting. At the meeting, local officials separated out the Tutsi, who were forced to stand in a line in the middle of the road. They stood there for hours. Oliva had the baby strapped to her back, and her four sons and two daughters began to complain of thirst and fatigue. Then the officials began to separate out the men and boys from the women and girls. Oliva begged them to let her leave with her sons, but the men refused. They led the boys away with the other men. Oliva managed to keep the baby by saying that he was a girl. That was the last that Oliva and her daughters saw of the boys. Oliva stopped her story there. It seemed that she did not feel that the rest of her survival story was important. She seemed to view her sons' deaths as her personal failure as a mother to protect them.

By the time of my return to Rwanda in 1999 to conduct research full-time for a year, virtually no one was willing to be interviewed directly about their experiences of the genocide with the exception of a few people like Oliva. Nonetheless, some women shared their stories on their own terms outside formal interviews. The moments when they would tell their stories were unpredictable. It seemed as if their stories chose to tell themselves. A place, a moment such as a time of day, or a presence, usually of a person but sometimes of a feeling or maybe a ghost (*umuzimu*), would inspire them to speak. Most often, their stories came to me in snippets or through silences evoked unwillingly by moments, places, or objects.

On one occasion, a genocide survivor who was standing in the yard of my house in my rural field site suddenly fell down and fainted. My research assistant and I ran to her side, and we tried to rouse her. She awoke quickly. We asked her what had happened, and she pointed at the gardener, who had just entered the enclosure carrying a machete. He had just come from cutting firewood. The woman explained that when she saw the machete an image from the genocide flashed before her eyes. She then lost consciousness and fell. Similar situations occurred on a regular basis. One evening several neighbors came to visit me at home. We were sitting in the living room. They were all genocide survivors, and two of them lived on a neighboring hill. A woman who lived next door to me began to recount part of her survival story—a moment after the massacre at the parish church had started and she was fleeing through a forest. She pointed at the man and woman from the neighboring hill: "I remember when I was in the forest in the valley, I saw the two of you. We were all running toward the Kanyaru [the river that forms the border between Rwanda and Burundi]. I hadn't thought of that moment before seeing you here." The group went on to recount other incidents from their flights toward safety in Burundi.

On a few occasions, women intentionally broke their silence and recounted their experiences at length. As with the stories that slipped out unintentionally in the course of everyday life, I was rarely prepared for these moments. One such story illustrates the unexpectedness of these narratives and reveals some of the motivations women had to share their experiences of violence. Seraphine was a member of a national women's organization that collaborated with me in my research. When introducing me to others, she positioned herself as my fictive kin, since she was a distant relative of a family with whom I had lived for a few months. For months, Seraphine insisted that I come to visit her at home, but it took us a long time to find a convenient date. Finally, one Saturday I made my way to her house at the top of a hill on the edge of Kigali. I had had a long and tiring week conducting surveys in the provinces, so I was looking forward to sharing a relaxing afternoon with Seraphine and her family and take a break from research.

Upon my arrival Seraphine offered me a drink while I sat in the living room with her husband. I attempted to make small talk with her husband, but he did not seem interested in talking with me. He drank his beer in silence and occasionally looked around nervously. In between her last-minute preparations for the meal, Seraphine came and sat with us. When her oldest daughter and son-in-law arrived, we sat down to eat. Toward the end of the meal, Seraphine's husband got up abruptly and left the table. A pained look crossed Seraphine's face, and she exchanged knowing glances with her daughter. I understood that something peculiar was going on but had no idea what. After the meal, we sat and talked for a while. Seraphine's daughter and son-in-law soon left. Then I started to make my own excuses to leave, saying I needed to go home to rest. Seraphine begged me to stay and invited me to take a nap. Although I did not particularly feel like staying, I accepted her invitation because of the tone of her voice.

She took me to a room where I could rest. She closed the windows, drew the curtains, and waited for me to lie down. She then lit a candle, which seemed to be an odd thing to do, since it was in the middle of the afternoon. Then she began talking: "Jennie, I've been waiting so long for you to come. We're [the members of the women's organization] so happy that you're here doing your research. We want to help you as much as we can. I have something to tell you—for your research project. It's something I haven't told anyone—not even the women at [name of the women's organization]. It's something hard for me to talk about, but it's important for you to know how it really was, what really happened." As she was talking, I started to feel a sense of dread. I was not emotionally prepared to listen to her story about what happened during the genocide—I was tired, and I had planned the afternoon to be a break from research. Seraphine spoke in French, and I listened to her story without taking notes because I did not have a notebook or a pen with me. As she spoke, I occasionally asked questions when I did not understand something. I reconstructed the narrative presented here later the same day in my field notes.

Seraphine continued her story:

> The day after Habyarimana's plane went down they called all the men in the neighborhood to a meeting. I was afraid for my husband to go because he's Tutsi, and the rumors had been going around for weeks that something bad was about to happen. In the afternoon, the Presidential Guard came to the house. They asked to see everyone's identity cards. They looked at them and asked whether anyone was staying with us. We said no, and then they left.
>
> By evening my husband still hadn't come back from the meeting, so I knew something terrible had happened. Late at night, I heard a quiet knock at the door. A neighbor whispered desperately for me to open the door quickly. He and another man were carrying my husband. At the meeting, they had separated out the Tutsi to kill them. My husband had been hit in the head with a spiked club, but he wasn't dead. My neighbors had found him and brought him home.
>
> We put him in a bedroom and bandaged his head. One of the men went and found a doctor we could trust. He came to the house and examined my husband. He said that he was in a coma. All we could do was to wait and see whether he woke up or died.
>
> We moved him to the kitchen storage room to hide him. I explained to the children that they must say that their father was dead if anyone asked. As the war continued, I stayed mostly here at the house so that when the Interahamwe and soldiers came, I could keep them from finding my husband.
>
> One day, General ———— came to the house with a group of soldiers. When he first came, I thought he was just visiting. But it became clear that he wasn't here for a simple social call—it was late, after all. He brought me here [*she pointed at the floor*]. He told me that I could have sex either willingly or by force—it was up to me.
>
> [*At this point in her story, Seraphine's voice began to quaver, and her eyes filled with tears.*] What could I do? My husband was still alive. My children were in the next room. [*Long pause.*] I took off my clothes and lay on the bed and waited for it to be over. Then he left with the soldiers. After that, the Interahamwe and soldiers stopped coming to search the house. The general came back whenever he wanted.

In her story as she told it to me, what Seraphine left unsaid but understood is just as important as what she told me. In the first paragraph, Seraphine reveals her husband's ethnicity to me, contravening postgenocide political correctness where it was forbidden to talk about ethnicity. Before she told me this information, I did not know the ethnicity of Seraphine or her husband. From her statement and the context of the rest of her story, I surmised that

Seraphine was Hutu and her husband was Tutsi. When Seraphine talks about the identity cards, it is clear that her and her children's identity cards were marked Hutu, or they would have been killed immediately. When Seraphine said that she remained at the house to prevent the Interahamwe from finding her husband, it was unclear how she managed this during house searches. Even if her husband was hidden in the kitchen storage room, the Interahamwe could have easily found him during a routine search. Thus, I assume, based on the testimony of others who did the same thing, that she bribed the Interahamwe to keep them from searching the entire house.

In the last paragraph, Seraphine explains her decision to have sex "willingly" with the general. When she said, "My husband was still alive," Seraphine seemed to imply that the general knew that her husband was alive and in the house and was using this situation to force Seraphine to comply. When she added that her children were in the next room, I understood that she did not want the children to hear a struggle because they would be frightened and upset or might try to defend her and risk being killed.

In the fourth paragraph, Seraphine refers to the genocide as "the war." When she recounted her story to me in 2000, it was common for ordinary Rwandans to refer to the genocide as either "the war," because they viewed the genocide as an extension of the civil war, or as "the events of 1994," because they intentionally wanted to avoid characterizing the violence as either a war or genocide. Over the years, Rwandans' language has become standardized under the influence of state discourse and nation-building practices. When I conducted interviews about the genocide and civil war in 2011, interviewees became visibly stressed when I used the words "civil war" to talk about the period between 1990 and 1993. In Rwanda today, citizens have learned to talk about "the Tutsi genocide" only, and the civil war is subsumed within it and erased from public discourse.

After Seraphine told her story, we sat in silence for a long time. Then I asked her whether anyone knew what had happened to her. She explained that her oldest son had tried to ask her what had happened after the general left, but she had refused to answer his questions. She suspected that the children knew ("They were in the house, after all," she interjected), but they never discussed it. She said that after the genocide, once her husband woke up from his coma, she told him. She said, "He's a good man. He said that it wasn't my fault. He understood that there wasn't anything that I could have done. I'm lucky." Here Seraphine referred to the reality that many husbands abandoned wives who had been raped in the genocide. She explained that probably the neighbors suspected what had happened, but she never told them, and they never dared say anything to her. Seraphine concluded her story by explaining why she chose to tell me:

I wanted you to hear how it was for us. [I understood "us" to be Hutu women married to Tutsi men.] I am a survivor even if people don't see it. Since the genocide, my husband isn't right in the head. That's why he acts so strange [referring to his behavior earlier that day]. He still has problems; he can't concentrate; he can't work. So everything is up to me. I have my husband— and I thank God for that—but it's up to me to find the children's tuition and everything else.

Seraphine's story and her deliberate and calculated choice to share it with me illustrate the complex relationship between narrative, time, and memory. Based on what Seraphine told me, I understood that she wanted to help me in my research, but this was not the only reason she spoke. Perhaps she was motivated by the desire for her story to be known, albeit anonymously. Maybe she was motivated by the Rwandan principle that every gift must be returned.[7] By sharing her story, she indebted me to her for a favor for which she has yet to ask.

Most women became less willing to recount their experiences the further the genocide receded into the past. Yet when they saw a reason for sharing their story, whether for justice, for history, or for setting the record straight, they chose to share it. Exercising their agency by controlling when, how, and to whom to tell their stories restored the dignity stolen from them. As a researcher, I did my best to respect these choices for ethical and moral reasons. Ethically, I could not push women to tell me their stories since I was not a clinical psychologist and was not qualified to engage in a therapeutic relationship. Morally, I felt compelled to grant them the little agency they had and to maintain the dignity of their memories. Despite Seraphine's decisions to remember and to tell, the lived memory of the genocide is not easily contained or cordoned off. It is embedded in everyday life, making it difficult for survivors to compartmentalize it. In the next section, I discuss how memory of violent experiences is an embodied practice.

Lived Memory

Lived memory consists of at least three different phenomena: physical scars on bodies, physical scars on the landscape, and metaphysical scars that connect people's emotions or mind and memories to space and time. Scarry (1985, 13) explains that the imagery of the physical injury to the body such as a broken bone is one of the ways that pain is expressed. Similarly, in Rwanda the physical marks that remain on bodies constitute an intrusion of the genocide into everyday experience. For survivors who bear the physical marks of the genocide in the form of scars from machetes, bullet wounds, or missing limbs, the genocide's empirical reality is inscribed on their bodies. Although always present, these markings can be forgotten or repressed: normalized by the routines of daily life, misread by observers, or hidden from view.

A woman I interviewed from a rural community in southern Rwanda was missing a finger and half her thumb on her right hand. Most of the time she hid her hand from view in the shawl she wore around her shoulders. I first became aware of her deficit when I met her. We crossed paths one day as I was walking home. As we shook hands in greeting, my hand tingled in recognition of her misshapen hand. Many weeks later, when I visited her, she shared her survival story with me. She explained that at some point when she was fleeing the massacre at the church where she had taken refuge, she was shot. A bullet removed her ring finger, and others injured her shoulder and her leg. She explained that she did not know at what moment she had been shot. In her fear, she ran through the forest. She eventually realized that she was covered in blood. As she continued her flight toward Burundi, a woman whom she did not know gave her new clothes so that she could take off her blood-soaked ones. When she arrived in Burundi, a "nice foreign [*umuzungu*] doctor," as she described him, closed the empty space between her remaining fingers with sutures. She laughed and held up her hand to show me the way in which her fingers curved in over the empty space. She told me that she could no longer hold a hoe, so she relied on her surviving daughter to cultivate. Despite what she said, I often saw her returning from her fields with a hoe in one hand and a heavy load of fire-wood or a jerrican of water on her head. The routines of everyday life hid her misshapen hand from view and normalized her deformity. Had we not shaken hands, I might have never noticed.

While some physical scars became hidden by routine, others were misread by the observer. A businessman among a group of friends I met regularly had scars on his scalp. I had noticed them, but I had assumed that they were due to a car accident. He had grown up in Burundi, so I assumed he was outside Rwanda during the genocide. One evening in 2001 someone in the group made a joke: "His head is so hard, even the Interahamwe's machetes couldn't break it." Confused, I asked what he meant. The man who cracked the joke fell silent, perhaps fearing his humor had struck too close to the quick. The businessman half grinned with obvious discomfort. He rubbed his scalp and sheepishly (and almost silently) admitted that he had been cut with machetes during the genocide. After a brief silence, someone abruptly changed the subject, as our friend looked like he was in pain. I felt ashamed that I had not recognized his silent suffering sooner, a suffering hidden behind a gregarious and gentle manner. His complaints about constant insomnia and his tendency to consume large amounts of alcohol on a nightly basis suddenly seemed like rational reactions to exceptional circumstances.

In 1997 I occasionally crossed paths with a beautiful young woman in Kigali. Half her face was covered with immaculately white gauze bandages, held in place with first-aid tape. I first saw her at the monthly meeting of women genocide survivors who had been raped, sexually mutilated, or sexually tortured. Most of these women's physical injuries were hidden from view by their clothing, but I interviewed a few of them and thus had some idea of the long-term physical consequences of their experiences. A sixteen-year-old girl had been so severely injured that doctors had been unable to save her vagina and uterus. An older woman had a severe vaginal fistula that rendered her incontinent. The young woman with bandages did not volunteer to be interviewed. Whenever I saw her walking in Kigali, I wondered how she managed to keep the bandages so clean, even in the dry season, when clouds of dust blanketed the city. When I left Rwanda in August 1997, I saw her on the flight from Rwanda to Brussels. As she passed me in the aisle, she recognized me with alarm in her eyes as if afraid I would speak to her. After the flight, I never saw her again, and I could only imagine what she hid beneath her bandages.

In addition to the sometimes obvious physical reminders of the genocide on people's bodies, the Rwandan landscape is pregnant with memories. Although I did not find a wealth of narrative signs of the genocide in 1997, many physical ones remained. Buildings all over Kigali lay in ruins from the battle between the Forces armées rwandaises (FAR) and the Rwandan Patriotic Front (RPF). In 1997 I attended a wedding reception in the shell of the parliament building, known as the CND, for Conseil national du dé-veloppement (National Development Council), the name of the parliament under Habyarimana. RPF troops had been garrisoned in the building in 1994 as part of the Arusha Peace Accords. During the battle for the city, the CND was the target for almost continuous bombardment by the FAR. Similarly, the main highways leading from Kigali to the outlying towns bore the scars of war in the form of enormous potholes that risked blowing out a tire if not swallowing a car. In addition, massacre sites—especially those in churches—throughout the country had been left in situ as a physical testa-ment to the genocide. When I returned to Rwanda in 1998, few physical landmarks of the genocide remained visible. The CND building had been refurbished, and the National Transitional Assembly met there regularly. The mortar holes in the exterior walls had been preserved and turned into windows. They served as a commemoration of the RPF's struggle and of the bombardment endured by the Tutsi survivors who managed to escape to the CND building during the genocide.

Even after the physical signs were covered over, the landscape remained charged with memories for survivors. Many survivors refused to return to

Figure 4. Rural house destroyed in the 1994 genocide, South province, 2000. Photo by Jennie E. Burnet.

the places they lived when the genocide occurred. When I asked them why, they explained that they did not want to relive painful experiences. In 2000 partially destroyed homes dotted the landscape in rural communities in southern Rwanda where I did my research. These constant reminders of all that was lost were too painful for some to bear. On one occasion, I visited a neighbor who had built a new house to replace the one destroyed during the genocide. As we passed by the remains of the old house, he motioned at them, shaking his head, and said, "Iyo mbonye iki kizu kintera ibibazo" (When I see that thing it causes me a lot of problems). I understood his statement to mean that the house reminded him of all he had experienced in the genocide and the wife and seven children he had lost.

Many survivors did not have any physical marks of the genocide inscribed on their bodies, but they remained scarred by embodied memories. While some Rwandans and most foreigners discuss these scars in the Western medicine discourse of posttraumatic stress disorder (PTSD), psychological trauma, or psychosocial trauma, ordinary Rwandans understood them otherwise; thus, I call them metaphysical scars, since they are very much connected to the physical world, to people's bodies, to objects, and to the landscape. In Rwanda today, the word "trauma" in French or English is synonymous with psychological trauma. In Kinyarwanda, the word is most often rendered as *guhahamuka*, meaning "to speak with a trembling voice" or "to be physically overcome by fear" (Jacob 1984, 432; Hagengimana and

Hinton 2009). For ordinary Rwandans, *guhahamuka* consists only of this erratic breathing that tends to overcome survivors when they are talking about their experiences or having a flashback. The many other symptoms and consequences associated with PTSD in Western medicine discourse such as depression, anxiety, hypervigilance, difficulty concentrating, loss of affect, and angry outbursts are not considered to be a consequence of genocide or experiences of violence. Yet the notion that the genocide lives in people's bodies and minds resonates with ordinary men and women.

From this perspective, Rwandans conceive of the genocide as the root of many health problems. Victorine, whose story I told in the introduction, suffered from measurable physical symptoms of stress for more than ten years after the genocide. She frequently awakened at night with her heart racing and feeling as if her chest were compressed by a heavy weight. Doctors at the National University Hospital attributed her high blood pressure and "panic attacks," as they diagnosed them, to "psychological trauma." They prescribed her sedatives, blood pressure medication, and a strict regimen of daily physical exercise.

In rural areas, many women I interviewed complained of suffering from *inzoka* (snakes or worms), the standard Kinyarwanda term for worm infestations of the intestines. The first few times I heard women, even old women, use this idiom, I was confused, since adults rarely contract intestinal worms. The women described *inzoka* crawling underneath the skin in their arms, legs, back, neck, or head. The *inzoka* provoked intense pain, frequently experienced as a burning sensation, in these areas. In 2001 the Polish nuns who ran a rural health center explained how they diagnosed adult patients who complained of *inzoka*: "We ask the patients to describe all their symptoms. Then we examine them. We then diagnose them according to their symptoms—malaria, high blood pressure, a rash, arthritis are among the most common" (author interview, 2000, South province). The same year, a Rwandan medical doctor who had studied medicine in the Soviet Union told me that he frequently diagnosed *inzoka* as high blood pressure, nerve problems, migraine headaches, myopia, or the somatization of psychological distress (author interview, 2000, West province). Among the survivors living in urban areas whom I have known for many years, many have been diagnosed with Type II diabetes. While epidemiological research identifies dietary change and sedentary lifestyle as the causes of this illness, virtually all the survivors attributed their illness to the genocide and stress of life in its aftermath. As a result they found it difficult to accept physicians' prescription for dietary change, exercise, and daily medication as suitable treatment.

For some survivors, embodied memories do not provoke physical illness; rather, they are experienced metaphysically, sparked by a conjunction of time, place, and objects. On April 7, 2001, I planned to attend the official national mourning ceremony in Gisozi. The night before, a close friend and genocide survivor, Veridianne, called and told me that we needed to go and visit a sick friend from a women's association. I explained my plans to Veridianne and apologized that I could not go. In the back of my mind, I wondered whether she invited me because of my car, since public transportation is limited on national holidays. She responded, "Why do you want to go there? Nothing ever happens. It's the same thing every year. Don't waste your time. You can watch it later on TV at my house. Trust me. You need to come with us to Annonciata's house." Her response surprised me. She was Tutsi and a founding member of a genocide widows' association. I had expected her to consider the national mourning ceremony as a worth-while commemoration of the genocide. Because of her insistent tone, I abandoned my "research plans" and agreed to go with her. Yet I was irritated that this friend, who understood my research and had helped me in the past, was interfering with my plans.

The next day, these annoyances melted away as we talked during the trip. Veridianne sat in the front with me, and three other women sat in back. At a certain moment, Veridianne fell silent, and tears welled up in her eyes. I asked her what was wrong, but she waved me away with her hands and then covered her face. As the other women had not noticed that she was crying, and as public displays of emotion are not encouraged in Rwandan society, I pretended not to see her and wondered silently what had upset her. It was at that moment that I noticed where we were on the road. I remembered an earlier conversation when she had told me part of her survival story.

Veridianne's husband, a Hutu, had been killed in the first days of the genocide because he was known to be a moderate member of the MDR and a supporter of Faustin Twagiramungu. After his death, Veridianne and their children remained at home for a few weeks until it was too dangerous for them to stay any longer. Veridianne decided to flee to her husband's home commune, where she hoped they would be protected. They left Kigali on foot. At each roadblock, Veridianne separated herself from the children in case the Interahamwe decided she looked "Tutsi." She imagined the children would be safer on their own. In his fear, the youngest child risked giving away their ruse at each barrier along the road. After twenty kilometers or so, the children became too tired to continue. Veridianne thought the children might have a better chance of surviving without her. Veridianne told them to leave the road and climb a nearby hill to ask for help. When Veridianne told me the story, she had explained where she and her children had parted ways. It was at that exact spot that Veridianne had fallen silent and begun crying during our trip.

Miraculously, following the genocide Veridianne had been reunited with her children, all of whom were alive. The children told her what had happened to them. They had gone and asked a family on a nearby hillside to shelter them. The old man and his wife protected them for the rest of the genocide while their sons manned the barriers on the main road below and killed Tutsi and other "enemies of the state." Months after her reunion with her children, Veridianne loaded a truck with food, clothing, household items, beer, and soft drinks. She drove to the house where her children had taken refuge. When she knocked on the door, the old man and woman hid inside and pretended not to be home. As Veridianne had seen them run into the house when she had pulled up, she started unloading the provisions that she had brought with her. Eventually, the woman opened the door and asked what she was doing. Veridianne replied, "I am bringing you these gifts to thank you—*Nje gukura ubwatsi* [I bring grass for your cattle]." The woman responded, "For what?" At that moment Veridianne stopped unloading the items and explained who she was. The woman went and got her husband. They invited Veridianne in and brought the gifts into the house. They spent the afternoon together, sharing the drinks and telling stories.

Veridianne and I had passed the same place on the road together several times before, and she had not noticeably reacted. But, passing by that point on a day when she had the genocide in mind, Veridianne found herself transported to a vivid memory of the genocide. The conjunction of time and place forced her to remember. From this perspective, spatiotemporal moments are accessible through memory; conversely, remembrances are accessible through places, sounds, smells, and moments in time. Veridianne's story highlights the complex relationship between time, place, and memory. It also shows the conflict between individual remembering of the genocide and attempts by the Rwandan government to manage memory.

Nationalized Mourning

The Government of National Unity, appointed by the RPF in July 1994, faced near insurmountable challenges. One challenge the new government faced was the (re)invention of a nongenocidal Rwandan state—the "New Rwanda." As part of its state-building project of national unity, the new government removed ethnic markers from national identity cards, created a new flag and national anthem, and promoted an ideology of National Unity (see chapter 5 for a discussion of these changes). Beyond the new national symbols, the government has made "re-membering" the genocide an integral component of its nation building for the New Rwanda.[8]

The RPF's portrayal of the civil war and genocide made clear distinctions between victims (presumed to be Tutsi) and killers (presumed to be Hutu.) Yet this version of events did not fit with individual Rwandans' experiences. Because of the country's diversity, which included many characteristics other than ethnicity, as discussed in the previous chapter, there was not a universal experience of the events of 1994. First, the genocide manifested differently in different places.[9] Some individuals took advantage of the state of war and chaos to settle personal scores, steal, or murder for reasons other than ethnic killing itself.[10] Furthermore, many people killed for a confluence of motivations.[11] Second, the *génocidaires* killed Hutu political opponents, journalists, and human rights workers in order to quash opposition to ethnic killing and keep the genocide "on track." Whether these victims are considered victims of the genocide remains a contentious political problem in Rwanda. In the civil war between 1990 and 1994, civilians of all ethnic categories were caught in the crossfire between the RPF and the FAR. How should these victims be remembered? Finally, unknown numbers of civilians were killed by RPF soldiers both in individual acts of revenge and in organized killings of Hutu and Tutsi. In short, the genocide in Rwanda includes a multitude of experiences of a highly differentiated populace. No single version of events can encapsulate all of them.

In the process of trying to contain the intense emotions and experiences of different Rwandan subjects, nationalized mourning minimizes and even denies the multiplicity of truths about the genocide. Nationalized mourning poses difficulties for genocide survivors who find that the dominant discourses do not fit with their own experiences. Other Rwandans find that the politicization of survivorship resulting from nationalized mourning denigrates their deeply personal memories of violence, loss, and trauma. While attempting to forge a new, unified national identity around a single understanding of the genocide and a single version of Rwandan history, national mourning homogenizes the diverse experiences of victims of the genocide, the civil war, and afterward. In this way, individual mourning becomes political and managed by the state.

Let me be clear. I am not denying or minimizing the genocide. Plentiful empirical data prove that the genocide happened and that it was planned in advance. I am also not saying that all Rwandan women suffered in the same ways or to the same extent. The diversity of Rwandan women's experiences of violence before, during, and after the genocide as well as their varied understandings of what happened during the genocide are at the heart of the social and political landscape in postgenocide Rwanda.

Month of National Mourning

As part of its national memory project, the RPF-led government declared the month of April as the month of national mourning. From 1996 until approximately 2003, the most intensive period of organized activities and changed routines began on April 1 and continued until April 7, a national holiday when a national commemoration ceremony was held. During these years, genocide survivors often complained that the ceremony did not respect reality, since the genocide began on the night of April 6, 1994. Most of Commemoration Week preceded the events being commemorated. In response to these complaints, the government moved the start of national mourning to April 7. During a visit to Rwanda in May and June 2011, commemoration pilgrimages of schools, universities, businesses, and government agencies appeared nightly on the news. When I asked why, survivors explained that the government extended the period for commemoration activities until the July 4 celebration of Liberation Day, commemorating the RPF's victory and end of the genocide.

Between 2000 and 2002, I participated in the month of national mourning each year. During these years, the national radio and television only broadcast programming related to the genocide or commemoration, including documentaries; survivor testimony; town meetings to discuss the genocide, reconciliation, or other topics relevant to national unity; appropriate music, that is, music that was sad or that honored victims; local-level genocide commemoration ceremonies; and cultural performances to honor and represent the (dead) victims. In the capital, nightclubs and other diversions remained closed for the entire month of April with the exception of local bars (cabarets), which remained open as long as they maintained a sufficiently quiet atmosphere.

Between 1996 and 2003, the first week of national mourning culminated in the National Genocide Memorial Ceremony held on April 7. After the change in schedule, the National Genocide Memorial Ceremony marked the beginning.of the national mourning period. Up until 2004, the ceremony was held in a different location every year. In 2004 the ceremony returned to Gisozi in Kigali, as it had been declared the national genocide memorial site. The government built a genocide museum on the site with support from the Aegis Foundation and the Clinton Foundation.

Between 1994 and at least 2002, citizens were called to *umuganda* (communal labor) in the weeks leading up to the ceremonies to search for remains and exhume them so that they could be reburied during the ceremonies. Each year, new bodies were recovered. Some Rwandans questioned, although not publicly, whether the bodies recovered in later years were genocide victims. In 2000 a genocide widow remarked about a story on the national news about exhumations, "I want to know where they keep finding these bodies," as she shook her head in disbelief. She seemed to be implying that these "new" bodies must not be victims of the genocide because all the genocide victims should have been recovered after so many years of looking. Many Hutu Rwandans quietly expressed the belief that many of the bodies recovered were victims of RPF-perpetrated killings.

Figure 5. Victims' names, Memory Garden, Kigali Memorial Centre in Gisozi, 2007. Photo by Jennie E. Burnet.

Despite these contestations, many survivors find these recovery rituals to be healing, especially when survivors are able to recover a family member. The lack of a proper burial for their loved ones was a constant source of grief for many survivors (Schotsman 2000). For those with Christian beliefs, a proper burial ensured salvation; while for those with traditional beliefs, it ensured the safe passage of the spirit into the spirit world. For most Rwandans, it probably eased anxiety on both counts. Most importantly, reburial ceremonies provided closure. As one survivor explained to me, "When we found my father and brothers and sisters, it was really difficult for me. I had to remember everything all over again, . . . imagine how they were killed. [He was not with them.] But now [over a year later], I realize that I feel much better" (author interview, 2000). This same man did not like the national ceremonies because they were too anonymous and impersonal to be meaningful for him. He also expressed skepticism about the identities of the bodies reburied in the genocide memorial sites. He suspected that some of them might be genocide perpetrators killed by the RPF.

National Genocide Commemoration Ceremonies

The national genocide commemoration ceremonies were an important site for the production of nationalized memory in postgenocide Rwanda. While the leaders of the postgenocide government promoted these ceremonies as a way to heal the nation and promote national unity, they served instead to divide the population. Through the ceremonies, the RPF-led government promoted a particular version of national history and narrative about the genocide. The ceremonies mobilized the dead as powerful, polyvalent symbols that divided those in attendance into two categories: victim and perpetrator. This dichotomous pairing of victim and perpetrator mirrored the pairing Tutsi/Hutu and erased Hutu victims of the genocide as well as Hutu and Tutsi victims of RPF-perpetrated violence from the national imagination. The national genocide memorial ceremonies were dense sites for the social production of memory and of nation building.

The first commemoration of the genocide in April 1995 was unique in that it promoted the ideology of national unity through representation of both Tutsi and Hutu as victims of the genocide. The ceremony was held at the National Amahoro Stadium in Kigali, and approximately six thousand anonymous victims of the genocide were interred in a consecrated grave just outside the stadium alongside several well-known Hutu victims, including Agathe Uwilingiyimana, who was named a "national hero" during the ceremony (Pottier 2002, 158; Vidal 2001, 6). President Pasteur Bizimungu, a Hutu member of the Rwandan Patriotic Front, and Vice President Paul Kagame, a Tutsi member of the Rwandan Patriotic Front, accompanied the coffin of a well-known Hutu victim and a coffin containing an unknown victim to their graves (Vidal 2001, 6). Additional unknown victims were placed in the graves, which were then consecrated in an ecumenical ritual by a Catholic priest, a Protestant pastor, and a Muslim imam. In this way, Hutu and Tutsi were given joint recognition as victims of the genocide. The association of Hutu and Tutsi victims of the genocide had powerful symbolism for the Rwandan population: "This [gesture] was to recognize that some Hutu had also been targeted by the genocide organizers. Such a recognition was not self-evident; it had emerged after debates in the government council [i.e., the ministerial cabinet]. The government, having nevertheless imposed [the inclusion of dead Hutu and Tutsi in the ceremony], was officially refusing to criminalize Hutu globally, was accepting that status as a genocide victim was not limited to Tutsi alone, and was not erecting a monopoly on suffering" (Vidal 2001, 7, my translation). Thus, the ceremony communicated that leaders at the upper echelons of the new government believed that building a durable peace should be the main political objective of state power (ibid.). This message was important to communicate to ordinary men and women who were overwhelmed by fears at the time. Hutu feared becoming the victims of a "second genocide," as some labeled it, at the hands of the RPF. Their fears were justified, as the RPA perpetrated extrajudicial killings of suspected Interahamwe and small-scale massacres against civilians in communities throughout the country (Degni-Segui 1996; Des Forges 1999, 705–14). In many communities, Hutu faced acts of revenge by genocide survivors and old returnees (HRW 1995, 1996b). Tutsi, on the other hand, feared that former FAR soldiers and Interahamwe would attack from their bases in refugee camps in eastern Zaire, close to the border with Rwanda, or that genocide perpetrators in the population within Rwanda would attack the survivors and kill them to eliminate witnesses. These fears were also justified, as attacks targeting genocide survivors, potential witnesses in genocide trials, and old caseload returnees were launched throughout 1996 and 1997 (UNHRFOR 1997a, 1997b).

Despite the messages of national unity communicated during the first national genocide commemoration, as time passed, Rwandan citizens began to doubt the RPF's commitment to an ethnically and politically inclusive society. Although the regime promoted national unity in speeches, the actions of its representatives, such as local government administrators and RPA soldiers, contradicted this policy. Three weeks after the national genocide ceremony in 1995, thousands of Hutu civilians were killed by RPF soldiers at internally displaced persons camps in southern and northwestern Rwanda (Lorch 1995; Médecins sans frontières 1995; Brisset-Foucault 1995; UNDHA 1995a, 1995b, 1995c; Pottier 2002). As a result of these events as well as death threats, prominent Hutu members of the transitional government resigned their posts, and many fled the country. In the resulting cabinet reorganizations, Hutu were appointed to key posts, but the real power lay in the hands of RPF members appointed at lower positions within the ministries (Reyntjens 1995).

The first ceremony in 1995 was well attended by representatives of the international media, but not a single minister or head of state from Western nations attended; only diplomats based in Kigali came (Vidal 2001, 6–7). To Rwandans this absence served to underline the lack of interest of the West in the Rwandan tragedy and replicated the complete lack of intervention by the international community to stop the genocide a year earlier. In this first ceremony, leaders of the new government from both ethnicities and multiple political parties, including President Pasteur Bizimungu, a Hutu member of the RPF, Vice President Paul Kagame, a Tutsi member of the RPF, and Prime Minister Faustin Twagiramungu, a Hutu member of the MDR, indicted the international community for its culpability in the genocide. As Pottier recounts, Vice President Kagame "reminded the world of its guilt, of how it had failed to stop the genocide, and said that this moral failure now needed converting into a moral commitment to help rebuild Rwanda. 'Everything we see here today is symptomatic of a serious sickness which had eaten our society for a very long time unchecked. . . . Despite all the speeches made here there is not a single person who has effectively answered for his involvement,' [Kagame] said" (2002, 158).

This theme of international complicity in the genocide played a central role in the annual ceremonies over the years. During his speech at the national ceremony held in 2001 in Kibungo prefecture, Kagame (now president) invoked the dead bodies as evidence of the genocide: "All these bodies that we just interred testify to what happened here and elsewhere all over the country." Later in the speech he offered the bodies as evidence of the international community's complicity in the genocide: "This world has no pity. Those who lie to you, those you call benefactors, they have no pity. If they had pity, all this [*pointing at the bodies*] would not have happened. This happened on their watch." Through his condemnation of the international community, President Kagame evoked the moral superiority of the New Rwanda, whose leaders had stopped the genocide. Kagame referred to the bodies a third time in his speech, this time as symbols of the government's moral correctness in its actions: "People cannot accept that what happened in 1994 can happen again [*motioning toward the bodies*]. That is why the Government of National Unity or the state in general has supported certain actions to keep it from happening again." Later in the speech he made it clear that "certain actions" referred to the RPA's participation in the Congo War and in killing Rwandans opposed to the new government whether they were inside or outside the country.[12]

The president's indictment had an added air of indignation, as the contents of a United Nations report on the illegal exploitation of Congo resources, which was to be officially released a few days later, had already been leaked to the international media (Ekoko et al. 2001). The report accused President Kagame and others in the upper echelons of power of continuing the Congo War in order to enrich themselves. Carla Del Ponte, prosecutor of the International Criminal Tribunal for Rwanda (ICTR), attended the ceremony in Kibungo. In the previous month, she had indicated her desire to bring charges against members of the RPF for crimes against humanity per the ICTR's mandate. The rumors circulating on the *radio trottoir* (French, literally "sidewalk radio," meaning roughly "word on the street") said that President Kagame's name was on the list of those under investigation. Although the president's speech focused on the national mourning, its subtext addressed these allegations.

While the indictment of the international community for its complicity in the genocide remained a constant theme of the national mourning ceremonies between 1995 and 2005, beginning with the ceremony on April 7, 1996, in Nyamagabe commune (now part of Nyamagabe district) in southern Rwanda, the symbolic use of the dead took a significant departure from the first annual ceremony, during which Hutu and Tutsi victims were honored and buried side by side. The 1996 ceremony shifted the emphasis to distinguishing between genocide victims, understood as Tutsi, and perpetrators, understood as Hutu, rather than honoring both Tutsi and Hutu as possible genocide victims.

Between August and October 1994, French troops of Opération turquoise were based at the École technique de Murambi, in Nyamagabe commune.

During the genocide, thousands of Tutsi had sought refuge at the school, which was still under construction, and most died in a massacre that began on April 21, 1994. Many Tutsi genocide survivors in the area accused the French soldiers of attempting to cover up the genocide. Indicative of this perspective was testimony given me by a Tutsi survivor when I visited the site in 2000. He explained that "UNAMIR troops," calling the soldiers UN peacekeepers instead of French soldiers of the Opération turquoise, had hastily buried the bodies in a mass grave and then built a "volleyball court" over it "to amuse themselves." More reliable sources allege that the French soldiers had no idea that their volleyball court had been erected over a mass grave dug by Interahamwe and FAR soldiers after the massacre at Murambi ended on April 22, 1994.[13] Regardless of its accuracy, this survivor's story captures the strongly negative feeling many survivors had toward both the UN peacekeepers who stood by while Rwandans were massacred and the French soldiers who gave safe passage to the genocide planners who fled the country.

In preparation for the 1996 ceremony held at the École technique in Murambi, 27,000 bodies were exhumed for reburial (Vidal 2001, 24). During the 1996 ceremony, the majority of the bodies were reinterred in consecrated mass graves, but more than 1,800 bodies were left on display in the classrooms of the school (Vidal 2001, 24). When I visited Murambi in 2000 and again in 2001 and 2007, they were still on display. Numerous genocide memorial sites prominently display victims' remains as a way to counter the claims of genocide deniers, but the presentation at Murambi is different. At Murambi the bodies were mummified through the application of lime. Thus, they appear not as collections of bones and skulls but rather as shriveled bodies—many still contorted in death poses, with hands covering faces or arms shielding an infant (fig. 6). When I asked the staff on the site as well as people living in the surrounding area about the display, I received various, conflicting stories as to when, why, and by whom the bodies had been mummified. Regardless of whether the RPF-led government made an explicit decision to mummify the bodies, it mobilizes these human remains to tell the story of the genocide. Most official diplomatic visits and other missions of international dignitaries include a stop at the genocide memorial in Murambi. These visits are then broadcast on the nightly television news with many images of the mummified bodies. This display of genocide victims was controversial and opposed by many genocide survivors and survivors' organizations on the grounds that it dishonored the dead (Schotsman 2000).

In precolonial times, Rwandans wrapped the bodies of the dead in mats and left them in the woods; no attention was paid to the bodies, and graves were not marked. As an object of horror, the cadaver was dealt with in a perfunctory manner. Instead, Rwandans focused on the spirits (*abazimu*) of the dead, who circulated in the world of the living and exercised their

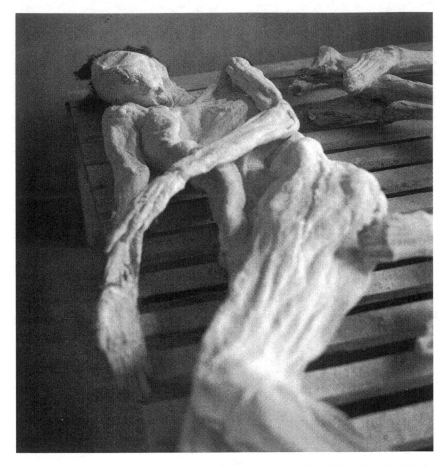

Figure 6. Murambi Memorial, ten years after the genocide, 2004. Photo by Paolo Pellegrin/Magnum Photos.

agency over them. Dissatisfied *abazimu* caused misfortune and trouble for the living—illness, failed crops, infertility—so they were honored through regular offerings of food and drink and consulted for advice through ancestor cults (*guterekera*). During the colonial period, these traditional practices were subsumed by or synthesized with Christianity, principally Roman Catholicism. While many families, especially rural ones, maintained the traditional ancestor cults, albeit discreetly so as to avoid excommunication from the Roman Catholic Church, they began to bury cadavers according to the imported idiom of European Christianity.

In this historical context, putting the mummified remains of the dead on display "put participants in a situation that excluded the possibility of giving the dead a human significance" (Vidal 2001, 24, my translation). The dead became inhuman embodiments of the terror of genocide for Rwandans and foreign visitors alike. Adding to this dehumanization were the memories of Interahamwe militiamen torturing and mutilating Tutsi bodies during the genocide.[14] Thus, the display of bodies, bodies with no living descendants to honor them either through Christian burial or through traditional ancestor cults, in a context that signifies them as Tutsi perpetuated the symbolic violence of genocide.[15]

Another important symbolic difference between the 1995 and 1996 ceremonies that was indicative of the shift in the government's ideological stance vis-à-vis the genocide was that the graves were not consecrated ecumenically in 1996. For many Rwandans, the absence of religious consecration constituted further violence against the dead: "In the African context, it is unthinkable to honor the dead without religion" (Vidal 2001, 26, my translation). In my own experience, mourning rituals among educated urban elites required a funeral mass and sacred burial followed approximately thirty days later by a "lifting of mourning" marked by another mass and a visit to the grave, where prayers were said.

As in 1995, the multiethnic government leadership presided over the ceremony. Yet unlike the 1995 ceremony, in 1996 attention was focused on Tutsi victims of the genocide. During the ceremony, a Tutsi genocide survivor gave testimony about how Tutsi had been assembled at the school and massacred. Then he began to point at people and accuse them of participating in the killing (Vidal 2001, 25). The crowd applauded as he continued his accusations. Finally, he turned to the dais, where the guests of honor were seated, and pointed at the Roman Catholic bishop of Gikongoro, Monsignor Augustin Misago, and accused him of genocide (Vidal 2001, 25).[16] Accusations against Hutu crowd members became a feature repeated annually at subsequent national commemoration ceremonies.

The national ceremonies reified ethnic categories and encoded them in a new language by separating the dead victims from the living and dividing the living into "rescuers," that is, the RPF, "victims," that is, genocide survivors, and "perpetrators," that is, the rest of the living. The ceremonies (re)produced the dead as "pure" (Tutsi) victims, but this symbolism problematized the positions of the living. If the dead are the only pure victims, then what about the living? This symbolic positioning in the ceremony had practical implications for survivors who faced implicit as well as explicit accusations from old caseload returnees that genocide survivors must have participated in the genocide in order to survive. The symbolic emphasis on victims created a dyadic relationship between victim and perpetrator whereby anyone not labeled "victim" in the ceremonies automatically fell into the default category of perpetrator. The national mourning ceremonies transformed the bodies of the dead and the injured bodies of living victims into powerful symbols of the nation and its moral superiority over the international community. The same symbolism was replicated in local-level commemoration ceremonies organized by genocide survivor associations and local authorities.

I attended one ceremony in a rural community in southern Rwanda that played on the same opposition of victims, both living and dead, with an "other," presumed to be "perpetrator." The ceremony began with a procession around the massacre site (an area of about a square kilometer). The cortège passed in front of the women and children lined up in front of the jail to bring food to family members imprisoned on genocide charges. Through the dialectic between polar opposites—dead/alive, pure/impure, victim/perpetrator—the ceremony produced the rest of the living, whether in the prison, waiting outside the prison, or hidden at home, as killers, abettors, deniers, and complicit bystanders to genocide. Through these processes, the ceremony purified who was remembered and how, who had the right to grieve and why. This symbolic purification, in turn, reinforced the government's "moral right," as the one who stopped the genocide, to continue its dictatorial rule.

Many Rwandan women refused to participate in genocide commemoration ceremonies organized by survivor associations and the government. Some women survivors explained that their memories of violence, loss, and trauma were so deeply personal that they could not be shared "with strangers." Others said that the master narratives that are dominant at these ceremonies did not fit their individual experiences. Hutu women desired the possibility to grieve the genocide as well as the loss of their loved ones killed in the war or at the hands of the RPF. Yet the reason they chose not to participate in the genocide memorial ceremonies was that they felt like the speeches and symbolism of these ceremonies implicated them as perpetrators.

Beyond the explicit shifts in symbolism of the national genocide commemoration ceremonies, the national ceremonies eclipsed community-level or family-level commemorations and precluded the public mourning of victims of RPA-perpetrated killings. As Vidal (2001) argues, the national ceremonies operated under a substantially different symbolic system than community-level mourning. Community-level and family-level ceremonies focused on the mourning of loved ones lost in the violence and fulfilling traditional and imported religious obligations toward the dead. The national ceremonies, on the other hand, emphasized national mythico-histories, many of which conflicted with individual Rwandans' heterogeneous experiences of violence during the civil war, genocide, and insurgency. These national narratives precluded individual, familial, and communal mourning. The community-level ceremonies, which were first conducted in early 1994 under the direction of Roman Catholic parishes, better served the needs of psychological healing and social reconciliation than the national ceremonies did (Vidal 2001). Given the prominence of the national ceremonies and the tendency to model local-level ceremonies after them, Rwandan citizens had little public space left to mourn in the fashion that best suited their needs.

Genocide Memorial Sites

Another attempt to fix remembrance of the genocide and its victims is genocide memorial sites. These sites have changed over time as the Rwandan government responded to pleas from survivors. In 1997 most "memorial" sites consisted of massacre sites that were preserved "intact" or mass graves marked with signs. The majority of memorial sites were in churches. As discussed in the previous chapter, churches, schools, and government buildings were used during the genocide to gather Tutsi together so that they could be killed more easily. While the genocide was still under way, government authorities organized the cleanup of many of these sites to hide the evidence of the ongoing genocide. Thousands of bodies were buried in hastily dug mass graves, septic pits, and irrigation ditches. At other sites,

Figure 7. Communal graves at Murambi Genocide Memorial Centre, 2007. Photo by Jennie E. Burnet.

Figure 8. Ntarama Genocide Memorial, December 2005. The bones and remaining debris of the victims who died in this church were left as a tribute to the eight hundred thousand Tutsis massacred in the 1994 genocide. Photo by Larry Towell/ Magnum Photos.

bodies were left in the open air because local authorities did not have time to organize cleanups before the areas fell to the RPF.

During my first trip to Rwanda in 1997, I visited only one genocide memorial site in Bugesera. At Ntarama, Tutsi and others targeted in the genocide took refuge in a small Roman Catholic church. The week of April 11, FAR soldiers, police, Interahamwe, and men recruited from the local community surrounded the church. Soldiers threw grenades in the church and then shot the men, armed with clubs, spears, and traditional machetes (*imihoro*), who were trying to protect those inside. Then the Interahamwe and civilians set about dispatching the rest with clubs and machetes. The massacre site was never cleaned up, and the postgenocide government decided to keep it intact in order to make the truth of the genocide undeniable.

When I visited Ntarama in 1997, I approached the church reluctantly, although I had rented a private vehicle and driven for almost an hour to reach the site. Just outside the church, leaning against the outer brick wall, was a small shelter constructed of thin tree trunks, green tarps, twine, and tin roofing. Inside the shelter, stacked neatly on tables made from tree branches lashed together with twine, were human bones. One table contained a collection of femurs, another arm bones, and another skulls. Based on the variations in size, it was immediately evident that the victims had included numerous children. My "guide," a tall, frail man in his late thirties, explained that the bones had been gathered from the ground in the churchyard and areas around the church. He explained that these were the victims who had tried to escape by running through the mob of local residents, militiamen, police, and soldiers who had mounted the attack on the church. I asked him how he knew what had happened. He said that he was a survivor of the massacre and had witnessed it from inside the church.

After pausing for a moment inside the shelter, I then moved toward the entry to the sanctuary. As I approached, I feared I might smell rotting flesh, as others who had visited the site had described to me. I smelled nothing, but a horrific sight came into view. Scattered amid the modest wooden planks that served as pews in the church were the remains of thousands of people who had died. Unlike the neat stacks of bones in the shelter outside, which I could detach myself from in some way, here I faced the horror of genocide. I saw clothed people clutching rosaries. My gaze settled on a cooking pot, still balanced on a pew, with its contents long dried in a crust on the bottom. It was the cooking pot that forced me to envision these men, women, and children facing the crazed mob outside. I did not stay for long.

When I turned away, the guide asked me if I wanted to take some pictures. Although I had my camera with me, the thought of taking pictures had not occurred to me. I explained that I was not sure it was appropriate to take pictures. The guide assured me that it was okay. All the foreigners did

Figure 9. Presentation of human remains, Ntarama Genocide Memorial Centre, 2007. Human remains and other debris were removed from the church. Photo by Jennie E. Burnet.

it. When I still seemed reluctant, he encouraged me. Despite my discomfort, I took a few pictures before leaving.

Many genocide survivors were opposed to sites such as this one because they deprive the victims of a proper burial (Schotsman 2000). In 1997 most of the genocide survivors I interviewed had very strong emotions, ranging from anger and frustration to deep anguish, because no "appropriate" genocide memorial sites existed. One woman, a prominent member of an association for genocide widows, expressed the following to me:

> A genocide memorial? Of course, we would like one. They [the government] say they are compiling a list of the victims, but who knows if they are really doing it or if it will be accurate?[17] No one has asked me [who in my family was killed]! The Brits or the Belgians or someone else gave money to the government to construct a national genocide memorial. Last year they held a ceremony at the traffic circle in town, where they laid the first stone. Since then nothing! It still sits there alone! (Author interview, July 1997, Kigali)

For many genocide survivors, it felt as if the government did not care at all about their needs. Particularly in 1997, when so many survivors were still homeless and destitute with little assistance, it was difficult for them to believe that anyone would do anything to help them. As early as 1995, the government had a "three-phase plan" to erect genocide sites around the country. The plan included a major memorial site in each of the eleven prefectures and consecrated burial of all remains (McNeil 1995). Yet survivors were either unaware of these plans or doubted they would ever become a reality. Indeed, the government lacked any significant financial funding from donors. Gradually over the years, genocide memorial sites emerged. Some were constructed by local survivors' associations, others by the Rwandan government, and some with financial support from international organizations.

The treatment of victims' bodies at the sites caused many genocide survivors additional pain. Not far from Ntarama, at a second, larger church at Nyamata, another massacre took place during the same week in April 1994. At Nyamata the government also preserved the site intact for many years. Although I never saw it myself, Nyamata was infamous for the display of a Tutsi woman's body as it had been left by the Interahamwe. The victim was impaled on a pike inserted through her vagina. Her body remained on display for many years while a few surviving relatives begged to be allowed to bury her (Alison Des Forges, personal communication, 2000). When I visited Nyamata in 2007, her body was no longer on display.

By 1999 genocide memorial sites had been erected in many communities. One, a large grave with a monument along a main highway connecting the capital to Gitarama town (now Muhanga), read: "Here are buried those killed for no reason from Musambira Commune and neighboring communes, killed during the genocide and massacres. More than 120 people were shot by soldiers and the Presidential Guard after seeking refuge at Kabgayi on 20th April 1994."[18] Twice in 2000 I visited another elaborate site under construction at Bisesero in Kibuye. During the genocide, thousands of Tutsi fled to the Bisesero hill and fought off the Interahamwe, police, and soldiers who came to attack them. From April 8, 1994, until July 1, 1994, they defended themselves and managed to kill several soldiers and Interahamwe (Des Forges 1999, 216–21). Around one thousand Tutsi survived out of the tens of thousands who had taken refuge on Bisesero hill.

In 1998 the national mourning ceremony took place at Bisesero. President Bizimungu, Vice President Kagame, and many ministers and other visitors came to Bisesero to honor the heroes who had fallen there. At that time, President Bizimungu promised the survivors of Bisesero that the site would become a national genocide memorial site. When I visited in 2000, several stone walkways, walls, and an arch had been built. Several well-constructed tin shelters held the remains of many victims. A dozen or so men came to greet us when they saw our vehicle arrive. They gave us a tour and explained how the Tutsi of the region, including our impromptu guides, had defended themselves in 1994 until the military reinforcements came from Gisenyi and launched a large-scale attack on June 2, 1994 (Des Forges 1999, 219). The Bisesero memorial site remained unfinished until October 2010.[19] The length of time it took for most genocide memorial sites to be completed demonstrated to many survivors the postgenocide government's lack of concern for survivors' plights.

In some cases, genocide survivors protested the burial of certain remains in genocide memorials. They claimed that among the dead were genocide perpetrators who had presumably been killed by the RPF. During its fight to take the country and stop the genocide, official RPF policy was to stop the killings, "to arrest the criminals and hand them over to the courts." Even young, recently recruited soldiers understood this policy and repeated it to foreign journalists (Des Forges 1999, 714). Nonetheless, the RPF made common practice of killing people suspected of participating in the genocide (ibid., 714–22). Presumably, these bodies, as well as the bodies of other Hutu killed in reprisal killings by survivors, lay in informal graves throughout the country. During the efforts to recover genocide victims' remains in preparation for genocide mourning ceremonies, these other bodies were sometimes recovered as well. On a visit in 2000 to a rural community in rural Kigali prefecture (now North province), I passed a monument. I asked my Rwandan companion who was from the community whether it was a genocide memorial. She laughed and said, "Well, we buried bodies there this past April [as part of the national mourning], but everyone around here knows that there were no Tutsi here before the genocide, so who knows whom we buried there."

A genocide survivor told me about an incident that occurred at the national genocide memorial ceremony in 1996. During the ceremony when they were placing remains in graves, a hysterical woman came forward screaming, "Don't bury those killers with the victims!" She was quickly subdued by audience members and sedated by a doctor. The genocide survivor told me the story to illustrate the ways genocide memorial sites may include the remains of those who were not genocide victims. He said he knew the woman who had screamed. She was a survivor from the community, and she later told him that she had recognized the clothing on some of the bodies. The clothing indicated to her that at least one of the bodies belonged to a notorious Interahamwe from the community who had been killed in July 1994 by RPF soldiers.

Like the mourning ceremonies, the genocide memorial sites purify the victims by distinguishing them from the perpetrators and memorializing them separately. The public mourning ceremonies and sacred public places contain, homogenize, and sanitize memory and emotion.

Mourning in Silence

The experiences and subsequent subjectivities or identity positions of genocide survivors are certainly unique. Living for months as the quarry of predators who sought to destroy them, genocide survivors have a heightened awareness of the single aspect of identity that made them victims. They were targeted because of who the *génocidaires* thought they were and not necessarily what genocide survivors claimed to be. Take, for example, the three-year-old child who begged the Interahamwe who had just killed his siblings in front of him, "Please don't kill me. . . . I'll never be Tutsi again" (Des Forges 1999, 212). This experience of survival is different from the experience of surviving war, although the two may share some commonalities. Yet Rwandans who resent the public silence surrounding their own experiences of violence and trauma have difficulty recognizing the uniqueness of genocide survivors' experiences.

Thus, although silence at times serves as a culturally appropriate coping mechanism of survival, when silence is mandated by an external state authority, it undermines ordinary men's and women's abilities to cope. As the next chapter explores in depth, the Rwandan government's politicization of the genocide and survivors' suffering amplifies the silence of Hutu and Tutsi Rwandans whose experiences of violence do not fit neatly into the categories produced in national mourning activities. As a result, many Rwandans, both Tutsi and Hutu, resist this political use of suffering and prefer to observe their own mourning privately in silence.

3

Amplified Silence

Hegemony, Memory, and Silence's Multiple Meanings

Understandably, the mass killing in the 1994 genocide lends itself to generalizations in which Tutsi are portrayed as victims and Hutu are portrayed as perpetrators. Indeed, many empirical realities support this ideological framework. Approximately eight hundred thousand Rwandans lost their lives in the genocide, and most of these victims were Tutsi. Thousands of Hutu civilians participated in the genocide by denouncing Tutsi who were in hiding, by looting property, by participating in *umuganda* to "clear the bush," by killing Tutsi with clubs, machetes, or guns, or by raping or sexually torturing Tutsi women and girls. These empirical data feed into simplistic understandings of Rwandan history as a struggle between two "sides," a struggle between "good" and "evil" where the "good guys" are the RPF, "Tutsi," and "survivors" and the "bad guys" are "Interahamwe," "Hutu," and "perpetrators."

A nuanced account of the genocide, the civil war, and the postgenocide period yields a much more complicated history. Individual violent experiences during the civil war, genocide, or insurgency do not fit neatly into the dyadic Hutu perpetrator/Tutsi victim logic. Many Hutu died in the genocide because they opposed the extremist regime that chose genocide as its policy, because they "looked" Tutsi, because they were married to Tutsi, or because they hid or protected Tutsi. Following the genocide, many Tutsi lived in the refugee camps in Zaire (now Democratic Republic of the Congo) and Tanzania alongside Hutu civilians, former government officials, soldiers, and Interahamwe militiamen who fled Rwanda and the advancing RPF. Tutsi who did not return to Rwanda survived the forced camp closures and subsequent massacres in eastern Zaire in 1996 and 1997. Some Tutsi were married to Hutu either through marriages that preceded the genocide or through marriages that were forced upon Tutsi women and girls during the genocide. Others had succeeded in passing as "Hutu," had escaped the genocide, or were afraid to return to Rwanda, where they might be targeted by the RPF-led government or RPF soldiers. RPF soldiers killed Hutu and Tutsi civilians in individual acts of revenge for the genocide, in military operations to eliminate "perpetrators" who lived in internally displaced persons or refugee camps, in small-scale massacres, or in counterinsurgency operations to eliminate opposition to the new RPF-led government. Tutsi women married to Hutu men faced pressure to divorce their husbands and take RPF soldiers as husbands (Twagiramariya and Turshen 1998, 112). As discussed in the previous chapter, the inherently political nature of national-ized, state-sponsored mourning practices and the RPF's paradigmatic history of the 1994 genocide have pushed individual memories and interpretations of the genocide and civil war into hidden places.

In postgenocide Rwanda, only certain social categories were allowed to speak publicly about the past or comment on government policies. Genocide survivor organizations, such as Ibuka and AVEGA-Agahozo, spoke freely in the public sphere, although the government maintained control over their leadership.[1] Survivors of RPF massacres, on the other hand, were silenced. In addition, these survivors had no public forum in which to mourn the victims. In many cases, the victims were buried in secret mass graves or in graves designated as genocide memorials. These "public secrets" were known by everyone but remained unspoken and contributed to the discur-sive regime that silenced RPF critics, whether Rwandan or foreign.[2] I call this intense public silence surrounding RPF-perpetrated violence experienced by Rwandans of all ethnicities "amplified silence." Just as the paradigmatic story of the genocide is amplified through loudspeakers at national mourning ceremonies, by radio and television speakers during the national mourning period each year, and through politicians' politically correct speech, the silence surrounding these excluded, individual, familial, and communal experiences of violence is "amplified" through its completeness. Amplified silence is simultaneously the state of silence and the action of silencing. Amplified silence is not an inconsequential byproduct of nationalized mourning practices. Fear is its foundation. Amplified silence drives a wedge between Rwandans and limits the possibilities for reconciliation.

In the seventeen years after the genocide, this phenomenon evolved and took on slightly different idioms, but at its heart it was the same process. In the months immediately after the genocide, people who spoke about RPF killings turned up dead or, if they were "lucky," were arrested and accused of genocide.[3] These actions were extremely effective. Amplified silence also functioned on the symbolic plane. The initial mourning ceremonies organized by local Roman Catholic Church parishes, by victims' family members or friends, and by local genocide survivor groups in 1994 were quickly replaced by state-led efforts to commemorate the genocide and turn it into powerful symbolic capital (Vidal 2001, 2004). On October 1, 1994, the new government declared a public holiday and organized festivities to commemorate the beginning of the RPF struggle to liberate Rwanda in 1990 and to celebrate its recent victory in 1994. The (Hutu) minister of justice, Alphonse-Marie Nkubito, thought this celebration was inappropriate and organized a Catholic mass to mourn "those who had perished" (C. Newbury and D. Newbury 1999, 292–93). Only a few people attended the mass, but its existence and the fact that a Hutu politician who had served in the Habyarimana government organized it point to the ways that the conflict over the national genocide memory does not fall along ethnic lines. These state-led commemoration practices have continued to shape the paradigmatic genocide history in public discourse and silent dissent.

These silences imposed a powerful moralizing discourse that shaped Rwandans' subjectivities—their understandings of themselves, of their place in the world, and of their possibilities to change it. The RPF government has fostered this discursive regime, which tends to classify all Tutsi as "victims" or (genocide) "survivors" (and thus morally superior) and to transfer guilt and blame to all Hutu and the international community. This discursive regime helped legitimate the RPF's dictatorship during the transition period (1994–2003) and to consolidate its continued control over the Rwandan political system. The genocide survivors' (presumed Tutsi) suffering served as the moral justification for government policies, especially when these policies oppressed civilians (whether "Hutu" or "Tutsi"). RPF critics were labeled "perpetrators," "killers," "Interahamwe," "Hutu extremists," "divisionists," and, most recently, purveyors of "genocidal ideology" (e.g., see Pottier 2002; HRW 2003a, 2004a).

The amplified silence surrounding RPF-perpetrated violence has a gendered component, as gender roles locate women at the articulation between nuclear family households and kin networks or the community. As coordinators of the domestic sphere, women maintained affective and exchange relationships with kin and neighbors, who provide the family's safety net in case of misfortune. Thus, women were at the center of decisions whether or when to break amplified silence by holding private mourning ceremonies with kin or neighbors. In addition, some women used their gender status as a form of protection to break amplified silence in public forums.

The best way to define amplified silence is to illustrate it in action. In June 2001 former president Pasteur Bizimungu, who had been a leading Hutu in the RPF, attempted to found a new political party, called the Parti démocratique de renouveau-Ubuyanja (PDR-Ubuyanja). The word *ubuyanja*, meaning "renewal" or "rebirth," immediately suggested connections to various Christian movements in the country, including an informal prayer circle led by Gen. Augustin Cyiza, a prominent Hutu intellectual who was former Supreme Court president and an RPA general who had been integrated from the FAR. It appeared that Bizimungu hoped to run as a presidential candidate at the head of a new political party. In him the RPF saw a formidable candidate. Bizimungu had been president for many years, representing the RPF. As such, many Rwandans viewed him as capable. As a Hutu, he would likely garner many votes among Hutu. Furthermore, he had recruited several prominent Tutsi genocide survivors as founding party members. He might also garner many votes among Tutsi genocide survivors. To prevent a potential challenge to its hold on power, the RPF-led government immediately declared Bizimungu's new party illegal, put Bizimungu under house arrest, and proceeded to suppress the new party (HRW 2002a). Throughout 2001, people associated with the Ubuyanja party or with Bizimungu faced harassment and threats by Rwandan authorities. A party founder, Gratien Munyarubuga, was shot and killed by unknown assailants in December 2001, and other party leaders were detained and interrogated (HRW 2002c). The government continued to suppress the party in 2002.

The state radio, television, and newspapers reported the story, labeling Bizimungu and party members as "divisionists." Voice of America and the BBC-Kinyarwanda service reported the stories as well, but they provided more balanced coverage. They interviewed Bizimungu and other party members and offered commentary from international human rights organizations. Party suppression became so total that people became afraid to use the word *ubuyanja*, and for good reason. In January two leaders of a local nongovernmental organization, Association modeste et innocent (AMI), were arrested because their newsletter had used the word *ubuyanja* in its masthead (HRW 2003a). The two men, one Hutu and the other Tutsi, had no connections to Bizimungu or his political party. Alison Des Forges, senior advisor to Human Rights Watch, commented, "If all these men have done

is publish a word that authorities don't like, they should be freed immediately. . . . To do otherwise violates the freedom of expression that the
Rwandan government has vowed to protect and suggests a troubling move
toward political repression" (HRW 2002b). One of the men, Laurien Ntezi-
mana, who had completed graduate studies in theology at the Catholic
University of Louvain in Belgium, had long used the word *ubuyanja* in his
own philosophy and theory of self-actualization, which served as the basis
of his approach to peace-building.

The government's campaign against the PDR-Ubuyanja political party
eventually passed into the broader culture. The suppression had a noticeable effect in Catholic churches, where *ubuyanja* was a standard part of the
theological vocabulary to talk about Christian rebirth through baptism.
Priests intentionally avoided using the word in their homilies. A few
Rwandans told me the following story when we were discussing Bizimungu's
problems in 2002. When they attended a mass in a rural parish in 2002, the
parishioners sang a popular hymn, "Ni wowe rutare rwanjye" (You are my
rock). In the first verse, the entire congregation fell silent in the middle of
the third line, "Uzangarurira ubuyanja n'imbaraga" (You will bring rebirth
and strength back to me). They dared not pronounce the word *ubuyanja*.

In April 2002 Bizimungu and Charles Ntakirutinka, the PDR-Ubuyanja
Party secretary-general, were arrested and "charged with endangering state
security, fostering ethnic divisions, and engaging in illegal political activities"
(HRW 2003a). In June 2004 they were found guilty of diverting public funds
as well as inciting civil disobedience and criminal association, but they were
cleared of the most severe charges of endangering state security. Bizimungu
was sentenced to fifteen years and Ntakirutinka to ten years in prison.[4]

Silence as Protection

During my field trips in 1997 and 1998, I found that the silence of Rwandans
who had lived in refugee camps in eastern Zaire, who had family members
in prison, or who had survived killings by the RPF was so complete that I
almost did not notice it. These women faced many obstacles in voicing what
had happened to them. I was aware of the general conditions under which
the new returnees came back to Rwanda, thanks to news reports and some
eyewitness accounts from foreigners who had worked in the camps in 1994
through 1996 or in Rwanda during the massive refugee return in late 1996
and early 1997. Yet the returnees themselves said nothing.

At first I thought their silence might be due to psychological trauma. In
1997 I visited an orphanage, where I met a young girl (seven or eight years
old). The girl said nothing and sat in the corner while the other children

played. The orphanage director explained to me that when the girl had arrived three months earlier, she had advanced symptoms of kwashiorkor, a type of severe malnutrition. The only thing she said was "Ibiryo, ibiryo, ibiryo" (Food, food, food). When orphanage workers honored her incessant requests for food, she had an insatiable appetite. She furtively ate dirt, chalk, and crayons when she did not have a protein biscuit to gnaw on. Eventually, her constant requests for food subsided, and a counselor who met with her frequently learned that the girl had witnessed her family's killing in Zaire. The girl had fled on foot with other refugees, first going farther west into Zaire and then back east toward Rwanda. She eventually walked all the way to Rwanda, a distance of nearly eight hundred miles.

While silence may be psychological protection for some Rwandans like this young girl, for others it is a culturally appropriate coping mechanism for their violent experiences. In 1998 I met a family who had survived attacks on their refugee camp in eastern Zaire in 1997. To call the household a "family" is a bit misleading, as household members were a hodge-podge of family relations. Patricia, the "mother," lived only part-time in Rwanda as her husband lived and worked in South Africa. Patricia came to Rwanda periodically to manage the family's property and business affairs. All but the youngest of Patricia's children, who lived with her father in South Africa, were scattered around the world in west Africa, Europe, and the United States. Patricia's goddaughters, Diane and Flore, lived in the household along with her four nephews. The girls' fathers had died in Zaire, and their mothers had not yet been able to reclaim their houses in Kigali, which had been seized and occupied (*kubohoza*) by old caseload returnees. Their mothers and siblings were scattered among friends; no one had enough room to accommodate the entire family. Patricia's nephews stayed with her because her brother, a farmer, was too poor to keep them at home and pay for their school fees. The final household member was a six-year-old named Mutara, an orphan.

Mutara rarely spoke, at least not while I was around. At night I some-times heard him cry out in his sleep. One day I asked how Mutara had lost his parents. Diane and Flore explained that Mutara's parents died in Zaire and that Mutara had seen his father, mother, and baby sister killed by soldiers. Mutara, only four years old at the time, had survived and followed the other refugees back to Rwanda. When he arrived at a transit camp in Rwanda, the International Committee of the Red Cross (ICRC) placed him in a center for unaccompanied children while they tried to locate a family member. Although Mutara was a distant cousin's child, Patricia searched for him because she had heard from a witness that the rest of his family had been killed. When Mutara was found and came to live with Patricia and the others, he did not say a word for months. At first, they were unsure whether he understood or spoke Kinyarwanda, since he had spent so long in Zaire. They eventually attributed his silence to psychological trauma; whenever Mutara saw a soldier pass in the street, he would shake, wet his pants, and cry. After several months, he started speaking.

After Diane and Flore told me Mutara's story, I asked whether they had witnessed any violence when the camps were closed. The girls opened their eyes wide, covered their mouths with their hand (a sign of shame or embarrassment in Rwanda), and then laughed. They fended off my questions with terse responses that were cut off by nervous laughter. "You don't want to hear about it." "Bullets and bombs were flying everywhere." "We saw everything." "It was terrible." They never told me anything more specific, but I learned from someone else that Flore's father and older brother were shot dead as they stood next to her.

One motivation of their silence may have been that Mutara, Diane, and Flore resisted talking about their violent experiences with me to help keep their violent memories at bay. More importantly, however, silence was a culturally appropriate coping mechanism for managing their violent memories. Rwandan children are taught that crying (or even complaining) to strangers is futile because only family members can understand and be truly sympathetic to a child's suffering (Mironko and Cook 1996). Thus, sharing their painful memories, especially memories that could provoke them to cry, with a relative newcomer in their lives was not a culturally appropriate form of expression.

In 2000 members of a women's cooperative spoke fairly openly with me about their husbands' deaths during the forced closing of the internally displaced persons camp at Kibeho in 1995.[5] A few weeks later I visited a group member, Honorata, in her home. She was visibly uncomfortable during my visit, although she still offered the culturally required hospitality. As my research assistant and I were leaving, Honorata whispered, although we were still inside her house, that following my meeting with the group, a supervisor had upbraided members for speaking too openly to "the foreigner" (umuzungu), that is, to me. The leader had warned members to avoid "saying too much." In future group interviews with other women's cooperatives in the same network, I found the women were unwilling to speak about violence or other political oppression perpetrated by the RPF, whether during the genocide or during the postgenocide period. In individual conversations, women intentionally refashioned their narratives to fit the paradigmatic genocide story and its aftermath. Husbands who died in prison after the genocide were said to have died "of illness." Husbands killed by RPF soldiers were said to have died "in accidents," "in prison," or "from life." Occasionally, other community members would let information slip, whether intentionally or unintentionally is impossible to discern, about the men's deaths. Through persistent listening to widows' and community members' stories, I gradually pieced together somewhat accurate information about the magnitude of RPF killings, which far outnumbered the carefully managed official descriptions of individual revenge seeking or "excessive use of force."

While some Rwandans' silence operated as a protection against traumatic memories or as a culturally appropriate coping mechanism, for many others silence was a survival strategy and "a powerful mechanism of control enforced through fear" as Green (1999, 69) described for the highlands of Guatemala. Rwandans (whether Hutu or Tutsi) who had experienced RPF-perpetrated violence maintained their silence for fear of incurring additional violence. Having already witnessed or experienced the concrete possible consequences such as interrogation, detainment, imprisonment, torture, "disappearance," or death, they remained silent about what they had already gone through and lived in silent fear of what they could go through if they attracted attention by speaking out.

Silence as Hegemony: The Amplification of Silence

Although the public silence surrounding the violence that Rwandans experienced during the civil war, in the refugee camps, during camp closings and the return to Rwanda, during the insurgency, and under RPF rule in postgenocide Rwanda was not immediately obvious when I began my field-work in 1997, over time it became a palpable presence. I learned to pay close attention to what went unsaid in interviews because the silence in people's stories was often the most important data.

Just as in individual narratives where the silence was integral to the story's truth, the public silence surrounding RPF-perpetrated violence was integral to the paradigmatic national history. The official narrative, which was amplified through radios, televisions, loudspeakers, and bullhorns, was made louder by competing narratives' absolute silence. Some Rwandans' social perceptions conformed to this paradigmatic national history, resulting in what can be "characterized as 'official lies,' where social knowledge is cast in dichotomous terms, black or white, good or bad, friend or enemy, without the nuances and complexities of lived experience" (Green 1999, 62). Amplified silence was part of the discursive regime that reinforced the RPF's hegemonic power.

The RPF regime harnessed this moral discourse to its rule and in the process produced a hegemony that controlled people's speech, actions, and even thoughts. This hegemony silenced potential opponents and terrorized the population into acquiescence or agreement with the status quo. A key to this hegemony's success was its reliance on words, actions, and practices that were ambiguous symbols and that could alternately be viewed as threats or as anodyne statements.[6] This hegemony linked individual and communal history-making processes to the national political plane where the government wrote its paradigmatic, official history. Amplified silence served as a wedge that separated these victims (presumed Hutu) from genocide survivors (presumed Tutsi).

In some places in Rwanda, victims of RPF massacres were exhumed, labeled "genocide victims," and buried in genocide memorial sites. This reassignment of RPF massacre victims (presumed Hutu) as genocide victims (presumed Tutsi) angered Rwandans from many different categories. Some genocide survivors did not want Interahamwe (i.e., RPF massacre victims) mixed with genocide victims. The RPF massacre victims' family members resented having their dead buried in genocide memorial sites that symbolically relabeled the dead as "genocide victims" and in the semiotic system labeled the living as "killers."

One woman, Savina, spent most of the genocide hidden behind a wardrobe in her own home, where her husband, a member of the MRND political party who refused to participate in the genocide, did his best to protect her. He told the groups of militiamen who came to the house looking for her that she had already been killed. Savina was the child of subsistence farmers from central Rwanda (Nduga). Luckily, the earnings from her father's coffee plantation had ensured that all the children studied through at least the end of secondary school. During the genocide, Savina's Tutsi father and brothers were killed. Her mother, Candida, a Hutu, was spared. After the genocide, Candida continued to live in her husband's home. One day Savina and I went to visit her. Savina explained to her that I was a researcher looking at the effects of the genocide on Rwandan women. Candida proceeded to tell me her story of survival, how she, her husband, and her children had fled to the commune office and how FAR soldiers surrounded the office and told the Hutu to leave. Candida had wanted to stay, but her husband told her to go. Candida lamented the deaths of her husband and her sons: "Here I am. All alone now. With no one. Savina lives far away. I'm here by myself."

After we left, Savina said to me, "I don't understand my mother. You know she cries all the time about her husband and her sons. But her entire family, all her brothers, were killed by RPA soldiers in 1994. After they took control of this area, they called all the men to a meeting. At the meeting they opened fire on them. They killed them all. My mother never talks about them. It's as if she forgot about them. She only cries for her husband, for her sons."

Hegemony and Culture

The postgenocide state extended amplified silence to other areas of public discourse as a way to mitigate political dissent. In some cases, this control was even exerted over genocide survivors, whose suffering was key to the RPF's moral discourse. In 1999 the Rwandan government identified a new threat to security—the *ingabo z'umwami* (army of the king) (HRW 2000). The Rwandan *mwami* (king), Kigeli V Ndahindurwa, had been overthrown by the Hutu opposition in 1959 and went into exile in 1961. For many years he resided in Kenya, but since the 1990s he lived quietly in Washington, DC. While the *mwami* insisted that he had no intention of returning to Rwanda via armed resistance, there were rumors in Rwanda in 1999 and early 2000 that the army of the king was organizing itself in Uganda. Whether or not this armed movement ever existed, many Rwandans inside the country began actively supporting the return of the *mwami*.

Unlike previous opposition movements in the postgenocide period, which were comprised primarily of Hutu, the monarchists included Tutsi who were dissatisfied with the RPF. In an effort to curb this movement, the RPF regime took several steps. President Kagame, who had only recently assumed the presidency when President Pasteur Bizimungu resigned, made numerous public statements welcoming the *mwami* as a private citizen but threatened: "Whoever will come (by [the] gun) will definitely die. . . . We are ready" (*Rwanda Newsline* 2000). In 2000 the government eliminated several public figures or politicians perceived to be a threat to RPF rule by threatening, detaining, or forcing them into exile. Two of the figures most widely discussed were the speaker of the National Assembly, Joseph Kabuye Sebarenzi, and a popular singer, Benjamin Rutabana. Rutabana and Sebarenzi as well as several other politicians rumored to be associated with the monarchists all originated from the same region in Kibuye prefecture. Former president Pasteur Bizimungu originated from the same region as well.

In early January 2000 the RPF's inner circle orchestrated the removal of Joseph Kabuye Sebarenzi from his position as speaker of the National Assembly. A Tutsi who had grown up in Rwanda, Sebarenzi was widely regarded and respected as a genocide survivor who protected the interests of other genocide survivors. Sebarenzi was accused of organizing genocide survivors against the government, supporting the king, and distributing cassette tapes that had been outlawed. In February 2000 he fled the country, first to Uganda and eventually to the United States.

Benjamin Rutabana, an RPF rebel soldier from 1990 until 1995, was one of the most popular singers in Rwanda. His songs and music videos were regularly played on the national radio and television stations in the late 1990s and early 2000s. Rutabana's lyrics promoted the RPF's ideology of national unity and its paradigmatic national history. His most popular song, "Afrika," blamed the ethnic divisions in Rwanda on Europeans and the Catholic Church. In late 1999 Rutabana was rumored to have associated with the monarchists in general and Sebarenzi in particular. Just before Sebarenzi's removal from power, Rutabana became afraid for his own life and reported to family members that he was being followed (HRW 2000). Rutabana fled the country in January 2000 along with a military officer, Lt. Bertin Murera, who claimed that he had been ordered to assassinate Rutabana but had refused to do it (HRW 2000). Rutabana and Murera were arrested in Tanzania in February 2000 by men purporting to be Rwandan policemen. The two were extradited to Rwanda and turned over to the military police. Rutabana was held in a military prison, but his detention was never reported by the government media.

Sebarenzi's flight and Rutabana's flight, arrest, and detention were widely discussed by Rwandan citizens, although discreetly in the privacy of their own homes. Rutabana's sudden absence from the public sphere was widely noted. Following his flight and during his detention, his songs and videos no longer played on the national radio or television. His audio and video cassettes were immediately removed from the markets. A Rwandan teenage girl explained to me that government officials regularly visited the markets and "sound studios," kiosks and shops that sold pirated music cassette tapes, to be sure that no one was selling the banned music.

Once rumors of Rutabana's association with Sebarenzi and the monarchists spread, the meaning of the lyrics of his second most popular song, "Imfura zirashize" (The people of integrity are dead), as well as the imagery used in the music video took on new meaning. In Kinyarwanda, *imfura* has two primary meanings: firstborn, as in the eldest son or daughter, and people of integrity, referring to the noble characteristics associated with firstborn children. Before Rutabana's association with the monarchists, most Rwandans interpreted the song to be about the Tutsi who had died during the genocide, and the music video showed a reenactment of Tutsi fleeing during the genocide and documentary footage of genocide victims' bodies. Yet this footage was interspersed with footage of the Rwandan nobility and *mwami* during the colonial period. In addition, the music video shows Rutabana singing at the Bisesero memorial site in Kibuye near his natal hill and the birthplaces of former speaker of the house Joseph Sebarenzi and former president Pasteur Bizimungu. Thus, once rumors of his support for the monarchists and Sebarenzi spread, the lyrics and the iconography of the video were reread as political statements: Rutabana supported the *mwami* and the politicians from Kibuye who pushed back against RPF dictates. Urban Rwandans who had seen the music video for "Imfura zirashize" reinterpreted the song as an endorsement of the *mwami* and his return to Rwanda.

Once the threat of the army of the king had died down by late 2000, Rutabana was released from military prison. According to the biography on his official website, he was "exonerated of all accusations" and released without condition.[7] The *radio trottoir*, on the other hand, reported that the government had negotiated the conditions of Rutabana's release. It was said that he agreed to sing his pro-RPF songs, to do a national tour sponsored by MTN Rwandacell (the only cell phone company in Rwanda at the time and owned by important RPF members), and to avoid associating with opposition members. Within a day or two of his release, Rutabana gave large concerts in several prefectures. Again, his popular song "Afrika" was played on the national radio and television. Yet his song "Imfura zirashize" never made a return to Rwandan national television or radio. In 2004 Rutabana went into exile in Europe.

Amplified Silence and Power: Resisting by Remembering

Despite the hegemony of this discursive regime, Rwandans resisted amplified silence by remembering their violent experiences individually and by sharing their memories quietly with intimates. Like the genocide survivors described in chapter 2, the survivors of RPF-perpetrated violence revealed their stories in snippets and snatches sewn together with large quantities of silence. They broke their silence spontaneously when inspired by a situation, a place, an object, a smell, or another person's narrative of suffering. Sometimes they broke their silence at calculated moments in order to bear witness for justice or for history.

For Rwandans living in exile, it was easier to recount stories of RPF-perpetrated atrocities because the speakers did not fear government reprisals.[8] One Rwandan man in his early thirties, Herve, shared his experiences during the genocide when he showed me his photo albums, which included pictures of his dead parents, brothers, and sisters. Herve had fled Rwanda in 1994 after the RPF's arrival. He first went to Zaire and then West Africa. He came to the United States through a UN-sponsored refugee resettlement program.

During our conversation in 2002, Herve asked about the new Rwandan government. He seemed surprised that I was not afraid to live in Rwanda. He had a very negative opinion of the RPF. I explained that things in Rwanda were not as bad as Rwandans in exile believed. Although the RPF government had its problems, it had made a lot of progress in rebuilding the country and restoring peace. Herve shrugged his shoulders in response and then declared, "I could never live in Rwanda again." Herve then explained that the RPF had killed his whole family:

> HERVE: The RPF killed everyone! You see, my mother was Tutsi and my father was Hutu. We had managed to survive the genocide. For all those months, we kept my mother hidden in the house. Then, when the RPF took control of our neighborhood [in Kigali], they went from house to house. They killed everyone.
> JENNIE BURNET: Why did they kill your mother?
> HERVE: You don't know the RPF! She was a collaborator to them. She was sleeping with the enemy. They [the RPF] killed them all. My mother, my father, my brothers and sisters. That's when I left [Rwanda]. I had no reason to stay, and I was afraid they would kill me too.

Herve's story was one of only a few that I heard of RPF-perpetrated killings. A Tutsi genocide survivor I interviewed in the United States in 2004 refused to state explicitly that she had witnessed RPF killings in 1994 and 1995, but she told me as much in coded language. Her fear of being heard was so great that she whispered her story to me and looked furtively over her shoulder (in her own house in the United States!) as she spoke. She only said, "Many bad things happened in 1994 and 1995 in RPF-occupied zones. It was best to not see anything, not hear anything, not know anything."

Rwandans still living in Rwanda were reluctant to tell their stories, but these stories sometimes slipped out unintentionally while the Rwandans were explaining something else about their lives. Women often revealed stories about the refugee camps when they spoke of their children. I pieced together the faintest outline of the story of one woman, Revocata, over two years of social visits and conversations between 1999 and 2000. Most often, we talked about her job, her son, who liked to play soccer more than he liked to study, or her husband's imprisonment, but pieces of her story slipped out during our conversations. The first time she ever mentioned violent experiences was when she related the difficulty she had helping her son, who was only three years old when their refugee camp was attacked by the RPF, understand why they had left his favorite pair of red shoes behind in the refugee camp. She laughed as she explained, "For days, then weeks, then months, he kept upbraiding me for leaving his red sneakers. He would ask me to go back and get them for him. He would cry. He would scream. Even now, he thinks about those sneakers from time to time."

Revocata had spent two years in the refugee camps near Goma. For most of that time, her husband, Edbert, languished in prison in Rwanda. In early 1995 Edbert had returned to Rwanda from the camps to see whether it was safe for the family to follow him. He and his family suffered severe harassment in the camps because he had worked for the UNAMIR forces before the genocide. Many Hutu extremists perceived the UNAMIR forces as RPF allies and thus MRND enemies. Edbert had decided that if he were to die, he would rather do so while breathing freely on his native soil than as an exile in Zaire, where the air was not fresh and clean. Within forty-eight hours of his return, he was arrested, nearly beaten to death by military police, and then imprisoned in the Kigali Central Prison. It took Revocata several weeks to learn what had happened to her husband. Given Edbert's fate, she decided to remain in the camps with their son and await the birth of their second child. When the RPF attacked the camp in 1996, she fled with her two children and her sister. Luckily, the attack began early in the morning before she had left the family's "home," a makeshift shelter constructed from thin wood supports and blue UN tarps, in the camp for her job with an international NGO. They were able to stay together, but in the chaos they left behind virtually all their belongings. They made the long trip home to a community a few kilometers north of Kigali on foot.

Revocata's story is similar to that of another woman, Pelagia. Pelagia explained to me that her three children, who were old enough to remember the time before the camps, the genocide and war, the time in exile, and the months of flight in Zairian forests, would sit around reminiscing about what they had seen. She said that sometimes, especially when they were younger and still living in the camps, her two sons would complain about the electronic game their uncle had sent them from Europe but that was left behind when they fled the advancing RPF in 1994. As her children grew older, she began to explain the harsh realities of the genocide, war, and refugee camps. They came to understand life's impermanence.

> PELAGIA: Now they say things to each other like, "Remember all those clothes we had in Rukomo? Wouldn't it be great if we still had them?" Other times they talk about what they saw in the forests.
> JENNIE BURNET: What did you see in the forests?
> PELAGIA: We saw things that no one, especially children, should see. Bodies with machete marks here [*she made a chopping motion with her right hand against her left arm*] and there [*another chopping motion on the back of her leg*], hacked to bits. Dead women shot through the face like this [*angling her hand in the shape of a gun at her cheek*] lying in the forest with crying babies still tied to their backs. (Author interview, 2000, Kigali)

Mothers often brought up the difficulty of explaining suffering to their children or watching their children suffer and being unable to do anything to comfort them. On another occasion, Revocata revealed more suffering while talking about her children. When I met Revocata, she lived in the remains of the house that she and her husband had been constructing before the war. The adobe brick walls covered with a thin layer of cement had numerous holes in them from shells and were pockmarked with bullet holes. A single, bare lightbulb lit the living room, where she received visitors on a few mismatched pieces of wooden furniture with no cushions. While we were sitting in her living room, night fell outside and seemed to emphasize the misery inside. Revocata sighed and said:

> The hardest part is when you have to put your children to bed without eating, so many nights, sometimes three in a row, when I couldn't find anything to give them and we would spend the night in the same bed, if you could call it a bed, it was just a pile of mats on the floor and one blanket to cover us, looking for sleep that never came.[9] Then Jacques or Zuzu would say, "Mommy, I'm hungry. I want something to eat. My stomach hurts." How do you explain to a three-year-old that there isn't any food? Sometimes they would cry and cry. I would just cry with them. What else could I do? They were breaking my heart. (Author interview, 2000)

It was over a year after I first met Revocata that she told me how she had been arrested, imprisoned, and tortured upon her return from the camps. Up until that point I assumed that the scars around her mouth and on her forehead were from a car accident, since I knew she was not a genocide survivor. During a visit she explained to me how she had been hurt. Our conversation began when I asked her about her house. She had just repaired the wall of a back room of the house and erected a wall in the hallway so that she could rent out two rooms to help cover her expenses. She had been working for several months for a UN-sponsored program in a government ministry, but the workers had not yet been paid due to a dispute between the UN and the Rwandan government. Renting out the rooms gave some assurance of food on the table. I asked her whether it had been difficult to reclaim her house when she returned from exile. She exclaimed, "Hard? That doesn't explain the half of it." Whether based on the months of slowly built trust or the spontaneous atmosphere of that moment, she began to recount the following narrative.

When she returned with her children from exile, they first had to report to her "commune of origin."[10] Although women automatically adopted their husband's commune of origin when they married, Revocata retained her own commune of origin because she and her husband were not legally married. Thus, she returned with her children to her parents' home in order to reestablish herself as a legitimate citizen.[11] When she reported to the commune office to register her return, seek a new identity card, and have her two children (who had been born in exile) inscribed on her identity card, she was arrested. She was held in the local jail and interrogated by soldiers and policemen for several days. During the interrogations, they "pressured" her into speaking, as she put it. They twisted her arms and fingers, kicked her with booted feet, and beat her with their fists, sticks, boards, and rope whips. She pointed to the scars on her face and explained that that was how she had received them. She then unbuttoned her shirt to show me other scars on her chest and back. After several weeks of mistreatment and torture, she was eventually released, thanks in large part to her mother, who courageously returned to the commune office every day asking about her daughter's well-being.

Another woman, Bibiane, told me more details of her story one evening in 2000 after we had visited a neighbor. Bibiane had grown up in a rural community in western Rwanda. She had completed secondary school and taught home economics in technical schools before the genocide. We had just visited an elderly genocide survivor in his late eighties. During the visit he showed us his "most precious possession," a traditional stool that had been passed down for at least four generations in his family.[12] He explained that when the genocide had started, the one thing he took with him was his stool. He had fled over eighty kilometers on foot in order to swim across the Kanyaru River into Burundi. As we left the house and walked toward our homes, I marveled to Bibiane:

> JENNIE BURNET: I don't understand how he made it.
> BIBIANE: What do you mean?
> JENNIE: How did he run so far? He can hardly walk from his house to mine [a distance of a quarter mile].
> BIBIANE: [*Excited*] Oh, Jennie! Ooh, ooh, ooh! You don't know what it was like! The things we've seen! In Zaire the elderly walked much farther than Mutama![13] You know my old mother-in-law? She walked through the forests from ——— to the transit camps [in Gisenyi, a distance of more than fifty miles]. The ones too old or too tired to walk anymore, they just lay down, one here [*motioning to the side of the path with her hand*], one there [*motioning to where the next hypothetical body lay, feet at the head of the last one*]. They just lay down, lined up in a row, to die. The path was lined with them. The rest of us just walked by them as if we didn't see [them]. All the way back to Rwanda.

As illustrated by these stories, individuals resist the paradigmatic story by selectively breaking the amplified silence in private spaces with intimates. Men and women each exercise agency in these decisions. In 1994 Rwandan women were legally emancipated, but in practice they were still widely perceived as legal "minors under the guardianship of fathers, brothers, husbands or sons" (Turshen 2001, 60). Although gender roles changed rapidly in Rwanda after the genocide, these cultural scripts were still powerful. In some instances, women used these infantilizing scripts as protection to break amplified silence in more public ways.

I asked a male genocide survivor whether it was possible that people killed by the RPF were buried in mass graves at genocide memorial sites. He laughed and said: "Possible? Not possible. *They are buried there.* The RPF executed the perpetrators they found right away, on the spot. They would bury them in graves with genocide victims to hide what they were doing [from the international community]. They still hide those bodies the same way. If you find a mass grave, you can't exactly say they were killed by the RPF, so they call them 'genocide victims' and bury them there [at the genocide memorial sites]."

Amplified Silence:
An Obstacle to Reconciliation

While amplified silence has served the RPF regime in the short term, in the long term it has undermined the state's legitimacy and perpetuated divisions in Rwandan society. Amplified silence prevented Rwandans from discussing the past openly. It created "more fear and uncertainty by driving a wedge of paranoia between people," as Green (1999, 69) wrote of the Guatemala Highlands. While Rwandans who lost family members in killings by RPF soldiers, who suffered together in Zaire, or who had family members imprisoned may have felt safe sharing their stories with other family members quietly in private places such as the home, they had trouble sharing their stories with friends and acquaintances who survived the genocide. As a result, from 1994 until the *gacaca* trials started nationwide in 2005, there was little meaningful communication between genocide survivors and Rwandans who had suffered during the civil war, in the refugee camps, or at the hands of the RPF.[14]

While the state's practices of amplified silence attempted to build national unity by creating a master narrative of Rwandan history that clearly separated "victims" and "perpetrators," the results were far from unified. Amplified silence perpetuated divisions within Rwandan society in four principal ways: it undercut healing, it impeded justice, it created competing discourses of innocence and victimization, and it perpetuated the social and political control of the state. While legitimate state control is an important component of a peaceful society, in Rwanda state control has played a detrimental role historically. In a sense, the genocide was possible because of the extent of state control over the population.

As will be discussed in chapters 5, 6, and 7, an important step toward reconciliation for many Rwandans was the sharing of individual narratives of suffering. Sharing individual narratives helped move people beyond ethnicity's essentialisms because the complexities and contradictions of individual experience helped people see beyond ethnic stereotypes. When only genocide survivors' stories could be told freely in public, the opportunities for empathetic sharing were diminished.

In a parallel manner, amplified silence impeded justice because there was no public assessment of who did what to whom before the *gacaca* process. Witnesses were reluctant to tell what they had seen during the genocide for numerous reasons. First, they feared attracting suspicion about their own actions. Whether or not the witnesses were perpetrators, others might have suspected them of complicity in genocide if they admitted to witnessing killing, looting, or raping. Second, they were sometimes reluctant to discuss the genocide because of their resentment over atrocities perpetrated against them or their family members by the RPF. Why facilitate justice for genocide survivors if RPF-perpetrated massacre victims could not have their own justice? Finally, for many Rwandans, distinctions between the civil war and the genocide did not exist, so they found it difficult or even impossible to talk about what happened in the genocide without also discussing what happened during the civil war or RPF-perpetrated violence before, during, or after the genocide. Although the *gacaca* jurisdictions were intended to overcome these impediments to justice, they could not succeed if people did not feel free to discuss everything that happened.

Amplified silence created competing discourses of innocence and victimization. Because the master narratives about the genocide established one class of victims (Tutsi) and another class of perpetrators (Hutu), it was logical for Hutu victims of violence to dismiss the master narratives about the genocide and national history as complete fabrications rather than as partial truths. Because Hutu victimization stories were not readily available in public discourse about the genocide and civil war, they were forced into private familial forums or into monoethnic group forums. In this way, the amplified silence around Hutu narratives of suffering became a competing discourse that supported the Hutu extremists' claims that the genocide did not happen.

4

Sorting and Suffering

Social Classification in the Aftermath of Genocide

In Rwanda the shibboleth of genocide forced a clear yet sometimes arbitrary demarcation between Hutu and Tutsi. This violent partition had an enduring impact on the lived experience of social classification in the aftermath of the genocide. The previous chapters described how the Rwandan Patriotic Front's (RPF) management of national mourning, its rewriting of national history, and its hegemony manifested in amplified silence produced a moral economy that equated "Hutu" with "killer" and "Tutsi" with "victim." As Geoffrey Bowker and Susan Star (1999) argue, all classification systems carry moral and ethical agendas. In their examination of race classification under apartheid in South Africa, Bowker and Star trace the ways that "the lives of individuals are broken, twisted, and torqued by their encounters" with the racial classification system (1999, 26). Gender and ethnic social classifications in the aftermath of the genocide affected Rwandan women in similar ways and increased the marginalization of citizens who did not fit into the social categories deployed in the dominant discourse about the genocide, civil war, and national history.

While many scholars have already tackled the meanings of ethnic classification in pregenocide Rwanda, few have written about ethnicity in postgenocide Rwanda. Investigating or writing about ethnicity in Rwanda today is not only extremely difficult, it is also dangerous. Under the RPF's policy of national unity, it is impossible to ask research participants direct questions about ethnicity. During the bulk of my ethnographic research in Rwanda between 1997 and 2002, this policy was a public secret, unstated but universally known. In 2001 the Law on Discrimination and Sectarianism codified this policy into law and defined "divisionism" as a crime punishable by one to five years in prison. The 2003 constitution stated that the Rwandan people should root out "genocidal ideology" everywhere and in all its forms. Neither law clearly defined "divisionism" or "genocidal ideology."

As a result, the government has used these laws to silence RPF critics and to suppress movements opposed to RPF rule. The first example was the 2004 parliamentary study of divisionism in international and national civil society organizations. The report resulted in a witch hunt of local civil society leaders of the organizations named in the report. The leaders of the Rwandan human rights organization Ligue rwandaise pour la promotion et la défense des droits de l'homme (LIPRODHOR) fled the country because of the threat imposed by the results of the reports (IRIN 2004a, 2004b). In 2005 the Rwandan Senate commissioned a study to identify divisionism and genocidal ideology among foreign scholars (US Department of State 2006). In 2006 a Canadian researcher was detained by Rwandan authorities who then revoked her research permit. They seized her passport and required her to attend an *ingando* (solidarity camp) where she would learn the "true history" of Rwanda before she was expelled from the country (Thomson 2011). She believed that it was the nature of her research, which attempted to gather a wide variety of perspectives on government policies from rural residents, that resulted in her detention and the suspension of her research (personal communication, 2011). Beyond this formal repression, the RPF has been extremely successful in selling its version of national history to the international community (diplomats, humanitarian workers, and journalists) (Pottier 2002).

In this chapter I examine the ways that systems of gender and ethnic/racial classification in postgenocide Rwanda make certain Rwandan women invisible. These social classification processes increased their suffering by bringing past violence into their present lives. Through a case study of three residual categories of women living in the borderlands of social classifications in postgenocide Rwanda (raped "maidens," Tutsi wives of prisoners, and Hutu genocide widows) I demonstrate that these categories do not fit into the dominant systems of social classification. The first category, raped maidens, consists of prepubescent and adolescent girls as well as unmarried young women who were raped during the genocide. The second category, Tutsi wives of prisoners (*abagore b'abafunze*), consists of Tutsi wives of (usually) Hutu men imprisoned on charges of genocide. The third, Hutu genocide widows (*abapfakazi b'itsembabwoko*), consists of the Hutu widows of (usually) Tutsi men killed during the genocide. Despite their marginalization, these women exercised their agency to rebuild their lives despite the structural and symbolic violence that sorting inflicted on them.

Sorting: Social Classification in Postgenocide Rwanda

As discussed at length in chapter 1, the classificatory systems of gender and ethnicity/race have been the product of changing constellations of social, economic, and political power and the violent sorting of categories throughout the 1990s. The violent demarcation of ethnicity/race during the genocide had an enduring impact on lived experiences of social classification. Yet the ethnic/racial classification system underwent further transformation in the years after the genocide. Under the RPF's policy of national unity, open discussions about ethnicity became taboo, and using the term "Hutu," "Tutsi," or "Twa" was considered politically incorrect.[1] Nonetheless, Rwandan society was far from unified, and ethnic distinctions remained salient. State practices of national memory and the attendant amplified silence maintained an ethnic dichotomy (Hutu/Tutsi) by politicizing victimhood and emphasizing the distinction between victim and perpetrator in national ceremonies commemorating the genocide (Burnet 2009).[2] The hegemony of public discourse and the state's power to define who was "innocent" and who was "guilty," who was "victim" and who was "perpetrator" undermined the RPF's professed ideology of national unity and reinforced ethnic categories of social classification.

Within this context, a new language for discussing ethnicity emerged. Rwandans and foreigners working in Rwanda began to talk about ethnic classification in terms of experiential categories focused on the 1994 genocide and two major refugee flows: the first, mainly Tutsi refugees who left between 1959 and 1973 and returned after the 1994 genocide; and the second, mainly Hutu refugees who left in 1994 and returned in 1996 or 1997. While this new set of categories may have been more accurate in that it focused on

Table 2. Social classification in postgenocide Rwanda

Tutsi	Hutu
victims (*inzirakarengane*)	perpetrators, killers (*abicanyi*)
survivors (*abarokotse*)	prisoners (*abafunze*)
genocide widows (*abapfakazi b'itsembabwoko*)	infiltrators (*abacengezi*)
old returnees (*abaturutse hanze, abarutashye*)	new returnees (*abatahutse, abahungutse, abatingitingi*)

individuals' experiences rather than on imagined, innate, ethnic essences, it maintained a polar distinction between Hutu and Tutsi. Terms synonymous with Tutsi included victims (*inzirakarengane*), survivors (*abarokotse*), genocide widows (*abapfakazi b'itsembabwoko*), and old returnees (*abaturutse hanze, abarutashye*) (referring to Tutsi who returned from long-term exile).[3] Terms synonymous with Hutu included perpetrators (*abicanyi*), prisoners (*abafunze*), infiltrators (*abacengezi*), and new returnees (*abatingitingi, abatahutse, abahungutse*) (referring to Hutu who went into exile in 1994 and returned in 1996 and 1997).[4]

While this new constellation of words may have been more accurate, it polarized discussions of the genocide by leaving no space in public discourse or mourning practices for Hutu genocide victims and by globalizing blame on Hutu, regardless of whether they participated in the genocide or not. For Rwandans in ethnically mixed families, this polarizing discourse excluded their experiences of violence: they could not be victims of violence at the hands of the genocide perpetrators because they were not genocide victims or survivors, and they could not be victims of violence at the hands of the RPF because in the hegemonic national discourses about violence, the RPF only committed violence against genocide perpetrators. Thus their experiences of violence were erased from the national imagination. Furthermore, this set of categories reinforced the distinction between Hutu and Tutsi among those Rwandans (Hutu, Tutsi, Twa, and those of mixed heritage) who grew up inside the country.

Vice President Paul Kagame summarized the double bind of Hutu opponents of the genocide in his response to a journalist's question about rumors of imminent massive reprisals against Hutu that were circulating widely in April 1995: "There are many ways to analyze this phenomenon. First is that this fear [of reprisals against Hutu] could be justified. A lot of people know that they committed or were complicit with some crimes, and they are afraid of being held responsible. The second explanation is a long history of intoxication—they always told the population that Tutsi are dangerous, that they wanted power."[5] In this statement, then vice president

Kagame deployed a linguistic device of coded ethnic talk that Rwandans heard clearly but that foreign observers could not detect. In his speeches over the years, Kagame has frequently opposed two terms: *abantu* (people) and Banyarwanda (Rwandans). In this opposition, the generic *abantu* is heard as "Hutu," while the more specific term, "Banyarwanda," literally "Rwandans" but which can also mean "the people to whom Rwanda belongs," is understood as "Tutsi." In this quotation, whether the first or second explanation proposed by Vice President Kagame was correct, the (Hutu) people were to blame—either for their participation in or complicity with the genocide or for their willingness to believe propaganda against Tutsi and the RPF. The vice president did not propose a third explanation: that the fears were justified because RPA soldiers had been killing civilians (both Hutu and Tutsi). Although these killings were well known among Rwandans inside the country, they were rarely reported by human rights organizations (author interviews, 1998, 1999, 2000, 2001, 2005). The most that international human rights monitors and humanitarian aid workers could do was report that the RPA tightly controlled access to local communities throughout 1994 (HRW 1995, 1996b). Rwandan citizens who opposed the killings—whether Hutu or Tutsi—kept their mouths shut in order to avoid becoming victims as well (author interviews, 1997, 1998, 2000, 2005). Under this discursive regime, even prominent Hutu dissidents who had been targeted for killing in the genocide were vulnerable to accusations of genocide. Numerous Hutu politicians included in the postgenocide government between 1994 and 2005 faced accusations of genocide when they criticized the RPF or when they were no longer politically valuable to the regime (*Dialogue* 1995a, 1995b; HRW 1996b).

To illustrate the contingency of ethnic classification, which begins to seem cut and dried when discussed abstractly, let me relate an ethnographic vignette about two brothers. The first brother, Petero, was in his late twenties and a student at the national university when I met him in 2000. He was also a soldier in the Rwandan Patriotic Front. Before the genocide, Petero had worked in a parastatal company in Kigali. Although Petero had wanted to go to the university and had excellent scores on national exams, he was not awarded a coveted place at the national university. Even though he had managed to change his official ethnic identity (meaning the one marked on his identity card) to Hutu, his parents did not have the necessary connections to secure him a place at the university. Under Habyarimana's patrimonial rule, having the "correct" ethnicity was not enough, as the state and its benefits were shared among a limited network of families and friends from the mountains of northwestern Rwanda.

In 1994 Petero escaped the killing squads by fleeing across the battle lines to the RPF side. His national identity card, marked "Hutu," did not offer him any protection from his prototypical "Tutsi" appearance. Like most able-bodied men and adolescent boys who managed to cross the front lines, Petero was conscripted into service with the RPF. In the years after the genocide, Petero tried to demobilize, but the army refused to release him and instead commissioned him as an officer. They sent him to study at the national university, which afforded him a civilian lifestyle, at least for a few years.

While Petero was classified as Tutsi, his older brother, Yohani, who had the same father and mother as Petero, was classified as Hutu. Before the genocide Yohani was a soldier in the Rwandan military, Forces armées rwandaises, known by its French acronym, FAR. When the genocide began, Yohani remained with his unit. The fate of most Tutsi soldiers in the FAR was execution by firing squad (Des Forges 1999, 266–70). However, Yohani, with a less obviously "Tutsi" physiognomy, had successfully passed for Hutu during his entire military career, and he managed to maintain this disguise during the genocide. Yohani remained with his unit and retreated into exile before the advancing RPF lines. Yohani eventually returned to Rwanda in 1998 after spending two years in refugee camps in eastern Zaire plus over a year in the rain forests following the RPF's attacks on the camps in 1996.

As a recently returned refugee (*uhungutse*) in postgenocide Rwanda and as a former FAR soldier, Yohani was classified as Hutu in the minds of most Rwandans who knew anything about his recent personal history. His siblings, on the other hand, were all perceived as Tutsi. In this ambiguity, Yohani returned to the community where his mother had lived before her death of natural causes in 1993.

Suffering:
The Torque of Social Classification

While in many ways highly ambiguous, this system of social classification played a foundational role in social interactions in the late 1990s and early 2000s. Especially among Rwandans without kin or friendship ties predating the genocide, these categories served as an initial filter of understanding (or lack thereof) among strangers or acquaintances. When combined with other categories of social classification such as gender, they created social capital—or, in most cases, the lack of social capital—that shaped individual agency. In the rest of this chapter, I explore the ways that the lives of certain female Rwandans were "torqued" and their suffering prolonged because they did not fit into the "Aristotelian ideal types of social classification" (Bowker and Starr 1999, 223) in postgenocide Rwanda. The gendered social classifications discussed in chapter 1 are at the heart of this discussion:

maidens (*abari*, unmarried Rwandan girls of marriageable age), wives (*abagore* or *abategarugori*), and widows (*abapfakazi*).

Raped Maidens

As discussed in chapter 1, cultural scripts placed women and girls under the protection of men: before marriage, that of their fathers, brothers, and uncles, and after marriage, that of their husbands, brothers-in-law, and fathers-in-law. Thus, the major preoccupation for a maiden in Rwanda, as in many other places in the world, is to get married, because it is the only way for her to gain some autonomy, albeit autonomy as the "heart of the household."[6] In the wake of the genocide, maidens faced a difficult terrain fraught with dangers. There were limited opportunities for them to enter into legitimate marriages.

As discussed in chapter 2, the genocide and war caused a demographic shift in Rwandan society that lasted for several years from about 1994 until about 2001. The targeting of Tutsi men and boys in the genocide meant that genocide survivors were disproportionately female. Male genocide survivors were mobilized as RPA soldiers to help fight the war. Hutu men and boys were more likely to flee the advancing RPF in 1994 for fear of being killed or imprisoned; wives sometimes remained behind in the hopes of retaining the family's property rights over homes and farmland and to prevent looting. As internally displaced persons and refugees began to return home in 1995 and as RPA soldiers shifted from combat to policing duties, the demographic situation began to return to a more normal equilibrium. The mass return of refugees in 1996 and 1997 quickly helped equalize the gender gap; however, the mass arrest of returning refugee men and adolescents on genocide charges meant that a significant proportion of Hutu men were part of the population but not accessible for social reproduction. Recruitment of Rwandan male youth for the RPA invasion of Zaire and ongoing RPA engagement in the Congo Wars (1997–2003) siphoned off many men of marrying age. In certain communities the gender gap remained significant, particularly among people of marriageable age. As a result, the demographic situation limited maidens' marriage opportunities in some communities more than others.

Beyond the demographic issue, the civil war and genocide's economic devastation reduced maidens' marriage opportunities. To enter into a "legitimate" marriage, meaning one recognized socially and legally, a bachelor needed to prove his ability to support a family. In rural Rwanda such proof entailed access to farmland and building a house. In urban Rwanda a stable job or solvent business sufficed. A bachelor also needed the required bride-price, which in the past had been furnished by his lineage. Since the vast majority of personal property, including bank account balances, and real estate were looted in the genocide or left behind in the flight to safety or into exile, most Rwandans, whether genocide survivors or not, had to begin their lives again from "less than zero," as one genocide widow put it, making a bride-price out of the reach of many bachelors and their lineages.

Beyond these material obstacles to marriage, maidens faced social obstacles that hinged on the symbolism of marriage in Rwandan culture. Many Tutsi maidens who survived the genocide had been raped or forced into so-called marriages with Hutu militiamen. Virginity, or at least the illusion of virginity, is a fundamental characteristic of a desirable bride in Rwanda. While brides today may rarely be virgins, they must have maintained the public illusion of virginity. For maidens raped during the genocide, entering into a legitimate marriage was virtually impossible unless they kept their rapes secret.

Maidens who were able to keep their rapes secret still had to cope with the psychological consequences of their experiences and, in some cases, the rumors about their rapes that circulated in the community. Maidens lucky enough to be courted faced difficult decisions whether to reveal what had happened to them. Caught in a true double bind, these maidens feared being jilted by their boyfriends or fiancés if they remained silent about their rapes because the men might assume they were "loose women" (a local term synonymous with "slut" or "prostitute") when the men discovered the maidens were not virgins. Or the maidens might be jilted if they revealed the truth about what had happened to them in the genocide because they could be perceived as "tainted" by their contact with Hutu militiamen.

Two categories of maidens found it impossible to hide their rapes: (1) those who became pregnant and (2) those who contracted HIV. After the genocide, these maidens were viewed and continue to be viewed today as tainted by the touch of Hutu extremists and the Interahamwe militias. Some of the single mothers faced rejection by surviving family members who denounced them as "collaborators" of the genocide perpetrators. The children who resulted from these rapes were also stigmatized: they remained as living reminders of their mothers' shame. Maidens who became single mothers faced a social dead-end: they could not advance to the next stage of life as wives and mothers and were stuck in a figurative no-woman's-land of single motherhood.

I met one such single mother, Placidia, along with her five-year-old son in 2000. Placidia was the sister of Petero and Yohani (discussed earlier in this chapter). I met Placidia when Petero invited me to attend Yohani's wedding celebration. On the morning of the celebration, we stopped to visit Placidia on the way to the event. After visiting with her, we went on to the reception hall, where I helped the wives and maidens prepare food. I noticed that Placidia was conspicuously absent from the preparations. Later during the wedding mass and reception, I again noticed that Placidia did not attend, although the celebration was taking place in her family's home community, where she continued to live with her son. At the time, I had no idea that Placidia's son was born of rape. It was only several months later that I had an explanation for her absence. Petero was lamenting the "trouble," as he called it, that Placidia was causing in their brother's marriage. I asked Petero why Placidia would want to cause problems.

> PETERO: I guess maybe it's out of jealousy. Placidia is stuck there in our mother's house. She can't get married—no one will have her.
> JENNIE BURNET: Why not?
> PETERO: Because everyone knows she was raped, even if we never talk about it. If she were a widow, it might be different. But they [meaning potential suitors] see him [her son]. Most survivors [read "Tutsi"] can't stomach the idea of adopting a Hutu bastard. It would take a really strong man to withstand all that.
>
> When I was trying to marry Jane [a woman with whom Petero had a son], Placidia meddled. She kept telling me that Jane wasn't a good wife for me. Now she's doing the same to Yohani, though he's already married . . . spreading rumors about his wife.[7]

Petero was sympathetic to his sister's situation even if he was exasperated. He added, "We try to be patient with her. She's suffered a lot. She continues to suffer. . . . It's not easy." While he did not say so explicitly, Petero recognized that a large part of his sister's problem, the root cause of her jealousy, was that she was cut off from traditional means of social reproduction. She could not be recognized as a legitimate wife and mother because she had never been married, and she probably never would be. As a result, she sought power when and where she could by influencing her younger brothers' marriages and courting decisions.

Tutsi Wives of Prisoners

In postgenocide Rwanda thousands upon thousands of Hutu men were imprisoned on accusations of genocide for years and years (table 3). At its peak in 1999, the Rwandan prison population was estimated to be 150,000, according to Human Rights Watch; the vast majority was awaiting trial on charges of genocide. While it is possible that the majority of prisoners participated in the genocide, as the government maintained throughout the late 1990s and early 2000s, many thousands had been imprisoned simply because they were Hutu and male or because someone had fabricated charges against them. In the years immediately following the genocide, it

Table 3. Prison population in Rwanda, 1995–2010

Year	No. of prisoners
1995	57,000
1996	83,000
1997	120,000
1998	126,000
1999	150,000
2000	125,000
2001	105,273
2002	108,000
2003	85,000
2004	86,000
2005	70,000
2006	87,000
2007	97,000
2008	65,415
2009	69,212
2010	68,430

Sources: Figures for 1995–99 and 2007 from Human Rights Watch, "Rwanda—Human Rights Overview," in *World Report*, 1996–2000, 2008; figure for 2000 from Hirondelle News Agency, "Rwanda/Prisons— Rwanda Wants to Relieve Congestion in Its Prisons," December 4, 2007; figures for 2001–6 and 2008–10 from International Committee of the Red Cross, *Annual Report*, 2002–6, 2008–10.

was extremely easy to get someone arrested on suspicions of genocide. Although officially accusations from three independent parties were required, in most cases a single accusation was enough to get someone arrested. Once a person was in prison, investigations moved extremely slowly due to the overload of cases and lack of personnel in the justice system. As a result, the falsely accused faced what appeared to be indefinite detention at the time. Thousands died while in prison awaiting trial due to the horrific conditions in the overloaded prisons, jails, and impromptu detention centers.

Regardless of whether they were guilty or innocent, many of these prisoners had families on the outside. In fact, their lives depended on their kin on the outside who brought them food, drinking water, and clothing. The Rwandan government provided minimal food rations at best and at times did not provide any food at all. Prisoners' families faced many difficulties. Their status as the families of prisoners left them marked as presumed perpetrators or at least as genocide sympathizers in the eyes of many Tutsi. When they took supplies to the prison, they were required to stand in long queues for hours outside. The weekly queues served to mark them symbolically as perpetrators in the eyes of community members who passed by. In many communities, genocide survivors heckled the families waiting outside the prisons and threw rotten food or rocks at them. Prison guards insulted them, mistreated them, and often exacted bribes in the form of cash or sexual favors from the women and girls.

Tutsi wives of imprisoned Hutu men usually found themselves marginalized from every traditional support mechanism, including their husbands' patrilineage, their own patrilineage, and the community. In some cases, the husband's patrilineage had opposed the marriage on the basis of ethnic difference in the first place. In other cases, the husband's patrilineage had come to oppose the marriage because they blamed the Tutsi wife for their son's imprisonment. They viewed their Tutsi daughters-in-law as RPF accomplices (*ibyitso*) or as cockroaches (*inyenzi*), expressing their dislike in the same terms used by the Hutu extremists to characterize Tutsi during the early 1990s and the genocide.

In many cases, Tutsi wives of prisoners were completely bereft of kin because their entire patrilineage was wiped out in the genocide. They often found that their few surviving kin blamed them for the genocide. Surviving kin viewed their Tutsi sisters as being both literally and figuratively in bed with the enemy. They saw Tutsi wives of Hutu men as collaborators in extremist Hutu politics and the genocide. Some of these Tutsi wives of prisoners knew or at least suspected that their husbands had participated in or even organized massacres during the genocide. They faced difficult decisions about whether to reveal what they knew about their husbands' actions (actions that sometimes had resulted in the wives' own family members—even children—dying terrible deaths), to promote justice for genocide victims and survivors, or to remain silent to preserve the sanctity of their marriages and what little kin support remained.

Beyond this marginalization at the hands of kin, Tutsi wives of prisoners were denied the moral, spiritual, and economic assistance some wives and widows found in associational life. Tutsi wives of prisoners were usually excluded from genocide survivor organizations because the members did not perceive Tutsi wives of Hutu men as "real" survivors. While associational life, particularly among Rwandan women, has flourished in the years since the genocide, prisoners' families could not create their own organizations because such efforts were perceived by the government as inherently political and were opposed on the grounds that they promoted "a genocidal ideology."

I met Dolores in 2001 when she worked for an American NGO in Kigali. Over several months I came to learn her story in snippets recounted here or there either by her or by a coworker. Dolores was in her forties and married, and she had several children. Her husband was imprisoned in the Kigali Central Prison on genocide charges. Under the Habyarimana government, he had been a member of the MRND and a highly placed bureaucrat. Each Saturday Dolores dutifully brought food to her husband, waiting in the long queues outside the prison, except for the last Saturday of each month, when there was *umuganda*. At work Dolores was usually cheerful although matter-of-fact and very direct in social interactions, not in typical Rwandan fashion. Occasionally, she would show exasperation as she exited the office of her direct supervisor, who was very demanding and, in Dolores's opinion, often unreasonable. Over coffee one morning Dolores's coworker recounted in Dolores's presence how Dolores's husband treated her during their marriage.

> Don't you know!?! Her husband was a notorious Interahamwe. He was a racist from the beginning [shortly after their wedding]. He always treated her badly, but things really heated up after the war started. He used to make her undress and stand completely naked beside the bed all night long so that he could look at her *if he wanted to*. If she would lie down in the bed to sleep, he would shove her out onto the floor and yell at her and make her stand there naked.
>
> [In the daytime] when he wanted something, he would order her around and call her *inyenzi*. All day she worked as a secretary [and gave her salary to him], and then at night she was a slave.
>
> They say he had a lot of people killed in the genocide.

On another occasion, when Dolores mentioned that her entire Saturday had been wasted waiting outside the prison, I asked her why she brought food and water to her husband if he had treated her so badly. She said, "I don't have a choice. You see, my in-laws have already taken one house. They would like to see me and the children put out on the street so that they can have the one we are in. I have to take care of my husband so that he will keep them from taking the house." What she did not say but what I could guess based on the experiences of other Tutsi wives of prisoners was that her in-laws demanded money from her, saying that she was rich because she worked for Americans. She had learned to explain away her earnings with stories of the children's tuition, uniforms, and other needs.

I lost touch with Dolores for several years, but I then learned she had immigrated to the United States. She brought her children to join her one by one. Then she died. According to a Rwandan woman who had worked with her, Dolores had been poisoned by her in-laws, who were furious that she had left Rwanda. I asked the woman how she knew it was a case of poisoning. She responded, "That's what everyone says. Who else would want to cause her harm?"

Months later I spoke with an American woman who had worked with Dolores at the NGO. I asked her about Dolores, pretending that I did not know Dolores was dead. The woman told me that Dolores had committed suicide. I explained that I had heard a rumor that she had been poisoned by her in-laws. The American woman explained:

She definitely killed herself. It's terrible. She worked so hard to get here [to the United States]. [Another American who had worked at the NGO] helped her to get the visa, then she stayed and applied for asylum. She worked really hard and then brought her sons. She escaped from her husband and in-laws.

It seems she started having problems. She became depressed. She started having flashbacks and other signs of [psychological] trauma. I think she must have believed that if she left Rwanda and came to the United States, all her problems would be solved and her life would be easy. When it didn't turn out that way, she ended it.

Committing suicide is an extreme way to exercise agency in difficult circumstances and is not an option that I would characterize as resisting systems of social classification. While Dolores's case had a tragic ending, other Tutsi wives of prisoners have fared better. Some managed to escape their husbands or in-laws. Others, who believed their husbands were innocent, did what they could to exonerate them. In some cases they failed, but in others they succeeded. These women faced the challenge of reintegrating their husbands into society—a society that scarcely resembled the pregenocide society they had known.

Hutu Genocide Widows

Following the genocide, many widows (whether they were widows due to natural causes, genocide widows, or widows due to RPF-perpetrated killings) found themselves in precarious situations because the male kin who protected their rights and guaranteed them access to land were absent.[8] Widows from ethnically mixed marriages faced the worst of it, as they often found themselves caught between the two families, with neither family willing to fulfill traditional kin obligations to the widow or her surviving children.

Intermarriage between Hutu and Tutsi was very common from the 1970s onward, especially in central and southern Rwanda. At the community level little distinction was made between Hutu and Tutsi until the start of the civil war in 1990. The genocide did not start until late April in this region, but then the killing was very effective because most Tutsi had gathered at government offices, schools, or churches. Because of the frequency of intermarriage as well as a greater representation of Tutsi in the population (around 40 percent, according to the 1990 census), the genocide decimated the population. Entire hills in Butare prefecture (now South province) remained empty because the few survivors were too afraid to live far from government offices or roads.

The situation of a woman's group in a rural area of southern Rwanda illustrates the impact of the genocide on social reproduction for women in ethnically mixed marriages. The group was comprised of Hutu genocide widows. Ranging in age from approximately twenty-three to sixty-six, the widows met weekly to study the Bible and work together. They shared many of the same problems, having dealt with social, political, and economic marginalization at the hands of kin and local authorities.

At a meeting in 2000 I asked the widows whether they had difficulties with their patrilineal kin. After a very long silence, one widow responded angrily, "All widows in our situation have problems with their family." The group leader interrupted her, saying, "You mustn't lie. There are also those who protected their families." Other group members then offered examples from the group where affinal kin had protected (or tried to protect) their Tutsi brothers-in-law, nephews, and nieces. Members of the group then explained that a Hutu genocide widow's relationship with her patrilineage depended upon how her brothers had behaved during the genocide: "There were Hutu men who protected their sisters' children; in these cases, there is no problem between the widow and her family. On the other hand, there were others who, instead of protecting their nieces and nephews, killed them, most of them indirectly—they went discreetly to call the Interahamwe from another hill [to do the killing]. The widows who lost their children like that—understandably, they have many problems with their families. Some have no relations with them at all." Some of the genocide widows' brothers were in prison accused of genocide. Those widows whose brothers had helped them during the genocide did not hesitate to take food to their brothers in prison.[9] As one widow explained, "I take food to my two brothers in prison each week. [Both brothers were single, so they did not have wives or children to bring them food.] They protected my children [during the genocide], but they went to kill others." Some widows who knew or believed that their brothers were responsible for killing their sisters' husbands or children would not take them food. Yet their resistance to kinship obligations came at a cost; they could not rely on their own patrilineage for assistance, whether economic, social, or emotional.

I asked the widows whether they had encountered difficulties with their affinal kin, such as disputes over land or property. The widows remained silent for a few minutes and looked down at the ground, a sign of sadness or shame. One widow finally spoke up. She said, laughing softly instead of crying, "You have to understand, for most of us there is no one left. They are all gone. There is no one left for us to have a conflict with."[10]

> WIDOW 2: Of course, for the few Hutu genocide widows who still have in-laws there have been problems, especially when the widow's brothers were responsible for killing her husband and children. In these cases, her in-laws will reject her. They refuse to let her cultivate. They take any remaining children and send her away.

> WIDOW 3: I know of one [Hutu widow] whose sisters-in-law survived. They were widows too, but they came home to their own patrilineages' land since all their brothers had been killed. They did not throw their sister-in-law out. They live together now as neighbors without any trouble. They help each other like sisters.

Following this group interview, my research assistant and I discussed whether these women were speaking in general or whether they were telling their own stories. In the end we concluded that it was probably a mix of the two, but, regardless, we did not have the detailed community information necessary to contextualize their narratives.

During another visit in 2001, the widows explained how they had been excluded from development assistance set aside for genocide survivors.

> WIDOW 1: In 1994 and early 1995 AVEGA gave us cooking pots, plates, cups, clothing, shoes, and seed. But when the foreigners [meaning international agencies] came to build houses for genocide survivors, we were not included. They built for other widows [of the genocide] first. Certain individuals [the widows intentionally did not name anyone] did not want us included on the lists. They said, "You have male kin [e.g., fathers and brothers]. They can build for you. You don't need any help." Even male genocide survivors received houses in the new villages [*imidugudu*], but we were forgotten.

The widows went on to explain that many of them were about to become homeless because the government building in which they had lived for four years was being reclaimed by the commune office to hold community food stores as part of a food security project sponsored by the World Food Program. The women were uncertain what to do and lamenting the fact that no one in the community seemed to recognize their difficulties.

The previous burgomaster who held the position from 1996 until 1999 was a genocide survivor. It was widely said that he took revenge against Hutu in the community. In 1999 he was removed from office by the Ministry of Local Affairs when many of his abuses of power came to light thanks to an investigative article published in a Kinyarwanda monthly news magazine. As he still lived in the community and wielded a great deal of influence, few people would state explicitly what he had done. Nonetheless, it was clear to my research assistant and me that the women believed that the burgomaster had excluded them from the original list of genocide survivors in need of housing assistance.

Because of their ambiguous status as "survivors" within the discourse promoted by the Rwandan government and its attendant, invisible classification system, community members felt justified in their "lack of pity," as the widows described it. Hutu neighbors remained complacent in the belief that the government or international aid organizations would help the Hutu genocide widows because only "survivors benefit from development assistance," as more than one rural Hutu said to me over the course of my research. Tutsi neighbors, on the other hand, believed that the widows' own patrilineages should take care of them. So these widows were left largely to their own devices, which were circumscribed by the customary law of land tenure and the widows' extreme poverty.

In a return visit to the same group in 2007, I caught up on news from the group. Six of the twenty members had died, leaving behind nine orphans whom the group did their best to help. Thanks to the assistance from Caritas Christi, the social support arm of the Roman Catholic diocese, the widows had received assistance in building houses in late 2001. Unlike most assistance projects coordinated by international NGOs, their houses were built with the free labor of prisoners on their own land on the hill rather than in a new village. During our brief meeting, I asked them about the progress of *gacaca*, and they told me that two of their members had been elected as judges (*inyangamugayo*), one at the cell (*akagari*) level and the other at the sector (*umurenge*) level.[11] When I asked them about the reintegration of perpetrators into the local community, they gave me what sounded like a rehearsed, politically correct answer; they said that everything went well.

> The prisoners had received awareness raising at a reeducation camp [*ingando*, required of all released prisoners] before coming home to the hill. We saw that when they arrived on the hill, they had changed a lot. They prayed a lot. You could see that they were true Christians. They approach the population to ask forgiveness from the people against whom they had committed genocide [meaning those whose family members they had killed]. They go help others. They go to explain to prisoners the benefits of confessing and asking for a pardon. (Author interview, May 21, 2007, Southern province)

I doubted that their account was complete, since many other people in the same community had explained that the reintegration of released prisoners and confessed genocide perpetrators was sometimes very difficult and tense. I then asked them whether they still had difficulty getting along with their husbands' kin or their own kin. They said that they had never had a problem with their husbands' kin. When I read to them from the interview transcript, they insisted that they had never told me they had problems with their families, and they said that I was mistaken.

Following the interview, I looked back again at my records and field notes from the interviews in 2000 and 2001 to check whether I could have mixed up the interviews. My research assistant and I discussed the situation. She also remembered the same women's group, and her recollection matched the information written in the interview transcript. We puzzled over the possible reasons for the widows' change in attitude and recollection. My assistant hypothesized that since the women had solved their most serious economic problems by receiving assistance to rebuild their houses, they no longer remembered the cold shoulder they had received from kin and neighbors in the years immediately after the genocide. Her hypothesis is certainly plausible. Another possibility is that the women did not feel comfortable responding as honestly in 2007. Given the rehearsed response we received to the questions about *gacaca*, I suspected the women again perceived me as an outsider and closed the veil of secrecy that shrouds rural life in Rwanda and obscures it from outsiders, whether foreign or Rwandan.[12]

Implications of Social Classification

The polarized system of ethnic classification in postgenocide Rwanda is logical given the shibboleth of genocide. Ethnic categories still mattered in everyday life. Yet the RPF's ideology of national unity and reconciliation forced ordinary Rwandans to invent a new coded language to talk about ethnic distinctions. The new social classifications became formalized, comprised of Aristotelian ideal types: a person was either a victim or a perpetrator, a survivor or a prisoner, an old returnee or a new returnee. Nonetheless, the life circumstances and experiences of many ordinary women did not fit neatly into the dominant system of social classification. These women inhabited a gray zone in the postgenocide national imagination; they stood at the point of "friction," a term I borrow from Tsing (2004), between lived reality and discourse.

Certainly, in the messiness of quotidian life, ad hoc accommodations were made: single mothers were called "wives," and mixed families maintained strained yet polite relations. Yet these women's marginal status prolonged their suffering and made it acceptable for people to exclude them from the balanced reciprocity of kin relations and communal life. The systems of gender and ethnic classification rendered these women invisible, so women in these categories manipulated their social invisibility and exercised agency to rebuild their lives in spite of this symbolic violence. Yet even women who fit neatly into postgenocide social classifications found that everyday life did not match up to their imagined social status.

I tell the story of cowives, Apollonia and Theodosia, who returned from exile in Burundi shortly after the end of the genocide, to illustrate this point. Apollonia was born during the colonial period in southern Rwanda in what was then part of Nyaruguru district, later became part of Gikongoro prefecture under Habyarimana, and now is part of South province. As a child, Apollonia fled with her family to Burundi around the time that large massacres targeting Tutsi took place in the region in 1963 or 1964.[13] In Burundi Apollonia married a Rwandan exile, Kabiligi, from the same region in Rwanda. Kabiligi was a wealthy man who had fled Rwanda in 1959 with his large herd of cattle.

Kabiligi built a successful business in Bujumbura. Although the family never explained to me how it happened, he eventually took a second wife, Theodosia. Apollonia and Theodosia lived together in a large house with their children. Each wife had seven children. They lived a good life, even though Kabiligi did not have a formal education. They had a car. The children, even the daughters, studied all the way through secondary school. Despite his many children, Kabiligi managed to provide for all of them, although Apollonia, Theodosia, and the children helped staff the family business. In Bujumbura they were considered wealthy and were well known among the Rwandans exiled there.

When the RPF attacked Rwanda in 1990, Kabiligi supported the cause by making monthly contributions to the RPF. When the RPF asked families in the diaspora to send their sons to fight for the liberation of Rwanda, Kabiligi sent two—the second son of each of his wives.[14] Shortly after the RPF victory in 1994, Kabiligi returned to Rwanda with Apollonia, Theodosia, and the twelve children who were still at home. He liquidated his business in Bujumbura and bought a house in Kigali. The family expected to be wealthy when they "returned home" (*abarutashye*). They expected to be rewarded for the sacrifices they had made in support of the cause. For the first several years in Rwanda, they did all right. Kabiligi started a new business transporting merchandise. A son found well-paid work with the United Nations. The other children continued their studies although with some difficulty since money was tight.

Life in Rwanda was expensive. One of Kabiligi's trucks broke down and could not be repaired. The United Nations left, and his son lost his job. In his seventies Kabiligi became sick, too tired to work. His sons kept up the family transportation business for as long as they could, but then the other truck died, too. The house began to fall down around them, but they did not have the money to fix it. As they became increasingly poor, Apollonia and Theodosia quarreled often. Their lives did not measure up to their dreams of returning home. Their connections to powerful people were not enough. The New Rwanda required high levels of education, but Apollonia had never been to school, and Theodosia had only studied through the end of primary school. Even though Apollonia and Theodosia were technically in a privileged social class in postgenocide Rwanda, their lives were torqued by social classification, albeit in different ways than raped maidens, Tutsi wives of prisoners, and Hutu widows of the genocide.

After coming to power in 1994, the RPF-led government pursued a "policy of reconstruction and development" framed in the "language of international donors: good governance, decentralization, gender mainstreaming, poverty reduction, rule of law, and transparency" (Straus and Waldorf 2011, 4). The government also attempted to "alter social identities, cultural norms, and individual behavior" (ibid.). A key principle within the RPF's approach to governance and development was an emphasis on formal education and employment practices that emphasized professional qualifications instead of social connections. Thus, Kabiligi, Apollonia, and Theodosia's belief that they would be rewarded for their loyalty when they returned home did not match the practical realities of an economic system that emphasized formal education. Furthermore, their plural marriage did not fit the RPF-led government's idea of a proper or legal marriage. The children felt disadvantaged by their family background although it was impossible for me to determine if their perception was based on empirical evidence. Not all old caseload returnees (*abarutashye*) have enjoyed success in the New Rwanda nor have they all experienced their repatriation as an improvement on their prior lives in exile.

5

Defining Coexistence
and Reconciliation
in the New Rwanda

In 2003 I presented a paper on grassroots perspectives on reconciliation at an internationally sponsored conference in Rwanda. The conference focused on microlevel studies of the 1994 genocide. My paper was scheduled for the last panel, so I listened to the other scholars' contributions. When commenting on papers from other scholars, several Rwandan participants questioned whether an "objective," "scientific" approach was appropriate to the study of genocide. In my presentation I highlighted the ways an inter-subjective approach might offer a viable alternative. I also outlined the main point of my paper: grassroots models of reconciliation that involved mutual sharing of survival stories helped women establish, or reestablish, mutually supportive social relationships in the aftermath of the genocide.

After my presentation in English, the first discussant, a Rwandan profes-sor from the National University who spoke French, attacked my paper for being "partisan" and "too emotional." As he spoke, I realized that he had either misunderstood or was intentionally distorting the main point of my paper. He indirectly accused me of being a genocide denier by stating that my "research risked denying the genocide." He recommended that I "interview some genocide survivors." As he continued, many Rwandan audience members, in particular the students, voiced muted exclamations of approval and exchanged triumphant looks. They seemed pleased to see my research attacked. As the discussant continued, I felt a growing sense of panic and dread, but I tried to maintain my composure before the crowd. The second discussant, a Rwandan who had been added to the program by the international organizers and subsequently removed from the program by the Rwandan organizers and added again by the international organizers, took a much more conciliatory approach. Since he had not read my paper as a result of the last-minute program changes, he applauded my courage for attempting to discuss such a sensitive topic, but he could do little to defend the research. In my five-minute response, I attempted to restate the main argument of my paper in French and defended my research and methods against the first discussant's accusations of partisanship and genocide denial. I explained that I had worked closely with genocide widows' associations and that more than half my interviewees were genocide survivors. Once the session finally ended, I was exhausted. Several foreign scholars expressed sympathy for my predicament.

I relate this experience to illustrate the highly politicized environment surrounding questions of reconciliation in postgenocide Rwanda. After the genocide, the RPF-led government made national reconciliation its exclusive political territory. As a result, anything related to reconciliation became a direct concern of the state. In this extremely politicized environment, efforts to define reconciliation according to realities at the grassroots level faced close scrutiny from the government. For a period of time between 1994 and 2000, women's civil society organizations were able to operate in relative freedom even when they were engaging in activities related to these sensitive issues. By 2001, however, government authorities began to watch women's organizations closely as well and occasionally intervened in their operations.

This chapter lays out the cultural and political terrain that Rwandan women navigated in their efforts to repair social relationships and build a peaceful society. In the first part of this chapter, I explore competing definitions of reconciliation in postgenocide Rwanda. Then I describe Rwandan cultural traditions of reconciliation and revenge that provide the cultural repertoires of signs, symbols, and practices on which ordinary Rwandans drew in forging their own reconciliation paths. Finally, I describe some of the state practices of reconciliation that left ordinary Rwandan women on their own to invent ways to live together again.

Grassroots Understandings of Reconciliation

When I began this research in 1996, I used the term "reconciliation" to refer to processes of reestablishing relationships between Hutu and Tutsi. During my first research trip in the spring of 1997, women in general and leaders of women's associations in particular reacted negatively to the term "reconciliation" and preferred to use the term "cohabitation" (*kubana*, "to live together"). As they explained, reconciliation was a matter of the heart and required genuine contrition, whereas cohabitation was a matter of necessity, since all Rwandans had to share the same country. At the time, it seemed the best women could hope for was for Rwandans to learn to live together without killing each other. Given the social and political landscape in 1997 just after the return of the new caseload refugees (see chapter 1), it is not surprising that women did not want to talk about reconciliation.

International Definitions

Similar to the indigenous definitions of cohabitation and reconciliation, a growing body of literature on peace building, conflict resolution, and what some call "coexistence work" (e.g., Weiner 1998) distinguishes between coexistence and reconciliation. Weiner (1998) defines coexistence as "an accommodation between members of different communities or separate countries who live together without one collectivity trying to destroy or severely harm the other." Weiner's definition allows for competition and conflict, as long as they are pursued through "legitimate channels" (quoted in Kriesberg 2001, 48). Applying the term "coexistence" to Rwanda requires some adaptation of the concept because, as discussed at length in chapters 1 and 4, Hutu and Tutsi are not distinct communities. Adapting Weiner's definition to the Rwandan case, I use the term "coexistence" to refer to the ad hoc accommodations made by Rwandans in the postgenocide period in order to live together without open physical violence among ordinary citizens. Thus coexistence is a state of relations where there is not widespread violence between groups in the public arena and where community members cooperate sufficiently for families to survive in a local economy that requires some interdependence.

Many international NGOs and intergovernmental organizations working in Rwanda adopted the term "coexistence" in their programming and planning. The Imagine Coexistence project, launched in late 2000 by the United Nations High Commission for Refugees (UNHCR), made the term more common. Inspired by the work of Martha Minow (1998), Sadako

Ogata, the high commissioner for refugees from 1990 to 2000, initiated the project to help bridge the gap between emergency assistance to refugees and development in the context of reintegrating refugees into divided communities (UNHCR 2001). A primary goal of the project was to foster peaceful coexistence in communities. In the peace-building literature, peaceful coexistence is defined as a "more sustainable" form of coexistence that goes beyond just living together without killing each other. Weiner (1998) identifies three elements to peaceful coexistence: (1) the parties formerly in conflict must accept that the other has the right to exist, (2) peaceful coexistence is a state in between open hostility and violence and reconciliation, and (3) peaceful coexistence has an ongoing dynamic that moves toward a durable peace. Whereas peaceful coexistence denotes a state of living together in relative peace, the peace-building literature defines reconciliation as the processes of rebuilding relationships between "parties that have experienced an oppressive relationship or a destructive conflict with each other" (Kriesberg 2001, 48).

The Imagine Coexistence project came to shape the language and ideological terrain in which reconciliation unfolded in Rwanda. The initiative implemented forty projects in twenty local communities, created a network of international and national NGOs involved in coexistence or reconciliation work, and held monthly workshops on thematic topics relevant to coexistence and reconciliation (Babbit et al. 2002; Laura McGrew, personal communication, 2001). Through these mechanisms its terminology and approaches spread to local organizations and communities. For example, some Rwandans, particularly those working for NGOs, began to use the term "coexistence" in place of "cohabitation" in their work.

State Definitions of Reconciliation

In the aftermath of the genocide, the Rwandan government had a vested interest in defining national reconciliation. Given that the RPF came to power through military conquest, it initially faced the challenge of establishing its legitimacy in the eyes of both citizens and the international community. The RPF legitimated itself internally as the saviors of Tutsi—as the only ones with the courage to stop the genocide in a cowardly international system (Pottier 2002, 1–2). It then used this guilt dividend to quell protests from the international community about any of its policies or practices (ibid., 81, 202).

Since its founding in the late 1980s, the RPF has promoted a nationalist ideology of ethnic inclusion, which it called "national unity." In 1993 the RPF taught new recruits that *"Inkotanyi* are Rwandans who aim to lead Rwanda to development after too many years of poverty and darkness.

Inkotanyi are not Hutu, Tutsi nor Twa. . . . The *Inkotanyi* party accepts everyone who believes in its goals" (quoted in Des Forges 1999, 694). The RPF emphasized the unifying aspects of Rwanda culture and blamed the country's ethnic problems on the divisive and racist policies of German and Belgian colonialism (Pottier 2002, 109–29).

In official discourse reconciliation was almost always discussed as part of the dyad "national unity and reconciliation" (*ubumwe n'ubwiyunge*). The Kinyarwanda term *ubumwe*, comprised of the root *-mwe*, meaning "one," and the class prefix *ubu-*, indicating "the (abstract) quality of," can be translated into English as "oneness" and very closely equates to the English word "unity." On the other hand, the term *ubwiyunge* has many connotations beyond its fundamental meaning, "reconciliation." *Ubwiyunge* is formed from the root *-unga*, meaning "to bring together by placing end to end" (Jacob 1988, 467), and has the connotation of government or military authority; it has the secondary meaning "to bring together several provinces, regions or countries under the same authority" (ibid.). With the addition of the reflexive infix *-i-*, the root becomes "to join oneself with, to unite oneself with, to reconcile oneself with" (Jacob 1984, 203).

In practice the joining of unity and reconciliation meant that government policy usually focused more on unity than reconciliation. In a 2004 speech, Fatuma Ndangiza, secretary general of the National Unity and Reconciliation Commission, made the doctrine equating reconciliation with national unity explicit: "In Rwanda's parlance reconciliation is short for National unity and national reconciliation. This is considered to be one of the four pillars of [the] rule of law, which are National unity, democracy, pluralism and respect for the rule of law. . . . We believe that reconciliation will not come through forgetting the past, but in understanding why the past led to political turmoil and taking measures, however painful and slow, which will make our 'Never Again' a reality." She also described national reconciliation as "a long-term painful process" (NURC 2004).

Another important component of the Rwandan state's reinvention of national identity was its refashioning of national history (Pottier 2002). RPF doctrine blamed the divisions in Rwandan society on colonialism without acknowledging that these divisions were politicized under Rwabugiri in the precolonial era. For example, the introduction of the National Unity and Reconciliation Commission's first annual report directly connects the arrival of colonialism in Rwanda to the 1994 genocide: "Ever since the arrival of White people, Rwanda has experienced bad governance based on the discrimination among and division of Rwandans which enabled leaders to maintain and reinforce their repressive regime. This policy of massive human rights violations eventually culminated in the genocide and massacres of 1994 which claimed the lives of more than one million people" (NURC

2000, 5). While colonialism further politicized ethnic categories by marginal-izing Hutu from political power and alleviating some of the worst aspects of corvée labor from Tutsi, Rwandan political leaders before and after colonial-ism also played a significant role in shaping the meanings of ethnicity in Rwanda.

Cultural Traditions Regarding Reconciliation and Revenge

Rwanda has numerous, sometimes contradictory, traditions vis-à-vis reconciliation and revenge. Unfortunately, many of the scholarly works documenting these competing traditions discuss Rwandan tradition and culture as part of an ahistorical (and idyllic) past, presumably before colonial-ism.[1] As a result, it is sometimes difficult to distinguish between interpreta-tions of tradition based primarily on empirical evidence, like Crépeau (1985) and Ntampaka (1997), and those based primarily on an ideological stance, like the National Unity and Reconciliation Commission (2000). Even portrayals based on empirical evidence sometimes misinterpret history. For example, Ntampaka (1997, 11) portrays the king (*mwami*) and chiefs (*abatware*) as being in the service of the collective masses, yet Vansina (2001) argues that the chiefs and the king were quite clearly in the service of the nobility at the expense of the masses in nineteenth-century Rwanda.

Crépeau's and Ntampaka's works are valuable for understanding cultural traditions because Rwandan men and women frequently use proverbs to justify their attitudes and actions. Particularly in rural Rwanda, proverbs provide material that structures men's and women's agency. Regarding the truth in traditional justice, Ntampaka cites contradictory traditions:

> *Aho kuryamira ukuri waryamira ubugi bw'intorezo*, literally, "instead of silencing the truth, you must let your head be cut off."[2] The *bagabo*, the witnesses, could only say what they had seen or heard. The opposite, *guca ibicuma*, was also said; it means "to testify for a profit," which was socially disapproved. The other proverb said *Ukuri guca mu ziko ntigushya*, "the truth passes in the fire and is not burned." There is another similar saying, *Ikinyoma cyicaza umugabo kuntebe rimwe ntikihamwicaza kabiri*, "a lie allows you to gain an advantage once, not twice."
>
> Rwandan society also said, *Ukuri wavuze uraguhakishwa*, meaning that in certain circumstances, it is not good to tell the truth to everyone. You must first know against whom you are going to testify and weigh the risks. It was in this way that the culture of lying for the benefit of the big men was able to install itself. You cannot testify against the powerful ones: they manipulate the truth to remain in power. (Ntampaka 1997, 13–14, my translation)

In short, Rwandan custom provides at least two contradictory precedents vis-à-vis the truth: (1) one must always speak the truth, and (2) sometimes it is best not to tell the truth. While the public information campaigns promoting the *gacaca* jurisdictions emphasized the tradition of always telling the truth, citizens who preferred to remain silent during *gacaca* mobilized the customary wisdom of remaining silent.

Similarly, Rwandan cultural traditions promoted both revenge and reconciliation. Sometimes revenge was a duty. As Vansina reminds us, "You can deplore collective revenge as the producer of ceaseless hostilities, but you can recommend it because it was the cement for solidarity touted by kin groups" (2001, 251, my translation). According to Rwandan proverbs, not seeking revenge is a sign of weakness: "Revenge may delay, but it does not miss the opportunity to exercise itself. . . . It waits for the opportune moment" (Crépeau 1985, 216, my translation). While acknowledging cultural traditions that mandate revenge, Crépeau notes that when the cycle of revenge decimated entire lineages, the *mwami* stepped in and forced the parties to reconcile (ibid.). Many Rwandans, particularly genocide survivors, view the RPF's role in stopping the genocide in this light.

One of the primary challenges in postgenocide Rwanda was that some survivors felt it was their duty to avenge what they suffered during the genocide. Their dissatisfaction with justice mechanisms like *gacaca*, the national courts, and the International Criminal Tribunal for Rwanda and their frustration with the slow pace of justice validated their desire for revenge. Poverty, solitude, and misery were constant reminders of everything they needed to avenge. Thus some survivors held grudges, exacted revenge in small ways, or waited patiently for their opportunity for vengeance. In this cycle a new set of (Hutu) victims was created who then awaited the opportunity to avenge wrongs done to them.

Yet counter to this tradition of revenge, traditional punishments in cases of social rupture emphasized the reintegration of the errant individual into good social standing. In short, justice could be conciliatory, according to Rwandan custom. The "delinquent should correct himself," and then the community should "pardon him for his actions and live in harmony again." This model of traditional justice was compensatory, as "it required several pots of beer that all should share together as a sign of reconciliation" (Ntampaka 1997, 14). Thus in postgenocide Rwanda both those seeking to reconcile with friends, neighbors, and compatriots and those harboring hatred and patiently awaiting the opportune moment for revenge found cultural antecedents to validate their actions.

An important basis for the promotion of peaceful coexistence in Rwanda was the tradition of mutual assistance (*gufashanya n'ukuzuzanya*, "to help each other and complement each other"). In the past, Rwandan traditions tended to emphasize corporate rights, whether those of the *inzu* (household) or the *umuryango* (lineage), over individual rights (Ntampaka 1997, 7–9). Despite the social, economic, and political transformations wrought by colonialism and the increasing privileging of individual rights during the postcolonial period (Jefremovas 2002, 59–78; Ntampaka 1997, 8), life in Rwanda still required a great deal of interdependence before and after the genocide. Rural families relied on their neighbors, who were sometimes kin but with increasing frequency in the second half of the twentieth century were not, to borrow salt, soap, household items, or farming equipment. In times of family crisis such as a death or serious illness, they lent money or contributed labor to help out a neighbor in need. While urban families tended more toward individualism because of their greater integration into a capitalist economic system, they also had a great deal of interdependence with other families in their social networks. For example, kin, friends, and colleagues are asked to contribute money, food, vehicles, or other goods for a marriage or a funeral.

In the aftermath of genocide, these practices of mutual assistance were disrupted. First, the massive displacements of the population, whether inside the country or across international borders, meant that for months or in some cases years Rwandan households had no neighbors or they had new neighbors. Thus they were required to build new relationships and not simply reestablish old relationships. Second, when Rwandans returned home, they sometimes mistrusted their former neighbors and their new neighbors as well. The genocide uprooted trust, as ordinary Rwandans found themselves betrayed by a brother, best friend, colleague, or other trusted relation. In some cases, this mistrust was built on empirical reality. In 1997 a genocide widow expressed her anger when asked about reconciliation, stating that it was impossible to reconcile with her neighbor who cooked in her pots, ate off her table, and wore her clothing—presumably all looted during the genocide.

State Practices of Reconciliation: Promoting National Unity and Erasing Dissent

In the years after the genocide, the RPF-led government undertook a program to rebuild the country; state building was a key component of this program. Beyond the national memory practices discussed in earlier chapters, the government initiated a number of projects to promote national unity and reconciliation. First, it eliminated ethnicity as an element in official government bureaucracy. Second, it created *ingando* (solidarity or reeducation camps) to teach the RPF's approach to national unity and to instill a sense of national identity in citizens. Third, it established the National Unity and Reconciliation Commission (NURC) in 1999. Fourth, the government adopted new national symbols, including a new flag and a new national anthem, in December 2001. These state-sponsored activities to promote national unity and reconciliation contributed to the political landscape that women and women's organizations navigated on their roads toward reconciliation.

Policing Social Categories
in an Ethnically Blind Society

Shortly after coming to power in 1994, the new government decreed that ethnic identity would no longer be an official factor in the bureaucratic life of citizens or the state. This move was a significant departure from the previous government's policy. In the 1970s President Habyarimana had instituted a policy of "ethnic equilibrium," which allocated positions in educational institutions and in the state apparatus on a quota system to correct the historic marginalization of Hutu in the Belgian colonial system. The RPF opposed the policy of ethnic equilibrium and advocated instead a system where each person was recognized for his or her individual qualities and skills (NURC 2000, 13, 20). Effective immediately, ethnicity was no longer considered as an official factor in employment decisions or in admissions to secondary schools or universities. In the second phase of this policy's implementation, the government eliminated ethnicity from national identity cards in April 1996 (IRIN 1996). As discussed in chapter 1, national identity cards played an important role in the 1994 genocide. At the infamous roadblocks, national identity cards determined who was killed. From the perspective of many genocide survivors, national identity cards were the physical manifestation of the ideology of genocide. The new identity cards eliminated the bureaucratic manifestation of this "genocidal ideology," as the postgenocide government has labeled it, in the form of an official record of a citizen's ethnic identity.[3]

At the time, no one questioned the new policy. If identity cards had been necessary to distinguish between Hutu and Tutsi, eliminating them was surely a good idea in a postgenocide society. Nonetheless, ethnicity as a social category still played significant roles in everyday life in postgenocide Rwanda. While the new national identity cards did not indicate a person's ethnicity, they still were used to police social categories in postgenocide Rwanda. The new identity cards helped to arrest suspected genocide perpetrators and to weed out infiltrators (*abacengezi*) who were hiding in the population. Both "perpetrator" and "infiltrator" were social categories that became conflated with the category "Hutu."

The new national identity cards issued in 1996 required all citizens to reregister in their communes of origin. At the time, most residents of Kigali were registered in the rural communities where they had been born. Kigali residents had to travel to these rural communes and secure documents from local authorities at every level, from the *nyumbakumi* through the head of the sector.[4] Then they had to wait in long lines at the commune office to file the paperwork and pay the fees. When their new identity cards were ready several weeks later, they had to return to pick up their cards. If they discovered a mistake on their cards, they had to start the entire process over from the beginning.

Security checks were a normal part of daily life in postgenocide Rwanda. At the entrances to most towns on national highways, police or military personnel verified the identities of all passengers going through the checkpoints. All taxi buses and most private vehicles were stopped at these roadblocks, while vehicles belonging to the United Nations or international humanitarian agencies, especially if they were carrying white passengers, were allowed to pass without stopping. In addition to security checkpoints along major highways, government officials, soldiers, policemen, or members of the local defense often stopped pedestrians to check their identities. These security checkpoints extended even into citizens' private homes, as families were obliged to register any overnight visitors with local authorities and record visitors' stays in a household registry.[5]

In 1997 I rented a car to travel from Kigali to Butare prefecture in southern Rwanda. The chauffeur, who came with the car, did not have an identity card, much less a new national identity card. It was unclear to me why he did not have a new card, as he had "returned" to Rwanda from Zaire, where he was born. In other words, he was an old caseload returnee and had served in the RPF while it was a rebel army. He told me that he had been embedded in a rural community in Kibungo in 1993, far outside the zone occupied by the RPF at the time. I suspected that his lack of identity card was probably tied to the story of how and why he was no longer an RPA soldier, since very few men in their late twenties or early thirties were able to demobilize from the RPF or the RPA between 1993 and 1997. In any case, his lack of an identity card slowed our travel considerably. We spent at least fifteen minutes at every checkpoint while he explained why he did not have a new national identity card.

The insurgency from 1997 through 1999 was concentrated in northern and western Rwanda in the prefectures bordering Congo (Ruhengeri, Gisenyi, and Cyangugu), in the neighboring prefectures of Byumba and Kibuye, and in parts of Gikongoro and Gitarama. During this period, men perceived to be of fighting age, roughly between the ages of fifteen and sixty years, left these regions to avoid getting caught up in the struggle between insurgents and the RPA (author interviews, 1999, 2000, and 2001). As the insurgency became widespread, ordinary Rwandans as well as government officials began to fear that *abacengezi* were spreading throughout the country and living among citizens. As a result, men, especially those of fighting age, faced increased scrutiny during identity checks. Young men who did not present a military identity card or a student identity card were often berated by soldiers or police for refusing military service. Some of them were even conscripted into the army, sent for military training, and deployed to Democratic Republic of Congo within a few months. Men who looked Hutu or who had national identity cards issued in the northwestern prefectures of Ruhengeri and Gisenyi, where the majority of the population is Hutu, faced the most intense scrutiny of all, as it was generally assumed that if they had not joined the RPF, they must support the *abacengezi* (author interviews, 1999, 2000, and 2001).

Thus, while the new identity cards abolished ethnicity as a fact in bureaucratic life, they also served to police identity and to sort between the categories "perpetrator/insurgent" and "survivor/RPF supporter." These distinctions fed into the classification system embedded in the national mourning and genocide memorial, where victims were separated from perpetrators. In this way, the new identity cards served to reinforce distinctions between the categories "Hutu" and "Tutsi" even though these labels had been erased from the cards.

National Unity in the Education System

The new government's policy of national unity removed ethnicity as an official factor from the education system, yet many Rwandans perceived ethnic discrimination in the postgenocide education system because of the perceived overrepresentation of Tutsi in institutions of higher education. Because ethnicity was removed from bureaucratic life, it is impossible to track whether this perception was accurate. If this perception was an empirical reality, it could be explained by structural factors in the economy.

Official government policy had mandated free universal education through the end of primary school since at least the 1980s. Nonetheless, many poor families, particularly in rural areas, encountered numerous obstacles to sending their children to school. Many families were unable to purchase required school supplies, including chalk, a slate, a uniform, and, in some schools, shoes. During my fieldwork in rural Rwanda between 1999 and 2001, students without the necessary supplies were sent home and instructed not to return to school until they had the supplies. If their families were unable to purchase the supplies, they did not return to school. In addition, many state-run primary schools charged enrollment fees even though primary school education was supposed to be free.

At the secondary level, students with the best scores on national examinations received priority admission to state secondary schools, where the tuition was much lower than at private schools. Yet secondary school students, who most frequently lived at school, required expensive school supplies, including books, notebooks, pens, pencils, mattresses, bedding, uniforms, shoes, personal care items, and pocket money for transportation. Although each commune had education funds to assist poor students, the demand for scholarships greatly exceeded the availability of funds. As a result, many well-qualified poor children remained "sitting at home with their arms crossed," as several rural families described it to me in interviews during 2000 and 2001.

While the rural poor included both Hutu and Tutsi, genocide survivors received financial support from the genocide survivors' assistance fund, known by its French acronym, FARG (Fonds d'assistance aux rescapés du génocide).[6] In 1998 the FARG was created by the Rwandan government and initially bankrolled by international donors, and its funds were intended to assist genocide survivors and, in particular, orphans of the genocide with education expenses, housing, and other basic necessities. The law designated 5 percent of annual domestic revenues to assist the "most needy" genocide survivors.[7] To access the funds, a person must be officially recognized as a genocide survivor by the local FARG administration, which requires signatures from local representatives of a genocide survivors' organization and two witnesses.

While the FARG was intended to help all survivors regardless of ethnicity, in many communities these funds were overwhelmingly channeled to Tutsi at the exclusion of Hutu survivors or survivors from mixed families. On the one hand, it would be reasonable to argue that Tutsi survivors suffered the most dramatic consequences of the genocide, since many of them were the sole surviving members of their families, and so they deserved to be privileged in the distribution of FARG funds. On the other hand, FARG funds became another way that Rwandans were divided along ethnic lines, because in practice although not by statute the FARG supported old case-load returnees, who were not in Rwanda during the genocide.

By 2000 the FARG was facing serious financial trouble. At the beginning of the second trimester, secondary school students supported by the FARG were sent home after a few days because the FARG had not paid schools for the first trimester. As one principal interviewed on Radio Rwanda explained, "We have no choice but to send the students home because we cannot feed them. We do not have money to buy food because the FARG has not paid us" (field notes, December 2000). Some university students who were genocide survivors stated that the FARG's insolvency was caused by the thousands of old caseload returnees who benefited even though they were not "direct victims" of the genocide. By "direct victims" they meant that the old case-load refugees did not face the threat of being killed, although they may have lost their entire extended families living inside the country. The students explained that in certain regions, notably Umutara and Kibungo, old caseload returnees bribed local representatives of genocide survivors' organizations to have their children added to the FARG lists. In 2000 the impasse between the FARG and secondary schools was finally resolved, but the widely circulating rumors of FARG corruption did not make it into the headlines.

Between 1999 and 2001 I encountered numerous instances of survivors who had difficulty accessing FARG funds. In one case, a Tutsi girl whose parents were killed in the genocide had been adopted by her godmother, a Hutu. The local representatives of the genocide survivors' association refused to add the girl to the FARG list. They said that her godmother was not poor, and so the young girl did not need assistance. Yet many other families in the community benefited from FARG assistance, including those of the local representatives who refused to add the girl to the list, even though they were not impoverished. In this case, it was clear that the root of the problem was the godmother's ethnicity. In another case, the children of a Hutu father and Tutsi mother were refused by the FARG authorities in a community in southern Rwanda. Their father was imprisoned on false accusations of genocide, and the family lived off the mother's small salary as a primary school teacher.[8] While the oldest son had found a scholarship to a Catholic secondary school, the children's mother was unable to pay for the younger children to continue their studies. When she sought FARG assistance, she encountered a bureaucratic runaround from the local FARG representatives. In one instance I witnessed a FARG representative refuse to sign the woman's papers; the representative insisted that she was no longer affiliated with the FARG. The next day I saw the same FARG representative sign another applicant's papers.

Whether rightly or wrongly, many poor, rural Hutu families viewed the availability of FARG funding to Tutsi survivors as a form of institutionalized ethnic preference (author interviews, 1999, 2000, and 2001).[9] While they acknowledged that many orphans of the genocide deserved financial assistance with education, they pointed out specific cases of genocide survivors who were not "needy" but who benefited from FARG money anyway. Many poor Hutu argued that it would be more just if the Rwandan government set aside money for needy children without distinguishing between genocide survivors and others.

The National Unity and Reconciliation Commission

In 1999 the government created the National Unity and Reconciliation Commission (NURC).[10] The 1993 Arusha Peace Accords had called for the creation of such a commission.[11] Aloisea Inyumba, minister of gender and women in development, was appointed executive secretary of the NURC. At the time, Inyumba was widely "regarded as the most senior female politician in the [RPF] party"; she was a founding member of the RPF and had served as director of finance for the RPF during the war. Inyumba's appointment to the NURC was perceived by some as an attempt "to give the commission political clout," but it was perceived by others as an attempt on the part of the RPF to control the commission and ensure that it promoted the RPF's vision of national unity (IRIN 2000).

Among the NURC's many duties was the organization of meetings and other activities to promote national unity and reconciliation, to "sensitize Rwandans on unity and lay it on a firm foundation," "to inculcate the culture of national unity and reconciliation," and "to denounce any written or declared ideas and actions aimed at, or based on disunity" (NURC 2000, 5–6). In its first year and a half of existence, the commission held seventeen consultative meetings and eleven solidarity camps where over ten thousand government officials, students, local defense forces, former infiltrators, and others were trained (ibid., 27–28). The NURC also monitored whether government organs, political parties, and national leaders respected the policy of national unity and reconciliation (IRIN 2000; NURC 2000). In 2002 Fatuma Ndangiza, executive director of the NURC, explained that the commission monitored appointments to cabinet posts and key positions in government ministries and private sector organizations for "ethnic balance" (field notes, April 2002).

Although in public they avoided saying anything negative, in private many ordinary Rwandans criticized the National Unity and Reconciliation Commission. Commenting on a wall calendar from the NURC, a priest and genocide survivor said with anger and frustration in his voice: "Unity and reconciliation. That's the problem. How can there be reconciliation without truth? They should have followed the South African model. What we need is truth and reconciliation, not unity. What we need is the truth. We need to know where our loved ones are, who killed them, how. [*Long pause.*] Then we can let them go. We can move on. What we want is the truth" (field notes, 2000). In a similar vein, the exiled former prime minister in the postgenocide government, Faustin Twagiramungu, promoted a truth commission in place of the NURC: "Reconciliation is not an administrative matter, and should be the business of the Rwandese. . . . A truth commission is an ideal way to allow people to give views about genocide and bad politics. . . . The problem is killers trying to punish killers" (IRIN 2000). By describing the government's reconciliation efforts as "killers trying to punish killers," Twagiramungu labeled the NURC as a political tool of the Rwandan Patriotic Front.

Another criticism leveled at the NURC was the controlled scripting of many of its events. For example, during the annual month of national mourning the NURC held town meetings to discuss national unity. Yet many attendees told me that there was little opportunity for genuine dialogue.

Formal presentations by invited speakers filled the meetings, and audience members were given few opportunities to ask questions or speak. Human Rights Watch leveled similar criticism at the 2000 Unity and Reconciliation Summit organized by the NURC (HRW 2001a). In April 2002 I attended a town meeting sponsored by the NURC in Ruhengeri prefecture. When describing the meeting, Rwandan employees of an international NGO called it an open forum for citizens to discuss unity and reconciliation. On the afternoon of the meeting, all businesses and organizations in town closed so that workers could attend the meeting. During the meeting, regional officials, including the prefect, gave speeches about unity and reconciliation. At the end of the two-hour meeting, the forum was opened for questions from the floor. A few anodyne questions came from audience members. Then an elderly man asked whether he would be allowed to return to his home now that the *abacengezi* had left. As described in chapter 1, the RPA had required much of the rural population to move into displaced persons camps, or *imidugudu* (agglomerations, meaning villages), as part of its counterinsurgency operations between 1996 and 2001. Instead of responding directly to the man's question, the prefect gave a general response along the lines that individual citizens sometimes had to make sacrifices for the sake of national progress. He then abruptly closed the meeting.

The meeting also did not touch on the issues raised by women from Ruhengeri prefecture during my interviews. During the insurgency, the population of Ruhengeri had been caught between the insurgents and the RPA, whose counterinsurgency tactics were "often brutal" (Prendergast and Smock 1999, 2). Many thousands of civilians, soldiers, and insurgents were killed. In interviews local women expressed concern over whether they would ever be able to consecrate the remains of their loved ones buried in mass graves throughout the region or whether they would ever be allowed to return to their own homes, which they had been forced to leave under the government's villagization (*imidugudu*) policy. Some women complained that justice was one-sided. Genocide survivors and the government had found their justice in *gacaca*, but women and their families could not seek justice against the RPA soldiers who had killed their loved ones or forced them to destroy their own homes during counterinsurgency operations.

Ingando (Solidarity Camps)

Another method that the new government used to promote national unity and reconciliation was through solidarity camps, known as *ingando*. According to Mgbako (2005, 208), an *ingando* in its contemporary form was an "invented tradition" used by the RPF to consolidate its power. Since it was first instituted in 1997, the *ingando* has existed in many different forms and appears to be modeled after the RPA's training for new recruits when it was a rebel movement; *ingando* participants engage in *muchaka muchaka* (running and singing military songs every morning), are taught Rwanda's national history from the RPF perspective, and are educated in the RPF's ideology of national unity. Refugees returning from exile in Zaire and Tanzania in 1997 were the first civilians required to attend *ingando*. Following the program's success in the eyes of government administrators, attending *ingando* became a requirement for all students admitted to state-run universities and for civilians appointed or elected to local governments. According to the government, the camps' mission is to promote unity and reconciliation among Rwandans, but some observers have criticized them for further dividing the population and consolidating the RPF's hold on power (see, e.g., Mgbako 2005; Thomson 2011).

Indeed, solidarity camps bolstered the government's ideology of national unity and countered the ideologies of genocide in several important ways. First of all, the camps disseminated a revised national history that supported the ideology of national unity, whereas the history taught in the pregenocide education system emphasized the Tutsi nobility's oppression of peasants under colonialism and the liberation of "the people" (some would say "Hutu") through a revolution. Second, the camps eliminated support for genocide deniers by providing participants with firsthand testimony from survivors as well as physical evidence and details about the 1994 genocide. Third, the camps provided Rwandan youth from all ethnic categories who were entering national universities and educational institutes with a common experience that served as a rite of passage and helped forge social bonds across ethnic distinctions.

Although solidarity camps were not deployed until 1997, RPF plans for the camps date back to at least July 1994, when RPF officers regularly spoke about the need to reeducate the population (Pottier 2002, 68). In 1994 Lt. Faustin Kaliisa, chief of the RPF's political department in Gisenyi, was reported to have said, "We shall re-educate the population on its return; lightly in the case of peasants, more profoundly for the educated, for instance through organizing a month-long seminar on the political history of our country" (quoted in ibid.). According to the NURC, the Ministry of Youth, Culture, and Sports first instituted solidarity camps following the war and genocide to "sensitize the youth on work and collaboration" (NURC 2000, 24). Yet I did not find evidence of *ingando* existing before 1997, when the government used *ingando* to educate, some would say "reeducate," returning refugees on "the policy of peaceful coexistence, security, mutual understanding and tranquility for every person" (ibid.). New caseload refugees who returned from exile in Zaire or Tanzania were compelled to attend *ingando*: they could not seek employment unless they could present an *ingando* completion certificate.

The refugee camps in Zaire and Tanzania were dominated by the same Hutu extremists responsible for the 1994 genocide. Their messages of ethnic hatred had propagated in the camps, including propaganda that denied that the genocide had occurred. Thus *ingando* for returning refugees were intended to counter ethnic extremism and "educate Hutu returnees about the country's goal of ethnic unity" (Drumtra 1998). They did achieve this goal to a certain extent. One woman who participated in a solidarity camp in 1997 explained to me: "It was good the way they explained how the genocide had happened. They provided concrete evidence to prove to those who denied the genocide that what had happened was indeed genocide." She went on to explain that this corrective measure was necessary since many people refused to accept that the genocide was a genocide that targeted Tutsi and not merely a "civil war where people on both sides died."

Another way that the camps promoted the government's vision of national unity was by the RPF's national history, which supported its ideology of national unity. As discussed in detail in chapter 1, the history taught in school under the First and Second Republics portrayed the three ethnic groups as the descendants of three waves of migration into the region in an adaptation of the Hamitic hypothesis, and independence was portrayed as a revolution that liberated "the people" from the oppression of the Belgian colonialists and the Tutsi monarchy. The RPF version of Rwandan history, on the other hand, emphasized the sameness of Rwandans and portrayed "Rwanda's ethnic divisions as a German or Belgian 'invention'" (Pottier 2002, 116). Yet from the RPF perspective, independence was not about abolishing the monarchy; rather, it was the first iteration of "anti-Tutsi" violence incited by "Hutu leaders" (ibid., 123). Some new caseload returnees responded negatively to the version of Rwandan history taught in *ingando*. One woman told me the following story when describing her experiences at solidarity camp:

> There was this one priest there with us. When they started teaching us about 1959, he couldn't take it. The organizers, they started talking about what *Kinyamateka* had done.[12] And this priest, he had worked at *Kinyamateka* at that time. When they started accusing *Kinyamateka* of having a genocidal ideology, he stood up and shouted all kinds of things in front of everyone. He said "Liars! *Kinyamateka* did not publish those things!" After that day he spent the rest of *ingando* lying on his cot in his tent. He refused to come out, not even to eat. He just lay there reading his books or muttering that they [the RPF] were liars. (Field notes, 2000)

Although some Rwandans, like this priest, contested this "new" version of Rwandan history, its dissemination via *ingando* was extremely influential on Rwandan youth who attended *ingando* before beginning university studies.

For several years after the genocide, until at least 2001, national history was not taught in school at the secondary and primary levels. While there was consensus that the national history taught under the Second Republic was distorted and needed to be revised, there was not consensus about what a revised history should include. Thus Rwandan youth who attended *ingando* had little knowledge of the country's history other than what they might have learned from family members or directly experienced themselves.

For Rwandan youth, *ingando* became an important rite of passage marking their change in status from minors to young adults. The camps helped forge social ties among Rwandan youth regardless of their ethnic identity, experiences of genocide and war, religion, background, or region of origin. Students who attended the camps wore military uniforms and learned how to handle weapons. When questioned about "the appropriateness of including weapons training among reconciliation activities, Rwandan authorities said that it is important to 'demystify' the 'myth about the army and the gun' for the 'self-defence and benefit of all Rwandese'" (HRW 2001a). In this way, *ingando* seemed to be partially modeled after the compulsory military service required in Israel. Most Rwandan youth who attended *ingando* remember their time at solidarity camp with nostalgia. Even when they attended different solidarity camps, they shared a common experience of *muchaka muchaka*, the early-morning run of soldiers, with its combined endurance training and repertoire of bawdy songs. The students also shared common stories of suffering through exhausting marches and runs, bad food, uncomfortable sleeping quarters, and dirty bathrooms. For Rwandan youth, *ingando* included activities to promote communication, mutual understanding, and reconciliation. Students wrote skits about various challenges they faced in their postgenocide lives and acted the skits out for each other. In forums that resembled town meetings, participants gave personal testimonies about their experiences during the genocide and asked questions of high-level government officials who visited.

In addition to *ingando* held for Rwandan youth and government officials, the NURC created *ingando* for children released from detention (HRW 2003b), for prisoners released after either completing their sentences or being found innocent in *gacaca* hearings (ibid., 38), for combatants from armed opposition groups captured by the government or who surrendered (Mgbako 2005, 210), and for those demobilized from the FAR or RDF (Rwandan Defense Forces, the name of the RPA after 2002). Although solidarity camps contributed to forging a common experience and patriotism among youth, *ingando* aimed at other audiences were not usually perceived as positively. Mgbako concludes: "Government officials have exaggerated the success of *ingando* as a reconciliation mechanism" (223). Nonetheless, *ingando* was effective in communicating the RPF's policies of national unity uniformly.

New National Symbols

The adoption of new national symbols in 2001, seven years after the genocide ended, and the creation of new national holidays were additional steps the new government took to promote national unity and reconciliation. The government first announced its intention to change the national symbols in June 1998. The 1998 announcement occurred only a few weeks after the RPF-led government extended the transition period for four more years. Some Rwandans viewed the timing of the decision as an attempt by the RPF leadership to put its own mark on its state-building activities. As with most activities connected to promoting national unity and reconciliation, the new national symbols and holidays contributed to forging a new national identity based on RPF ideology.

According to Rwandan government officials at the time of the new flag's unveiling in 2001, the flag needed to be changed because the old flag represented "Hutu tyranny." As one government official told Reuters News Agency in 1999 shortly after the design competition was announced, "It was high time we carried out these changes for not all sections of Rwandans were identifying themselves with the flag . . . which was a eulogy to the Hutu supremacy."[13] The old flag consisted of red, yellow, and green vertical bands equal in width, with the letter *R* in the middle. According to the website of the Rwandan Embassy in Washington, DC, the red stood for the blood shed during the struggle for independence, yellow represented peace, and green symbolized agriculture. Many other African nations used similar color symbolism in their flags adopted at independence.

The new Rwandan flag consists of light blue, yellow, and green horizontal bands of varying widths with a sun. Whereas the old flag included the color red, emblematic of the blood shed in the struggle against colonialism, the new flag included a more "positive" message, with yellow and green representing the "light of the sun . . . and Rwanda's lush vegetation" and sky blue representing hope for the future (Vesperini 2001). According to the Rwandan Embassy in Paris, the green represents the hope of prosperity through the rational exploitation of the country's natural and human resources, the yellow, along with the sun's rays, symbolizes economic development and the gradual enlightenment of the Rwandan people, and the blue represents peace.

At the same time that the new flag was unveiled a new national anthem was officially inaugurated. The government justified replacing the old anthem by stating, "Many believe the old anthem—adapted from a traditional folk tune 30 years ago—glorifies the Hutu as they fought to throw off Tutsi oppression" (Vesperini 2001). Like the national flag, the new anthem was written as part of a national competition. Entrants submitted their creations, and a national committee, appointed by the cabinet, selected the winner. Entitled "Rwanda Nziza" (Beautiful Rwanda), the lyrics were written by Faustin Murigo, and the music was composed by Jean-Bosco Hashakimana. It replaced the original national anthem, "Rwanda Rwacu" (Our Rwanda), written by Michael Habarurema and Abanyuramatwi, a choral group, in the early 1960s.

As with most government policy, few Rwandans were willing to voice an opinion about the new national symbols in 2001 other than to state that the new flag was "beautiful." Indeed, the new flag's imagery is striking and works very well in media images surrounding new holidays such as Liberation Day. In 2001 the majority of Rwandans that I asked about the new flag and anthem smiled wanly or made a comment to the effect that the state does as the state sees fit, and the citizens wait to see what will happen next. The few Rwandans willing to speak more openly wondered why, if the country was the same, the people needed a new flag and a new national anthem. They viewed the new symbols as representing RPF dominance in the New Rwanda.

Conclusion

For ordinary Rwandans, the major flaw in the government's approach to reconciliation was that it banned open discussions of ethnicity. Many women, particularly those who had experienced violence or marginalization at the hands of the RPF, asked how people could reconcile if they could not discuss what happened. Under the RPF's policy of national unity, discussions involving ethnic difference had to be encoded in the new language of experiential categories—genocide survivors, old caseload refugees, new caseload refugees, and so on—as discussed in detail in chapter 3. On the one hand, these new categories fit ordinary Rwandans more accurately than ethnic categories did. On the other hand, these rubrics oversimplified the complexity of women's lived experience. The ethnic subtext remained unspoken, but it continued to structure women's perceptions and to reinforce prejudices; most importantly, it undercut government efforts to foster reconciliation. In this context, ordinary women were largely left to their own devices to discover ways to live together (*kubana*) again. In the next chapter, I explore some of these idiosyncratic paths from coexistence to reconciliation.

6

Paths to Reconciliation

One of the most significant consequences of the 1994 genocide was the rupture of the social fabric. As Donatia described in the introduction, "I was consumed with hate. . . . I didn't trust anyone, not even those who helped save me." Nonetheless, little by little Rwandans began to repair the social fabric, many times unwittingly, as they muddled through the dire material circumstances in which they found themselves. Women, in particular, reached out to former friends, neighbors, and colleagues. While many might portray women's central role in rebuilding Rwandan society as the natural consequence of women's biology, this outcome was not a foregone conclusion. Women's central role in rebuilding Rwandan society was the result of their social position in the kin group and in the community as well as Rwandan women's embracing of feminist ideals drawn from both international and Rwandan sources.

During the genocide, many long-term relationships (friendships, marriages, business partnerships, etc.) that transected ethnicity were destroyed or seriously eroded by distrust. Nonetheless, the possibilities for reconciliation at the individual level were greater than at collective levels because of the shared history and memories predating the genocide. Because government-sponsored memory-making and reconciliation activities prohibited the kind of honest exchange of experiences that ordinary Rwandans needed, women were left to forge their own paths. As I discuss in this chapter, this journey began with finding a way to live together (*kubana*) again. From this cohabitation out of necessity, some individual women as well as some women's associations invented their own ways toward reconciliation. I describe five examples of reconciliation in this chapter: three of individuals and two of women's associations. Understanding these idiosyncratic paths to reconciliation can contribute to developing reconciliation programs better adapted to the needs of ordinary people in conflict zones around the world.

Cohabitation: A Matter of Necessity

Everyday life in rural Rwanda requires the accommodation of difference and negotiation of conflict even when people are not living in a postwar context. In the aftermath of the genocide and war in Rwanda, the transition from a state of warfare to a state of coexistence was a slow and uneven process. Because Rwandans had experienced earlier periods of communal conflict within living memory, some of them already had experience with rebuilding communal life with little outside intervention.[1] Nonetheless, the level of physical, social, and emotional destruction of the genocide far surpassed anything that any community had previously experienced.

In the weeks and months following the genocide, acts of revenge were fairly common in many Rwandan communities. Some genocide survivors took the opportunity to exact revenge against their neighbors by killing them, destroying their houses, taking their property, or falsely accusing them of genocide. In addition, RPA soldiers engaged in acts of violence against civilians (Des Forges 1999, 702). While the evidence gathered by human rights organizations indicates that RPA operations against civilians may have occurred on a large scale, the RPF "was remarkably successful in restricting access by foreigners to certain parts of the country"; thus it was "extremely difficult to prove wrongdoing" (ibid., 692). As the new state established its authority and as the army units responsible for local policing began to prevent acts of revenge, ordinary Rwandans turned to the work of rebuilding their lives.

Rural subsistence peasant farmers had little choice but to find ways to establish a local truce of some sort so that minimal amounts of cooperation and exchange could occur. In the beginning, neighbors lived together with little to no interaction or only thinly veiled hostility. Slowly over time, communities began to establish some kind of normalcy in their everyday interactions. This transformation moved slowly from the cessation of open acts of hostility, to exchanging terse greetings, to inviting neighbors to parties, to borrowing household items or farming equipment. In 2001 women in a rural community of southern Rwanda explained how astounding it was that at a recent wedding Hutu and Tutsi neighbors had come and sat next to each other without any open conflict. They explained that they could never have imagined that this would be possible in 1997, when many of the Hutu community members returned from exile in Zaire. Despite this progress, not all community members accepted these changes.

In the same community, a group of genocide widows complained bitterly that a neighboring association of prisoners' wives had tried to "steal" their fields in the valley. When I met with the group of prisoners' wives, they explained that an international NGO had implemented a project to improve the marsh in the valley so that it could be cultivated. The prisoners' wives, among "other community members" (their language implied Hutu as opposed to Tutsi), had contributed their labor for the project. After the project was finished, the genocide widows had complained to the local authorities that their fields had been stolen. In this way, according to the prisoners' wives, the genocide widows had stolen the new fields in the valley from everyone else. The genocide widows hired (Hutu) community members, the same people who had worked to improve the marsh and make it suitable for farming, for the equivalent of less than a dollar per day to cultivate the fields for them. This single story is emblematic of dozens of others I collected.

Whether intentional or not, a more common but less obvious form of exacting revenge was through structural violence that limited opportunity for certain categories of people, such as prisoners' families. In the same rural community in southern Rwanda, I found many examples whereby Hutu community members faced obstacles to economic mobility. For example, virtually all the salaried positions in the community were held by genocide survivors between 2000 and 2001, including the local government office, the Roman Catholic parish church, the government-owned primary school, and the private secondary school. While the majority of educated elites who returned to the community following the genocide were genocide survivors, the few Hutu who had returned and found positions had been accused of genocide and imprisoned for years awaiting trial. Although it was impossible for me to know whether these accusations were true, I suspected some—perhaps even many—of them were false, since the well-known perpetrators in the community, the ones everyone named, had never returned from exile in Zaire. Regardless, community members felt that the local government "belonged" to "the genocide survivors" (the members' language implied Tutsi) and that no one else had a chance of winning in a dispute.

Beyond its symbolic implications, this ethnic exclusivity had concrete, material consequences for other community members' access to the cash economy. As Jefremovas (2002) documented for the pregenocide period, access to paid labor and the means of production was frequently controlled by commune officials. Community members relied on patron/client ties to local officials or wealthy merchants to gain access to employment. In my own household, I discovered that one of my guards was giving half his salary to the genocide survivor who had recommended him for the position. The guard asked me to begin paying him with food, clothing, or other goods rather than cash. As he explained it, his "patron" was not interested in "sharing" these items, so the guard preferred them as a way to safeguard his pay.

This sort of structural violence extended beyond the labor economy. For instance, genocide survivors were the only ones to frequent the local bars. As one man who had spent three years in prison accused of genocide and was then released for lack of evidence explained: "A man can't enjoy himself there. If you go to have a beer, they [genocide survivors] bother you. They insist that you buy them beers. If you don't, they'll cause you problems. Maybe they'll follow you home and beat you, or maybe they'll go to the commune and accuse you [of genocide]. It's best just to stay at home" (field notes, March 2001). For this man, it was preferable to withdraw from community life than to risk problems with his Tutsi neighbors. In another example, released prisoners often "thanked" genocide survivors with beer and money to avoid being thrown back in prison. One family in Gisenyi prefecture explained that they made large payments to the burgomaster, who was a former RPA soldier, when the husband was released from prison. In my rural research site in southern Rwanda, released prisoners migrated to Kigali or provincial towns soon after they were freed from prison. As one explained to me, he preferred to live in Kigali, away from his family, where he could "live freely," avoid "problems" with "certain neighbors," and have some hope of finding work.

Individual Paths toward Reconciliation

Individuals can find their own paths to reconciliation if they are given the right circumstances, including freedom from fear of immediate violence, a minimum of economic independence, and a desire to reconcile. These ad hoc processes of reconciliation are highly contingent upon individual character and circumstances. Individual capacities for reconciliation vary greatly, and they do not seem to coincide with how much one has suffered. Often I have heard the most hardened opinions against "perpetrators" or against Hutu coming from people who grew up in exile and who did not directly experience the genocide. At the same time, several genocide survivors whom I interviewed had reestablished close relationships with Hutu friends or family members after surviving terrible atrocities during the genocide.

Part of this difference of experience could be attributed to the differing degrees of adherence (or not) to a collective Tutsi identity. Some Rwandans fit their individual experiences into master narratives of ethnic oppression. Thus they perceived their relationships with their neighbors of the other "group" as a constant interplay between wrong done and revenge taken. Because of their marginalization in their places of exile, many old caseload refugees experienced their "Tutsiness" more deeply than Tutsi who grew up in Rwanda and who had maintained long-term relationships with Hutu. Malkki (1995) has documented a similar phenomenon among Burundian Hutu refugees in Tanzania. Malkki found that refugees who had integrated into life in Tanzanian towns did not adhere strongly to a notion of self grounded in "Hutuness" but that the refugees living in camps and not integrating with Tanzanian society experienced a strong sense of "Hutuness."

To some extent these variations in capacity for forgiveness seemed to coincide with the degree to which a person had established long-term intimate relationships such as friendships, marriages, and business partnerships that crossed ethnic lines. As one genocide survivor explained, "It is easier for us because we have lived together before." Rwandans who grew up inside the country have a lifetime of experiences of living together in relative peace.

In one community I found an elder who had survived the genocide but had lost his wife, several of his children and their spouses, and more than ten grandchildren. Yet he often spoke with a "forgiving heart" and expressed sympathy for the "difficult position" that many Hutu community members had found themselves in during the genocide. On one occasion he explained that the burgomaster in power at the time of the genocide had "little choice" in preventing the massacre at the commune office and church. In the same community I heard some of the most vengeful and unforgiving commentary from a man whose wife and children had survived the genocide more or less unscathed. Although his family was spared the worst physical consequences of the genocide, he continued to harbor hatred for Hutu in the community, regardless of whether they participated in the genocide. Several community members (both Hutu and Tutsi) recounted instances where this man or his wife had acted maliciously toward Hutu or toward Tutsi married to Hutu.

At the individual level, the obstacle of amplified silence can be overcome because the requirements for reconciliation between individuals vary a great deal based on the specific histories of the individuals involved. In this context, the challenge is to find a way to switch from the cycle of blame, grudge holding, and revenge to open communication and mutual empathy. The end of open hostilities and the reestablishment of basic social norms (a state of coexistence) are necessary first steps in this process. Once this minimal state of coexistence was achieved, some individuals and families found paths to reconciliation through the ad hoc process of "muddling through" the aftermath of the genocide. Here I outline five examples of reconciliation as a process that requires discovery, nurturing, and reaffirmation: three between individuals and two involving members of associations. As a process, reconciliation is influenced by the wider sociopolitical/economic context. Insecurity, remembrances of the genocide, and the national political scene all affect how individuals experience their worlds, perceive others, and interpret other people's actions.

Sharing Narratives of Suffering

One woman, Epiphanie, related the following story to me in the course of a longer and more general discussion of reconciliation. She recounted the narrative as an illustration of the ways that Rwandans may be unaware that they need to reconcile with each other. In 2000 Epiphanie went home to visit her parents after her father was released from prison. Although Epiphanie's father was well respected by the genocide survivors in the commune because he had tried to intervene to protect them during the genocide in 1994, he had spent four years in prison accused of genocide. Thanks in large part to years of lobbying by genocide survivors, he was released in 2000. While she was home visiting her parents, a childhood friend and neighbor, Richard, whom she had not seen in years, came to visit the family to help celebrate her father's release.

Richard, a Tutsi, had gone to join the Rwandan Patriotic Front rebel movement in exile after the massacres of Tutsi in the community in 1990. A few months after the massacres he had disappeared. No one knew where he was, not even his own family, although everyone assumed that he had gone to join the RPF. During the genocide in 1994, his family was decimated, as they were among the first that the local Interahamwe had sought out to kill.[2] Since his disappearance in 1990, Epiphanie had not seen Richard again until 2000 at her father's release celebration.

During his visit Richard shared some of his experiences during the war, and Epiphanie explained what she and her family had lived through in the camps and forests in Zaire. At this point in recounting her story to me, Epiphanie became very animated and seemed to jump to another topic entirely:

> The world really is an amazing place. Back in 1993 when we [Epiphanie, her husband, and her children] lived in Byumba, the RPF made a sudden advance, and we found ourselves in the middle of a battle. Bombs [mortars] were falling all around us. I ran with the children to the hospital where Eugene worked. Eugene decided that we should flee in the hospital vehicles. We loaded the children into an ambulance with what things we had grabbed from the house. Eugene was driving as we sped out of the hospital compound. We drove at full speed all the way to Kigali.

As she told me this story, I did not understand what any of this had to do with Richard. As I had become accustomed to the circuitousness of Rwandan storytelling, I waited to see whether the relevance of this story would become apparent. Epiphanie then explained that Richard had been at the battle at the hospital fighting with the RPF. During the fighting he and a comrade had taken up a position just outside the hospital compound gates. As the hospital vehicles pulled out of the gates in a convoy, he took aim at them. Epiphanie continued: "He was taking aim at *our* ambulance! His comrade said, 'Let them go. They are civilians.' Can you imagine how amazing it was when we realized this?!? Richard shook his head with shame, lamenting what he might have done. I told him [Richard] that it was all right. He hadn't shot us, and besides, he didn't have any choice, since he was a soldier." Epiphanie had recounted this story to me to illustrate the way that reconciliation worked for her with a long-term friend. For her, it was important that Richard acknowledged his individual responsibility in her suffering. With his story offered in exchange for her description of her escape from the massacres in Zaire, she felt that he had acknowledged his (albeit negligible) role in the months that her family had spent in the rain forests in Zaire as well as the very tangible close call at the hospital in Byumba. Most importantly, they had found common experiences, she as a refugee in the rain forest and he as a RPF (rebel) soldier—lack of food, lack of water, poor sleeping conditions, and so on.

Epiphanie indicated that a key element of this instance of reconciliation for her was the mutual and empathetic exchange of stories about their individual suffering. In her telling of the story, Epiphanie implied that she too had expressed her remorse at the senseless massacre of his family and the ways that he suffered as a soldier with the RPF. As she explained it, although neither one blamed the other for what he or she had suffered, each had needed the other to recognize his or her role in the other's suffering. Yet they had not comprehended the full extent of their roles before their encounter. Epiphanie continued to explain that since their exchange Richard had become an important source of support for her and her parents.

Being Heard in Silence

This second ethnographic vignette illustrates that the mutual exchange required in reconciliation is not necessarily limited to face-to-face encounters. On a visit to Grace's home, I noticed that she had new cushions on the furniture in her living room. I complimented her on how pretty they were. Grace explained that an old friend, Agnès, had given them to her. Grace commented, "At least once a year, she makes some kind of gesture like that." Her tone seemed to imply that these gestures had some deeper meaning than simple generosity or the balanced reciprocity of gift exchange between friends. She then offered an explanation, which initially seemed to have nothing to do with the cushions.

Before the genocide, Grace and Agnès had been the best of friends. Grace, a genocide survivor, had lost her husband and several of her children during the genocide. Only she and her youngest son, who was only a few weeks old when the genocide began, survived. During the genocide, she had sought assistance from her friend Agnès, whose husband held a position of some importance in the provincial government. Grace explained:

> In 1994 my children and I were hiding at friends' houses.[3] These friends lived next to each other, so we would switch houses at night to avoid the searches.[4] In one house we hid in a tiny space behind a false wall in the closet. In the other the boys and I hid in the ceiling, while the younger children hid in the dining room hutch.
>
> You know that at that time, while the genocide was going on, the RPF was fighting the government troops. Secretly, we listened to Radio Muhabura, which reported where the RPF had reached. By June we heard that they weren't far from here. We also heard on RFI and BBC [on shortwave] about the Zone turquoise. I decided that we should try to get to the liberated zone or the Zone turquoise, so I discreetly sent a note to Agnès. Her husband was in a position of power, so I knew that she could help us. She never responded, so I sent her another message and pleaded with her, but still no response. As it was becoming too dangerous for us to stay where we were, I decided that our best bet was to flee toward the Zone turquoise anyway, so I made other arrangements as best I could.

Although they had managed to get false identity cards saying they were Hutu, most of Grace's children were killed during their flight.

After the genocide, Grace went to live with Agnès and her family, although Grace's "heart had hardened against her," since Agnès had refused them assistance during the genocide. Grace blamed Agnès for the deaths of her children, but she did not have anywhere else to go with her baby because she had no money, her house had been burned to the ground, and she had lost everything. Grace explained her relationship with Agnès after the war: "We never talked about the genocide. We pretended that nothing had happened between us, but we both knew otherwise."

As she was educated and spoke French, Grace found a job with an international NGO shortly after she returned home. When she was paid, she built a small annex next to the shell of her former house. Once it was habitable, she moved in with her son. Grace went on to explain that during the genocide, she had kept a journal: "Every day I would write down what had happened. After the war, I continued writing in it. In that book I wrote *everything*. Things that I can't say to anyone. What happened to me. What happened to my children. What I thought about what Agnès had done." When she left Agnès's house, Grace left behind her journal. Initially, I thought she had left it accidentally, but as her story continued I began to wonder whether she had left it on purpose. A few weeks later, Agnès came to visit Grace in her new "home." Agnès brought her the journal. When she handed it to Grace, she said to her, "I read it."

When Grace told me this, I expected her to be angry with Agnès, but her reaction was completely the opposite: "No, I wasn't angry with her. I was glad that she had read it because then she knew exactly what had happened, exactly what I felt [about her]. I could have never said those things to her or to anyone else. We never talked about what was written in my book. It was enough for her to know what I had lived through, what I thought, and for me to know that she knew." Grace's conclusion to this story and her tone of voice indicated to me that this brief exchange had laid the groundwork for her reconciliation with Agnès. Somehow it provided her with the sense that Agnès acknowledged her role in Grace's suffering and in the death of her children. Perhaps it was because Agnès had not tried to defend herself for her inaction.

And so what does the journal have to do with Grace's new sofa cushions? Grace's explanation of reconciliation is very difficult to untangle because of the multiple levels on which her exchange with Agnès operated. Before Agnès knew Grace's story, Grace hid her anger and bad feelings toward Agnès because she needed Agnès's generosity to survive. Since the entire infrastructure of her former life was destroyed in the genocide, Grace did not have the economic possibility of refusing Agnès's generosity. Thus she accepted Agnès's gifts out of desperation instead of as part of the normal reciprocity between friends. Grace's total dependence on Agnès and her bad feelings transformed their relationship into an economic transaction in Grace's eyes. In the prereconciliation situation, Grace felt that by accepting

Agnès's generosity, she was accruing a debt that she would have to repay monetarily. After Grace had moved out and their brief exchange over the diary, Grace no longer felt obliged to accept Agnès's generosity in bad faith. Grace could reject her gifts now, if she wanted. Yet because she felt like she had been heard and her pain acknowledged, Grace again saw Agnès's gifts as part of the normal reciprocity between friends.

The journal opened the door to rebuilding their relationship anew. Would their friendship ever be the same as it had been before the genocide? Probably not. But how could it have been? They were different women, re-made by their losses and their suffering, and they were rebuilding their lives in the wake of tragedy. For Grace, the fact that Agnès had "heard" Grace's story and her anger, even if from her pen instead of her lips, allowed Grace to open up the possibility of friendship again. Although Grace claimed that she and Agnès had "never" talked about the genocide again, their brief discussion about the journal made it possible for Grace to recognize the possible limits of Agnès's ability to have intervened. As Grace explained, "Now I understand that maybe she couldn't do anything to help us. Maybe she and her husband were vulnerable. Maybe they had been threatened." Furthermore, Agnès's gifts served as a reaffirmation of her solidarity with Grace. Modeled in part by Rwandan cultural idioms of gift exchange, the sofa cushions and other gifts were tangible evidence of Agnès's desire to repair their relationship and make amends for the past.

(Re)conciliation among Strangers

Delphine and Clementine were coworkers for a government project sponsored by the United Nations Development Fund. They spent most of their time traveling in the field with a team of three men. Since they were the only women, Delphine and Clementine usually shared a room on over-night missions so as to save their per diems to augment their salaries. They began working together in 1999 shortly before I first met them. In the beginning, Delphine and Clementine found it difficult to work together.

A devout Catholic who prayed regularly at home and at church, Delphine was married and in her forties. Both she and her husband, Firmin, were Hutu. When the genocide began in 1994, Delphine's family was living in Kigali. Interahamwe from the neighborhood, who suspected Delphine was Tutsi because of her physical appearance, harassed her and her family. The family went to stay with Firmin's brother, an officer in the FAR, at the Camp de Kigali. When the RPF advanced on the camp in June 1994, Firmin, Delphine, and the children fled toward the north and eventually crossed the border into Zaire. They lived in the refugee camps until 1996, when their camp came under attack. Again the family fled, this time into the rain forests.

In the forests they saw "many terrible things," as Delphine put it. They lived for several months in the forests, occasionally cultivating Congolese's fields in exchange for food, until, exhausted and starving, they returned to Rwanda via Goma. Upon their return to Rwanda, Delphine and Firmin again found themselves living off the benevolence of family members. As returning refugees, they were required to attend a reeducation camp (*ingando*) before they were qualified for employment either with the government or with international NGOs. Even after attending the camp for a month, it still took the couple over two years to find employment. In 1999 Delphine finally found her position with the international NGO. Firmin still had not found a government position, so he worked part-time in a merchant's shop.

Clementine was single and in her twenties. Clementine was a devout *umurokore* (born-again Christian) who still attended Catholic mass but who went to an *umurokore* prayer group where most members were Protestants from evangelical churches. She was Tutsi, a genocide survivor from the eastern prefecture of Kibungo. A graduate of the National University of Rwanda, Clementine had had trouble finding a permanent position in her field of study. She explained to me that she suspected the problem was that she had refused a political position as mayor of her native commune when local RPF officials asked her.

Clementine had survived the genocide with her family in Kibungo. Because her father was well respected by many Hutu in the community, their neighbors helped them hide for the few long weeks until the RPF liberated their commune. Clementine once explained to me that "some people" believed that Tutsi in her region had not suffered because the genocide did not last very long. She explained that although the genocide did not last very long, the massacres began immediately and were widespread because several prominent local officials and businessmen supported the Interahamwe and the Hutu Power political parties, CDR and MRND.

During her studies at the university, Clementine was a member of the genocide survivors' organization on campus. Yet she sometimes came into conflict with other members of the organization because of her membership in the *abarokore* prayer group on campus, which had numerous Hutu members. Some survivors called her "Interahamwe" because she prayed with Hutu.

When I first met Delphine and Clementine in 2000, they appeared to get along well. I saw them frequently during my fieldwork, as they worked in the same region as my field site. By 2001 I noticed that they frequently engaged in mutual teasing and seemed to be the best of friends, no longer just colleagues. One week they stayed at my home while they worked in the region. I was happy to have some visitors to entertain me in the evenings. One evening, the subject of reconciliation came up. Both Delphine and

Clementine had strong opinions about it. They both asserted that in order for reconciliation to be possible, "all sides" had to admit what they had done. Each then enumerated the "crimes" committed by the "other" side—for Delphine the RPF and for Clementine the Interahamwe and FAR. The discussion shocked me, as I had never heard Rwandans from so-called different sides who were not lifelong friends speak so openly about the country's history or about what they had suffered.

A few weeks later, I asked Clementine how she and Delphine had managed to become such close friends. Clementine explained:

> When we first began working together, it was difficult. We were together all the time, but we were guarded. And Delphine would always make statements to me: "You survivors think this," "You Tutsi think that." It was "Hutu-Tutsi" all day with her. So I finally got tired of it, and I confronted her. I asked her what her problem was.
>
> She told me that she was sick of hearing about how Tutsi had suffered. She said, "We've suffered, too" [*with an angry tone*]. I then asked her to tell me how. That's how it started. For nearly a week, all we did in the evening was tell each other what we had lived through. We said everything—all the details. She told me what she saw in Congo; I told her what I saw during the genocide. That's how it happened.

The way that Delphine and Clementine built their relationship, a new relationship across ethnic, generational, and status (married woman/wife versus unmarried woman/girl) lines, illustrates some of the obstacles Rwandans face in postgenocide Rwanda. Because Delphine and Clementine did not have a shared personal history that predated the genocide, they needed to build a basis of trust for their relationship. In the beginning, Delphine viewed Clementine principally as a "survivor" and assumed Clementine believed that only Tutsi had suffered during the genocide. By both women's admission, their shared faith and regular prayer served as an initial stepping-stone for them down the path of reconciliation.

Through the sharing of their suffering, Delphine and Clementine built a framework for mutual understanding and honesty. Once they had gotten past the assumptions of prejudice associated with ascribed identities, they were able to see the similarities in their experiences. Delphine's father spent five years in prison accused of genocide. Clementine's brother, a soldier in the RPF, was in military prison, accused of killing a superior officer in Congo. Thus, they shared the stigma of having a family member in prison. Both had felt the invisible barriers of discrimination in postgenocide Rwanda, Delphine due to her status as a Hutu and new returnee from Congo and Clementine as a genocide survivor who refused to join the RPF.

So what can we glean from these examples of reconciliation in practice? First, individuals need to have some economic self-sufficiency in order to engage in the process of reconciliation. If they are still beholden to the charity of others, they are not free to disclose the true feelings in their hearts. Second, sharing personal histories of suffering can help move individuals toward solidarity. To be effective this sharing must remain focused on the individual and detached from the master narratives of ethnic oppression. Thus individual narratives avoid falling into generalizations and globalization of blame. Third, the parties involved must feel that the emotions expressed are genuine. At the heart of them all is the move beyond the essentialisms of ethnicity through the sharing of individual stories that challenge the master narratives of ethnic oppression and violence. Once two individuals have reconciled with each other, the possibility for renewed exchanges and the rebuilding of relationships between kin groups opens up. These strategic anti-essentialisms can be the catalyst for a process of communal reconciliation when undertaken in a community that has achieved a minimal state of peaceful coexistence.

Communal Paths toward Reconciliation

From the examples of reconciliation in practice, we see that individuals can find their own paths to reconciliation given the right circumstances. Once two individuals have reconciled with each other, the possibility for renewed exchanges and the rebuilding of relationships between kin groups can be opened. Although the reconstruction of social relationships operates differently between individuals than it does at the community or national level, this first step can be the beginning of the process of communal reconciliation when undertaken in a community that has achieved a minimal state of peaceful coexistence.

To a limited extent, some women's organizations, youth associations, church congregations, and church-based organizations in Rwanda have achieved some success in developing models for fostering peaceful coexistence and even reconciliation in communities. Many of the organizations that I found engaged in reconciliation or coexistence work did not set out with reconciliation as their goal. They originally set out with more specific goals such as helping victims of sexual violence, assisting genocide widows, improving the socioeconomic conditions of women, or helping youths to worship Christ. In the process of helping people rebuild their lives after the genocide and war, these organizations realized that rebuilding had to start with economic well-being and then move to the psychological health of the individual. In their work they discovered that an important aspect of psychological health included the rebuilding of the social self, which could not be accomplished without reestablishing relationships with others in the community.

First, they built on the processes of reconciliation at the individual level by promoting peaceful coexistence among their own members first. For some, their original membership only included genocide survivors or widows of the genocide, most of whom were Tutsi. Other groups included both Hutu and Tutsi, but they often worked with these members separately in the period immediately following the genocide. Here I present two case studies of peace building by Rwandan women's organizations, the first a national organization of elite women and the second a rural network of women's groups organized by a Catholic priest.

Reintegration First, Reconciliation Second

Association des femmes pour le développement rural (AFDR) was a grass-roots network of over three hundred women committed to assisting rural Rwandan women.[5] Founded in the mid-1980s by young professional women, the organization brought together women with the capacity to analyze and address the problems of Rwandan society, in particular those problems associated with sexual discrimination. Originally conceived of as a "circle of reflection" to discuss women's issues, by the late 1990s the organization emphasized direct engagement of its members in rural women's development. AFDR members were expected to initiate projects at the grassroots level, to organize association activities in their regions, and to take leadership roles in Rwandan society.

Association des femmes was devastated by the events of 1994. Its membership was decimated by the massacres and flight of refugees to Zaire and Tanzania. In September 1994 AFDR found that it had only three of its eight staff members, as two had been killed and three others had left the country. The volunteer leadership had shrunk by half, and regional bodies were similarly affected. The formerly vibrant regional network of Gikongoro and Butare found that only three members from before the war were still alive and in the country. Beyond the loss of human resources, AFDR members who formerly implemented the association's programs had suddenly become potential beneficiaries in need of the basic necessities. The infrastructure of the association had also been devastated. The association's offices had been looted of all equipment, including two vehicles, furniture, and computers, and the regional bodies had lost everything, including funds for extending microcredit loans to members. Fortunately, the national association's modest bank accounts remained intact as well as its relationships with its principal foreign sponsors, the Belgian government and a Canadian aid agency.

The remaining members, many of whom were genocide survivors, recognized that Rwandan women had suffered some of worst consequences of the genocide and war. The average Rwandan woman had become a head of household weakened by the consequences of genocide. She had lost even the most basic material possessions; she was physically exhausted and psychologically traumatized. Perhaps the most challenging obstacle was that she was socially isolated because the traditional social supports such as extended family and neighbors had been destroyed.

As many members explained, the organization chose to transform "problems" into "opportunities for positive change." The national coordinator, Beata, frequently said, "Are you the problem or are you the solution? Choose to be the solution!" (author interviews, 1999, 2000). Beata's words became a rallying cry for association members whenever new challenges arose. The organization developed and implemented a postgenocide strategy, including three major elements: recruitment, training, and reintegration.

Association des femmes was successful in recruiting new members following the genocide. In 1993 the organization had 151 active members; by 1998 the membership had more than doubled to 305. Several factors contributed to their recruitment success. First, there was a surge in interest in Rwandan women's organizations following the war. Many women who returned from exile in 1994 had been active members of women's associations in their countries of exile in Africa, Europe, and North America. They brought experience and a strong desire to rebuild their country. Second, international aid to Rwanda increased dramatically after the genocide, and many of these organizations' programs directly targeted women. The increased resources attracted new members to women's organizations, which launched new programs that benefited members. Finally, many Rwandan women had become widows. According to AFDR members, widows turned to associations for the emotional and social support they would have received from kin or neighbors in the past. AFDR intentionally recruited widows as part of its reintegration strategies.

Before the genocide, AFDR members had developed leadership capacities beyond many other women's organizations. Realizing the importance of capable leadership, AFDR decided to reinforce the leadership capacities of newly recruited members. The association launched an extensive training program on a wide range of subjects for its members with support from its international sponsors. The training program helped to consolidate the associative life of all members and to infuse the membership with a sense of unity and cohesion around the AFDR vision.

Figure 10.   Grassroots women leaders, North province, 2007. Photo by Jennie
E. Burnet.

Figure 11. Grassroots women leaders with the author, South province, 2002. Photo by Jennie E. Burnet.

As part of its postconflict strategy, AFDR set aside reconciliation as a goal and instead focused on reintegrating women into economic and social life. Beata firmly believed that reconciliation was impossible if women lacked the basic necessities. The organization concentrated its initial efforts on helping members get back on their feet. AFDR helped members with the basic necessities like food, clothing, cooking utensils, soap, and so on. The association relaunched its microcredit program so that members could start or renew entrepreneurial activities for income. In Gikongoro and Butare AFDR created a trauma counseling center for genocide survivors, old caseload returnees, and new caseload returnees. Trauma counseling was vital for members suffering from mental health issues that prevented them from resuming their activities.

As part of its reintegration activities, AFDR initiated an outreach program for genocide widows. One genocide widow described her experiences:

After the war I was incapacitated with anger. I sat there [*motioning to the corner of her living room*] in the only chair I had, unable to move. My hair was a mess, my clothing was dirty. I was dead.

Then this woman, you know her, Beata, came here to see me. She was my savior. She's the one who brought me to AFDR. When she first came here, I yelled at her, told her to get out of my house. Seeing her with her Hutu face made me even angrier.

She said she couldn't leave me because she "loved me." [*She made a spitting sound.*] Love!?! I didn't know what that was anymore. I had lost my husband, my family, everything. For me, love didn't exist anymore. Besides, how could a stranger love me? She asked me to tell her what happened, but I didn't say anything.

She continued to come to see me. She would come and just sit there. Silently. Sometimes she would bring something with her. Soap. Powdered milk. Sugar. A dress. Once she came and told me to get dressed. She took me out to have my hair washed and braided. It may seem like nothing, but these little things . . . a clean dress, presentable hair, they make a difference. I started to feel human again. And then I started talking. And she listened. (Field notes, 2000)

The widow went on to explain that Beata eventually brought her to an AFDR meeting. Joining the association was a transformational experience for her. As she explained it, the association gave her a "new family" and helped her heal from the trauma of genocide. AFDR members became the people with whom she shared the joys and difficulties of life.

Beyond reaching out to widows within the country, AFDR made a concerted effort to communicate with members who had gone into exile. It sent members to visit exiled members and invite them to return to Rwanda to rebuild their organization and the country together. Many returning members stopped at the AFDR office first when they arrived in Kigali. During the massive return of refugees in late 1996 and early 1997, the organization developed a program to welcome women returning from the camps. The program was based at the Nkamira Transit Center in Gisenyi, where almost all returning refugees passed when entering Rwanda. AFDR volunteers and staff welcomed the returning women, gave them information on the situation in Rwanda, and offered trauma counseling.

Several members of AFDR became widely recognized for their success in promoting reconciliation. Intriguingly, these women were recognized individually and not as representatives of AFDR, although they all told me that their actions were born within AFDR and succeeded because of the association. Several members explained that a key to AFDR's success was the creation of *isangano* (a place where people feel comfortable expressing themselves) in the organization's offices. Whenever I visited the office, I found members greeting each other (and me) warmly. AFDR members frequently stopped by the office to "gather morale," as they put it. Many members credited AFDR's success in promoting reconciliation to the "energy," "patience," and "love" of the former national coordinator, Beata, who died in an accident in 2000.

Despite the organization's success, it faced numerous challenges after the genocide. At times conflicts arose between "old members," those who had joined before the genocide, and "new members," those who joined after. Old members sometimes felt that the new members did not share the same vision of the association's mission or lacked commitment. Like all civil society organizations, AFDR had to negotiate the complicated and sometimes difficult politics around ethnic categories. As members explained it, old members were less likely to be divided along ethnic lines than the new ones. Most old members, especially those who had founded AFDR, saw it as their mission to safeguard the organization against accusations, whether generated internally or externally, of "ethnic favoritism" or "playing the ethnic card." In one instance I witnessed an emergency meeting to confront just such an issue.

At a director's meeting, a staff member accused a founding member who was on the board of directors of encouraging ethnic division within the organization. The accused member, Natalia, was devastated by the accusations and had told several members that she planned to resign her position. Natalia was a Hutu from central Rwanda, and her husband was Tutsi. He survived the genocide thanks to Natalia's network of friends and kin, but he died in 1998. A group of armed men attacked the family's business and shot Natalia's husband and her oldest daughter. They both died. The crime was never solved, but local authorities blamed it on *abacengezi* (infiltrators). Given her background, Natalia was well respected in her community and among AFDR members. None of the old members could believe there was any truth to the staff member's accusations. A few days after the meeting, six founding members visited Natalia at her home to reassure her. During the visit they tried to identify why the staff member had made this accusation and what should be done to preserve the association's integrity. The women determined that the staff member had been motivated by jealousy and fears over her job security. They also speculated that the staff member might have been sent by government authorities to destroy the organization.[6] Two women suggested that the best course of action was to fire the staff member, but the others disagreed because they thought it could escalate the problem. They worried that firing her could be turned around and used as evidence that AFDR was ethnically biased. In the end the group decided that the best way to deal with the problem was to surround the staff member with "love and support" and eliminate the fears that had motivated her in the first place.

While AFDR survived this particular challenge without a public scandal, it did not fare so well after 2003. The 2003 Constitution reserved one-third of all decision-making positions in government bodies for women. AFDR, along with many other women's organizations, lobbied for gender quotas to be included in the final constitution. Following its adoption in 2003, women's civil society organizations faced a brain drain as their leaders left civil society to become senators, deputies, mayors, and local government administrators (Burnet 2008a). AFDR lost its executive director, national coordinator, and many members of the board of directors to government positions. While a new generation of young women leaders was hired to run AFDR, these women lacked some of the commitment of the organization's founding members. As many members were busy with demanding jobs and studying in the evenings to earn university degrees, the organization struggled to implement projects. In 2008, an executive director embezzled tens of thousands of dollars from AFDR and destroyed its reputation with its international sponsors. Near bankruptcy, a few founding members banded together to save AFDR with the help of one of its international sponsors. By 2011 AFDR still existed, but it was only a tenth of its former size, few members paid their annual dues, and the organization had little capacity to conceive or implement projects.

Reconciliation as an Organic Process

A second case study from rural Rwanda illustrates the possibilities and challenges of fostering reconciliation at the community level. A principal attraction of this rural research site was the presence of a women's organization that had brought together genocide widows, other widows (including widows whose husbands were killed by the RPF and widows "from life"[7]), and women whose husbands were in prison. The organization had grown out of the work of a Catholic priest first sent to the community following the 1994 genocide.

Father Félicien was Tutsi and a genocide survivor himself. When he first arrived at the parish in late 1994, he found the church and neighboring primary school occupied by genocide widows and their children. The women and children had nowhere else to go, as their homes had been looted and destroyed during the genocide. Having no formal training in psychology or social work, Father Félicien improvised. He asked the widows to come and speak to him individually. Once they started speaking, "they couldn't stop. . . . They told their stories from beginning to end, gushing like a flood." He asked the women to tell him their problems. Each time he visited the parish, he continued in the same way, speaking to one widow at a time. He arranged for some food aid from Caritas Christi to help the widows.

After a few months he realized that he wasn't making much progress because the widows were too numerous. In addition, he had come to understand that the women shared many of the same problems—no food, no shelter, and no family members to help them. The widows were *indushyi* (vulnerable or neglected people), but without any family support network. Father Félicien's solution to this seemingly intractable problem was to call a meeting of the parish widows. A genocide widows' group described the meeting to me:

> Father Félicien called all the widows of Musozi. He held mass, he taught us the Bible. Afterward he said to us, "I see that you're widows. Widows have always existed, but you are different. In the past, a widow lost her husband, but she stayed with his property, with his children, his family, his brothers and sisters, but you, you have nothing, no children, no husbands, no houses. . . . I ask you to go find among yourselves companions, brothers, and sisters. If not, if you stay there like that with your arms crossed, you won't survive much longer. I ask you to form groups, to go cultivate together in the valleys. I will give you seeds, I will find you help. If you form groups, we will be able to find you easily. (Field notes, November 15, 2000)

In general, Father Félicien's approach was not unique. In many places around the country, efforts were made to bring together genocide survivors and especially genocide widows and orphans into organizations or "mutual assistance" groups. As early as May 1994, the RPA asked genocide survivors and other civilians in displaced persons camps to form groups (Des Forges 1999, 702). Men and youth were conscripted into military service to continue the fight against the FAR and the genocidal government, while the injured, elderly, women, and young children were grouped in the camps so that aid could be distributed to them more easily. Once the RPF took power and people began returning to their home communities, efforts to regroup orphans and widows of the genocide continued.

What was unique about Father Félicien's approach was that he called all widows, regardless of their origin, life status, or social category. Given Musozi parish's proximity to Kibeho, many widows in the parish had lost their husbands in the killings at the Kibeho camp in April 1995. One group, comprised of widows "of life" and women whose husbands had been killed by the RPF, described the difficulties they faced early on because the genocide widows did not want to associate with them: "Father Félicien asked us [the widows from Musozi] to bring ourselves together, but the genocide widows did not want to unite with us. They said that Hutu widows had their children, their property, unlike the genocide widows. But according to Father Félicien, the only thing that mattered was to be a widow. It was then that we formed our groups" (field notes, August 14, 2000). Another group of widows "of life" and women who lost their husbands in RPF killings described the tension between themselves and the genocide widows: "After the war we were afraid and ashamed. It was hard for us to get on the same road. Even if we had problems, we felt really ashamed to look at those genocide widows, without children, without a place to sleep" (field notes, October 10, 2000). While the women felt ashamed, they did not know what to do. They had their own immediate concerns and material problems. Plus, they feared how the genocide survivors might react if the widows attempted to speak to them.

Father Félicien had noticed a similar problem. As he explained it to me in 2001, the genocide widows could not "see beyond their own misery. They continued to retell their harrowing stories, over and over again. But it did not seem to help them very much." As members of one widows' group described it: "Every time we were praying, the genocide widows would cry a lot, and Félicien decided to bring a man named Dennis to try to heal [their] trauma [meaning psychological trauma]. He also brought a mother from Save [a parish in southern Rwanda] who had lost her husband and her ten children to try to witness to these widows that she too had problems [as serious as theirs] but that she tried to calm herself down" (field notes, August 14, 2000). In addition to the professional intervention, Father Félicien hoped that by bringing different kinds of widows together they might be able to "see beyond their own misery," empathize with the other widows, and begin to rely on each other.

Since his initial efforts to organize the widows into groups, Father Félicien emphasized the principles of mutual assistance and self-reliance. Given the harsh conditions that rural Rwandans found themselves in at the end of the war (i.e., no food stocks, unplanted fields, no agricultural implements, etc.), they were in dire need of humanitarian assistance. Nonetheless, humanitarian assistance educated some Rwandans to depend on others. As the leader of one women's group explained:

> During that time, each one of us was only interested in our own problems. After many days, the priest, Félicien, who was at Musozi, called us. When someone called us, we would bring a sack with us, thinking that he was calling us to give us aid. It was difficult for Félicien to convince us to accept the biblical teachings. He told us, "Don't think that I have aid to give you. I don't even have ten francs. Only those who want to study the Word of God should come." He asked us to create groups according to the people who had the same problems. . . . A few days later, he asked us our wishes. The first wish that we gave him was spiritual assistance so that our hearts could find their places again. As for physical assistance, he gave us potatoes for planting and we also received a cow. (Field notes, October 10, 2000)[8]

Father Félicien encouraged the groups to develop communal labor projects. The majority of them secured access to marshlands from the commune authorities and cultivated together. The groups all had different arrangements of labor and harvests. Some divided the harvests, or the proceeds from the sale of the harvests, evenly among members. Others deposited the proceeds from the sale of the harvest in a group bank that members could borrow from in cases of emergency. A few groups even began to assist other vulnerable community members. The leader of the same women's group explained:

> What I can tell you is that the Word of God helped us a lot. Before, everyone thought only of her own problems, but with the Word we have been able to do a lot of things. For example, these elderly widows I told you about live from our assistance. That old woman I showed you who never had a child, she has the child of one of our members who spends the night with her, who draws water from the spring for her, and if she is seriously ill, it is we who go look for additional assistance. This woman, who has an orphaned infant, received three thousand francs to help buy milk for the baby. She was able to receive this amount from the group leaders who meet each Thursday at the Musozi church. In our group, we gave her sorghum for porridge, and we hope that each one according to her ability will continue to make a contribution to find something to feed this baby. If it weren't for the Word of God, no single one of these acts [of charity] would have been done. (Field notes, October 10, 2000)

As did this group leader, group members frequently cited Bible study and prayer as key to their transformations and healing. Many group members, Father Félicien, and Donatia all told the same story to attest to the transformational nature of the groups' Bible study.

Worse than the initial tensions between genocide survivors and the neighbors who had not fled into exile were the conflicts that erupted when the flood of refugees returned from the camps in Zaire and Tanzania. One group of women whose husbands were in prison described their return from exile:

> JENNIE BURNET: When were your husbands imprisoned?
>
> WOMAN 1: As soon as we returned here in the country, our husbands were arrested directly in front of the commune office without our feet even touching the hills. They got into trucks. First, they were held in Nyanza, but for the moment they are in Butare or here [in the jail] at the commune office. It was the [RPF] soldiers who were behind us who said, "You women, you continue home, and the men are going to stay here."
>
> JENNIE: How were you received upon your return here in the country?
>
> WOMAN 2: It was a catastrophe. The survivors beat us. They took our things by force. We weren't even able to send our children to draw water at the spring. When the children went, they [the survivors] hit

them or even killed them. We were very frightened by the state of affairs at that time.

OLD WOMAN: For example, me, I was beaten by young survivors who were with their parents. They [the parents] watched and admired. They never came to help. (Field notes, October 28, 2000)

Several community members described to me how their houses were torn down or burned by the genocide survivors who were living in them. The survivors preferred to destroy the houses than give them to the returning refugees as demanded by the local authorities.

Over a thousand men and a few dozen women accused of genocide were imprisoned in a makeshift jail, in what had been a boardinghouse for teachers at the nearby secondary school. Each Thursday, the families of detainees would line up in front of the jail to bring them food. They waited in line for hours in front of the genocide survivors who were still living in the parish church, primary school, and other buildings. In the beginning, the genocide survivors would hurl insults at them and encourage their children to throw rocks or rotten food at them. Father Félicien and Donatia brought up the survivors' actions in the groups' meetings. For several weeks, the members discussed the Christian principle of forgiveness and studied relevant passages from the Bible. Slowly, the members stopped insulting the prisoners and forbid their children to throw things at the prisoners' families. After several months, a few group members proposed that they should prepare food one week and take it to the prisoners to help relieve the burden on the prisoners' families. Seeing the example of the widows, other community members eventually stopped harassing the prisoners' families as well.

Some of the prisoners' wives were deeply touched by the transformation in the genocide survivors. They went to Donatia and asked her if she would teach them the Bible. At first, Donatia, by her own admission, was suspicious of the women's motivations. She feared that they might be hoping to benefit from material assistance without truly wanting to study the Bible. Donatia discussed the proposition with the widows' groups. Some members wanted to allow the prisoners' wives to join them, but others were opposed. Initially, Donatia began meeting with the prisoners' wives separately, but they soon formed women's groups, like the widows, and the group leaders began meeting on Thursdays with the widows' groups' leaders.

Association members were not unanimous about the degree of reconciliation that had occurred among the various categories of members. In one of my first visits to the group leaders' weekly meetings in 2000, a few of the women admitted that there continued to be conflict among some group members. I later discovered that after I left the meeting several group members chided the ones who had spoken out for revealing "secrets" that should remain within the group. One woman whom I spoke with individually said: "Anger is not lacking, and we do not succeed in understanding each other completely" (author interview, February 17, 2000). She added that the group leaders had succeeded in reestablishing relationships much more than the other group members. As she explained: "Only the group leaders have arrived at that level. They are meeting often [every Thursday] to study the word of God, but the women in the groups do not meet all together to study the Bible. They each meet within their own groups, which gather together women from the same category [i.e., genocide survivors, widows "of life," prisoner's wives, etc.]" (field notes, February 17, 2000).

On one occasion, I encountered these conflicts when I had set an appointment to meet with a group from a particular sector and cell without realizing that there were several groups. When I arrived at the designated meeting place along with my research assistant, we found three groups waiting to meet with us. We immediately noted that there was a lot of tension between the women, but it was unclear to us what had caused it. We proposed to meet with all three groups at the same time, but the women refused. After some debate among the women, it was decided that we would meet with two groups first in someone's home and then with the third group down in the valley near the field where they did communal labor. During the group interviews, we realized that the first two groups were comprised of genocide widows, while the third consisted of prisoners' wives (field notes, October 2000). In the interviews, the women in all groups made clear that they had serious, ongoing conflicts with women of the other category.

Some community members opposed the reconciliation efforts of this network of Catholic women's groups. While community members were reluctant to admit their opposition, as doing so could be viewed as being against the policy of "national unity," some community members appeared to be jealous of the women. On one occasion, I asked the commune-level leader of the grassroots women's structures whether the sector-level or cell-level development councils, which were elected administrative bodies, were active. She responded with anger: "What would they do!?! Any aid that comes into this community goes to Donatia's women." In late 2000 a new parish priest was appointed to Musozi during an unexpected reorganization within the diocese. The women's groups had complained that the new priest did not want to help them. In an informal conversation during a social visit to his home, the priest said to me, "I am the priest for all the Catholics of Musozi, not just those women. If I pay too much attention to them, the other Catholics will lose faith."

The most significant evidence of opposition to the women's groups activities were political problems that Donatia and Father Félicien encountered. In an interview a former diocesan lay minister described how he had been called in for questioning by the police on numerous occasions. A Hutu who had worked closely with both Hutu and Tutsi in peace-building efforts since before the genocide, the man indicated that anyone working across ethnic lines risked attracting attention and being accused of involvement in "politics." He gave Donatia and Father Félicien, both Tutsi and genocide survivors, as examples. I later asked Donatia whether she had ever encountered problems with the police or government authorities. She explained:

> I had problems with the authorities who believed that I was involved in political activity, that I was against the government, that I was encouraging ethnic segregation, that I wanted to divide Rwandans, in short, and that I was against national unity.
>
> When they brought me in for questioning and started accusing me of all these things, I didn't know what to say. I didn't know how to prove to them that I was innocent. I felt innocent, but I didn't have solid arguments to defend my position or to deny the accusations. I explained to them that for me every Rwandan is a child of God who may redeem himself one day without any other consideration, whether ethnic or otherwise.
>
> In the end, they required me to work in the open, during the daytime, in public places, never in private homes. Now I don't have those problems anymore, and the women have managed to live together without problems and to help each other. (Field notes, February 17, 2000)

In the long term, it seems that the women's groups in Musozi parish succeeded, more or less, in building relationships among themselves, overcoming community opposition, and helping the community to begin to rebuild social interactions. These tentative steps demonstrate the ways that the individuals facing the extraordinary circumstances of the postgenocide succeeded in lieu of, and sometimes in spite of, state intervention.

Conclusion

In the aftermath of the genocide, Rwandan women were left to find their own ways to muddle through the suffering, ambiguity, and complexity of life in a postgenocide society. Because of their unique position at the interface between the nuclear family and the social world, women began to reach out to former friends, neighbors, and colleagues. In the journey to find a way to live together (*kubana*) again, some Rwandan women and women's associations discovered their own paths toward reconciliation.

These individual and communal paths to reconciliation suggest a common process and set of conditions to move from coexistence toward reconciliation. First, open violence in the community has to be brought to an end and people need to have a sense of basic physical security. Second, community members need to have their most basic needs met: water, food, shelter, and clothing. Ideally, once these basic needs have been met, they need to establish economic self-sufficiency. If people are beholden to the charity of others, they are not free to express their true feelings for fear of losing the aid on which they depend. Third, a space where people feel comfortable expressing themselves (*isangano*) needs to be created so that individual stories of suffering can be shared. Sharing individual stories with people from different social categories creates the opportunity to recognize common experiences of suffering that transect social categories. This sharing of individual stories can help establish a new basis of trust between people. Yet in this exchange the narratives must remain focused on individual experiences and avoid globalizing blame to categories of people as the globalization of blame reinforces divisions. Fourth, as illustrated by the reconciliation stories of Grace and Agnès and Delphine and Clementine, participants need to recognize the suffering of others and accept responsibility for their own role in the others' suffering—whether they caused it intentionally or unintentionally. Fifth, participants need to demonstrate their desire to move forward and establish new (or renewed) social relationships through culturally appropriate means, for example Agnès's gifts to Grace or the Musozi parish genocide widows' preparation of food for prisoners. Throughout all stages of this process, movement toward reconciliation remains tentative and can be easily thwarted by renewed violence or by parties who wish to disrupt the process. Thus, people engaging in reconciliation processes and peace-building activities must remain vigilant to mitigate the potential negative effects of spoilers and must make intentional decisions to continue their journey.

While many observers, especially members of the international feminist movement, portray the centrality of women in rebuilding Rwandan society as a consequence of women's "natural" tendency toward "nurturing kindness" and "peace," this outcome depended on the decisions of individual women in the course of everyday life as well as on the efforts of women's organizations. These lessons made it possible for the courageous steps some ordinary women took during the RPF-led government's largest unity and reconciliation activity: the reinvented "traditional" *gacaca* courts that adjudicated over one million cases of genocide crimes between 2001 and 2008 using ordinary citizens instead of lawyers as judges. I examine ordinary women's roles in these courts in the next chapter.

7

Reconciliation, Justice, and Amplified Silence

Moving forward in the wake of the genocide required Rwandans to face material, emotional, and social realities unknown in living memory. Women in particular were forced to (re)invent a world that accommodated their unique circumstances—widows bereft of male kin and children, girls with limited (or no) marriage prospects, female heads of household with full economic responsibility but limited experience negotiating the public sphere. In postgenocide Rwanda, women had to learn self-reliance in a context of dire material circumstances. In many cases, they faced a double burden of marginalization, first as girls, wives, or widows and second as ethnicized targets of violence whether before, during, or after the genocide.

The practices of state building in the New Rwanda contributed significantly to the construction of postgenocide subjectivities and conscribed the agency of ordinary women. In part, these state-building practices fostered reconciliation. Yet certain aspects of the RPF-led state-building practices hindered reconciliation. By emphasizing national unity as the core of reconciliation, the state excluded certain Rwandans' (i.e., Hutu) experiences of war and genocide. The amplified silence resulting from this situation was an obstacle to "meaningful," as defined by ordinary women, reconciliation. As discussed in the previous chapter, ordinary women and women's associations have found their own paths to reconciliation through the mutual sharing of individual narratives of suffering.

In this chapter I discuss the largest government initiative to promote reconciliation to date: the use of so-called traditional *gacaca* courts to try over one million cases of genocide crimes. The *gacaca* courts had a profound effect on ordinary women's lives. In the short term, the *gacaca* process disrupted women's efforts to reestablish normal social relations in local communities and destroyed the progress women's associations had made toward reconciliation. In the long term, *gacaca* delivered justice for some and established at least a partial truth about what happened during the genocide in local communities. However, since the *gacaca* courts did not have jurisdiction over crimes perpetrated by RPA soldiers, many Rwandan men and women felt they were denied justice. The "quest to establish 'the truth'" of the genocide through *gacaca* was "circumscribed by political considerations" that limited who was heard, what information was reported, and what the final verdict was (Hinton 2010, 14). Since the *gacaca* courts did not have legitimacy in the eyes of the population, they were often viewed as another imposition of the central government on local communities and as another venue in which local power conflicts worked themselves out while appearing to conform to central government policies.

The Search for Justice

The RPF-led government adopted a stance of maximal prosecution vis-à-vis the genocide: every single participant in the genocide from the central planners down to coerced peasant farmers or opportunistic looters would be prosecuted and punished for their crimes. Article 2 of the 1996 genocide code delineated four categories of responsibility in the genocide: (1) "planners, organizers, instigators, supervisors and leaders of the crime of genocide or of a crime against humanity," persons in positions of authority in the government or political parties, "notorious murderers," and "persons who committed acts of sexual torture"; (2) perpetrators or "conspirators of accomplices" of intentional homicide or physical assault causing death; (3) persons guilty of "serious assaults against the person"; and (4) persons who committed crimes against property.[1] Subsequent amendments to the genocide code, including the laws establishing the *gacaca* courts and amending their structure and statutes, maintained this hierarchy of responsibility, with punishments varying in severity by category.[2]

The first genocide trials began in Rwanda's Belgian-style court system in December 1996. The Rwandan justice system, itself destroyed in the genocide and its personnel decimated, was overwhelmed, and trials moved forward slowly. By March 2001, the national courts had tried only 5,310 people (HRW 2002a, 79). Yet prison and local jail populations in Rwanda had soared to over 130,000, almost all imprisoned on charges of genocide. Even if Rwanda had had the best justice system in the world, it would have been overwhelmed by the problem of trying genocide suspects. Under pressure from the international community to solve the problem, the Rwandan government turned to *gacaca*.

In its traditional form, *gacaca* brought together *inyangamugayo* (people of integrity, usually respected elders), the people in dispute, and residents of a hill to establish the facts of the conflict and find a solution. *Gacaca* takes its name from the patch of grass found in the inner courtyards (*ibikari*) of traditional homesteads. Inner courtyards were the most private place in the family home, and usually only family members entered them. Thus, *gacaca* in its traditional form was a private rather than a public affair. The deliberations in *gacaca* were considered confidential, and even the "judgment" or decisions of *gacaca* were reported publicly only if such reporting was a specific decision of the *gacaca* process.

Under Belgian colonialism, tribal courts overseen by local chiefs handled disputes among the indigenous population, while "modern" Belgian-style courts handled legal disputes involving the foreign (mostly white) population and Rwandans who qualified as "civilized" under colonial law. Colonial law applied to only Europeans and certain categories of other foreigners, while customary law applied to Rwandans and other Africans. *Gacaca* continued to operate during this period, but its decisions were only enforced by local chiefs if these chiefs recognized the legitimacy of a specific *gacaca* and its decisions. In the postcolonial period, the Belgian-style modern courts replaced the tribal courts, yet in some communities, local administrators held *gacaca* sessions to resolve disputes among rural peasants without involving the modern legal system (Reyntjens 1990). While *gacaca* was used by local officials under the Habyarimana regime, this practice was never codified by Rwandan law, so the exact format and function of *gacaca* varied widely from community to community. In addition, families continued to resolve intrafamilial conflicts through *gacaca* when necessary.

Exactly when *gacaca* was proposed as a possible remedy for Rwanda's postgenocide judicial woes is unclear. In 1996 the UN Human Rights Mission to Rwanda commissioned a study of *gacaca* by several professors from the

National University of Rwanda in Butare (Karega et al. 1996). The report documented several forms of *gacaca* throughout the country and even found a few communities that had applied it to solve local disputes in the absence of a functioning judiciary in 1995 and early 1996. Yet the report concluded that *gacaca* was not appropriate as a judicial remedy for the genocide. Political scientist Timothy Longman dates the *gacaca* solution to a conversation between Michelle Wagner, a historian of the region and then a researcher for Human Rights Watch, and some professors from the National University of Rwanda on the terrace of the Hotel Ibis in Butare in 1995. Regardless of the idea's origins or initial negative studies, *gacaca* emerged as the only possible solution in the eyes of the Rwandan government and many members of the international aid community despite widespread opposition from the international human rights community. International human rights organizations opposed the *gacaca* courts because the accused were prohibited from having legal counsel and did not have the right to cross-examine witnesses or call witnesses for their defense (Penal Reform International 2006, 26–37). As Peter Uvin and Charles Mironko state, "Perhaps the strongest element in favor of gacaca is the lack of an alternative" (2003, 277).

In January 2001 the parliament passed the law creating the *gacaca* courts. These reinvented courts changed many of the fundamental aspects of the traditional *gacaca*. The first and most important difference is that the *gacaca* courts made the proceedings a public rather than a private affair, with the entire community participating. Second, the foundation of *gacaca* court proceedings was the testimony of prisoners who had confessed their crimes. In traditional *gacaca*, testimony usually began with the aggrieved stating their case, followed by impartial witnesses providing testimony. The accused gave their testimony last, while participants cross-examined them based on the accounts provided by the impartial witnesses. Thus, the *gacaca* courts changed the order in which truth was established, putting the offenders before victims. Third, the foundation of traditional *gacaca* was not punitive justice but rather restorative justice. Although the recommendations (or "judgments") of a traditional *gacaca* might have included some punishment (e.g., the gift of a cow, goat, or other livestock), these punishments were focused on reestablishing social equilibrium between the aggrieved parties. When a *gacaca* judgment included the gift of livestock, such a gift was to be made with all the attendant ritual ceremony normally accorded to such a gift and followed by all the subsequent countergifts required. Thus, the dialectic of "normal" social interactions was reestablished. The *gacaca* courts attempted to include aspects of restorative justice through the inclusion of "works of general interest" (known by its French acronym TIG, or *travaux d'intérêt général*), portrayed as a sort of community service but in practice more like prison work camps, and the payment of reparations to the victims' families or to the genocide survivors' assistance funds as part of perpetrators' sentences. In most communities the *gacaca* courts were perceived as focused solely on punitive justice. The *gacaca* courts imposed sentences ranging from "civil reparation of damages caused to other people's property" to life imprisonment.[3]

Despite this reinvention of a private conflict resolution mechanism as a public punitive justice mechanism, the Rwandan population, including survivors, the accused, and families of the accused, maintained hope that the truth might emerge, justice might be served, and the falsely accused might be released. Elections for *inyangamugayo* were held in late 2001, and a pilot phase of *gacaca* began in 2002. Following its pilot phase from 2001 through 2002, the *gacaca* statute and entire Rwandan judiciary were reorganized based on the results of the pilot phase. Organic Law No. 16/2004 was promulgated on June 19, 2004, and the *gacaca* courts began operating nationwide.

In public statements the Rwandan government expressed hope that *gacaca* would help with the problem of mass incarceration of people accused of genocide. The prisons would be emptied, and the drain on state and community resources would be stopped. In early 2003 President Kagame ordered the provisional release of several thousand prisoners who were elderly or sick or who had been minors in 1994. Again in July 2005, in August 2006, and in February 2007 authorities released tens of thousands of detainees who had confessed to participating in the 1994 genocide and had already served the maximum sentence for their category of crimes (HRW 2006a; IRIN 2005). Many others were old and in poor health or had been children at the time of the genocide. Released prisoners attended a six-week *ingando* (solidarity camp) before returning to their home communities. Despite these steps to reduce the prison population, *gacaca* resulted in an exponential increase in the number of accused genocide suspects. In January 2005 the secretary of state in the Ministry of Justice announced that approximately 761,000 suspects had been identified in the investigation phase of *gacaca* (Reyntjens 2005, 13). From the beginning of 2006, the number of detainees in Rwandan prisons and jails rose from 60,000 to around 90,000 in May 2007 (Hirondelle News Agency 2007a). In December 2007 Domitille Mukantaganzwa, executive secretary of the National Service of Gacaca Courts, announced that 712,723 genocide cases in the *gacaca* courts had been completed out of a total of over 1.12 million cases (Gakwaya 2007).

By May 2009 most prisoners had either been released or moved into TIG camps. Many of those who returned home were still required to participate in TIG three days per week. Prisoners in TIG camps worked on TIG projects six days per week and lived in miserable conditions in large structures made from tarps, wood poles, and tin roofing. The stench rising from one camp along the road from Kigali to Muhanga (formerly Gitarama) in May 2009 was stunning. TIG projects were highly visible and included the rehabilitation or construction of roads, the improvement of marshes to increase arable land, and the terracing of hills to increase arable land and reduce environmental degradation.

Putting Justice before Truth

Gacaca courts were portrayed as a way to uncover the truth about the genocide, and in some communities they served this purpose. Chakravarty (2006, 28–29) has documented the complex ways in which the logic of genocide was deconstructed in some sector-level *gacaca* hearings. Some survivors recovered the remains of their loved ones thanks to testimony given before the *gacaca* courts. Others learned more precisely how, when, or where their loved ones were killed. Yet for many others, the truth remained elusive. The accused were offered reductions in sentences for confessing to their crimes, and thousands did confess. Yet, given the benefits of confession, an unknown number of people confessed to less severe crimes than the ones they committed. Others confessed to crimes they did not commit so that they could be liberated.[4] Many *gacaca* courts rejected the confessions as incomplete or untrue (HRW 2007c, 1; Penal Reform International 2003, 8). In some communities, clandestine groups, referred to as *ceceka* (keep quiet), organized a code of silence before the *gacaca* courts (Reyntjens 2005, 13). Thus, the *gacaca* process did not restore the truth to many genocide survivors.

The accused, prisoners' families, and other Hutu feared that the *gacaca* courts would be used for ends other than justice for the genocide. In some communities genocide survivors and others organized false testimony against certain people. In some cases they appeared to be motivated by the desire for reprisal or revenge. They felt as if they knew certain people had been involved in the genocide, and they wanted to make sure those people were found guilty. In other cases, they fabricated testimony to settle long-term personal conflicts or family feuds as well as disputes over land or other property. Some RPF soldiers whose families were targeted first in the genocide sought revenge against anyone they knew who was Hutu.

Another issue is that *gacaca* was perceived as one-sided, as victors' justice (Carroll 2000, 185; HRW 2007c, 2). The *gacaca* law limited the courts' jurisdiction to crimes related to the genocide. Thus killings and other atrocities perpetrated by RPF soldiers, whether during the civil war before 1994, during the genocide and its aftermath in Rwanda, or in Democratic Republic of Congo, were off the table. Although the documentation of RPF abuses committed in 1994 was sparse, several sources reported indiscriminate killings of civilians, extrajudicial executions of suspected or accused *génocidaires*, and expropriation of houses, livestock, and other property (Amnesty International 1994; Des Forges 1999, 702–22). As the RPF took control of new areas, it set about separating civilians from "Interahamwe zariye abantu" (literally, Interahamwe who ate people, meaning those who killed a lot). It relocated civilians to camps and then killed the suspected Interahamwe. Gen. Paul Kagame explained the policy on Radio Rwanda: "Harmful elements were hidden in the bushes and banana plantations. Therefore a cleaning was necessary, especially to separate the innocent people with the killers" (UNAMIR, notes, Radio Rwanda, 19:00, July 27, 1994, quoted in Des Forges 1999, 716). The RPF called these campaigns of indiscriminate killings *gutwika ahantu* (to set a place on fire). When refugees returned en masse from Zaire and Tanzania in late 1996 and early 1997, the RPF again sorted the "big killers" from other civilians and often killed suspects on the spot. As a result of these campaigns to root out "real Interahamwe," many Rwandan citizens felt that "Interahamwe nyanterahamwe ntizikiba mu Rwanda" (the true Interahamwe are no longer in Rwanda, meaning they are either dead or in exile). Thus to many Rwandans, the people accused in *gacaca* courts were not "the big killers"; at best they were small-time participants who were coerced, or they were wrongly accused.

Up until 2008 the official language to name the 1994 genocide in Rwanda was *itsembabwoko n'itsembatsemba* (genocide and massacres). This language included and recognized the thousands of Hutu victims of the genocide. However, a 2008 law replaced this language with *jenoside yakorewe abatutsi* (genocide against Tutsi), codifying the long-term symbolic erasure of Hutu victims of the genocide from national mourning activities (see chapter 3; Burnet 2009). Beyond their inability to publicly mourn their dead, the families of Hutu victims of the genocide or of Hutu victims of RPF killings lived with other people's assumptions that their dead loved ones were genocide perpetrators—even those who died at the hands of the Interahamwe during the genocide. In *gacaca*, these families sometimes faced accusations that they aided and abetted their so-called genocidal kin.

The Injustices
of Local Justice

Integrating released prisoners and *génocidaires*, meaning those who had confessed to and been sentenced for crimes of genocide, into local communities was a serious obstacle in the *gacaca* process. Following the provisional prisoner releases outlined earlier, releases continued as *gacaca* courts started operating nationwide in January 2005. During *gacaca* many more prisoners were convicted and released for time served.

In preparation for *gacaca*, the government waged a public awareness campaign to educate the population about the need to accept released prisoners, whether innocent or guilty, back into the community. These types of "sensitization campaigns," as they are called in Rwanda, have a long history and are a common technique employed both by the government and by international nongovernmental organizations to change or shape local knowledge. In focus groups conducted in 2007, I frequently heard various versions of the "official" response to prisoner releases:

> Once they [the released prisoners] arrive on the hill, they get along very well. They try to ask for forgiveness from people whose family members they killed. (Female respondent, South province, May 2007)

> The prisoners had received training sessions in *ingando* [reeducation camp] before coming onto the hill. You can see, once he [a released prisoner] arrives on the hill, he has changed a lot. First of all, he prays a lot. You can see that he is truly Christian. Second, he approaches people to talk and to ask forgiveness from people against whom he committed genocide, whose family member he killed. Third, he goes to help others. (Female respondent, South province, May 2007)

> I went to visit a freed man at his home who lived really close to my house, and he came to visit me at home too. We have exchanged ideas, and I've seen that this is someone who has totally changed. We should have the courage to approach these people. This man of whom I'm telling you, he killed my family, he asked forgiveness, and I forgave him. I find that it's good if someone truly accepts these actions and asks forgiveness. At this time he is relieved, and you, too, you feel something like peace in your heart. (Female, Tutsi, genocide widow, South province, June 2007)

In focus groups including Tutsi (or Hutu) genocide widows and Hutu wives of current or former prisoners in South province or including Tutsi returnees and Hutu women in North province, the vast majority of respondents were very careful to stick to this official, idyllic version of prisoner reintegration into local communities. In many cases, the very same respondents would recount in more private contexts an entirely different version of what was happening. Some women waited for others to leave so that they could add to or change what they had told me.

In more homogeneous groups of women, I heard less rosy depictions of prisoner reintegration. Genocide widows (whether Tutsi or Hutu) explained the difficulties of accepting known *génocidaires* back into the local community.

In general, the prisoners integrate themselves without any trouble. But there is one who came who did not change. He, he stays at home, he talks to no one. Since he did very bad things in the genocide, killed a lot, we leave him alone like that. We've put him in quarantine. (Female, Tutsi, genocide widow, South province, May 2007)

We can't look into men's hearts; certainly, there are those who are happy and others who are not happy. In general, we pretend to get along. (Female, Tutsi, genocide survivor, South province, May 2007)

Some Rwandans are tricky. You hear them on the radio saying, "The man who killed my children came and asked for forgiveness. I gave it. Now my daughter will marry his son." That isn't the way it is. Since *gacaca* started, we [genocide survivors] live in fear. . . . Since they [the prisoners] came home, I can no longer walk every morning by myself. When I used to get up at five a.m. to walk by myself in nature, I felt confident, I felt alive. I had removed the fear. Now the fear has returned. [*She put her hand on her chest.*] (Female, Tutsi, genocide widow, Kigali, June 2009)

The sentiments expressed here are not surprising. It is not hard to imagine how difficult it must be for genocide survivors to live as neighbors with people responsible for hunting them like prey, looting and burning their homes, or killing their family members.

What I find striking about the first two cited passages is the subtle differences in the attitudes behind them. The first statement was made by one of the leaders of a church-based women's organization. She herself was an *inyangamugayo* in the *gacaca* court in her sector, and she had courageously served as an unbiased leader in the *gacaca* process by helping to ensure that the innocent were released and by punishing false testimony. Yet she freely admitted that certain *génocidaires* do not have the right to rejoin the community, because although they asked for mercy (*basabye imbabazi*) before the courts by pleading guilty and admitting the acts they committed, they had not shown remorse (*baticuza*).

Many Rwandans, whether Tutsi genocide survivors or Hutu who did not participate in the genocide, pointed out this qualitative distinction in the confessions made by *génocidaires*. To confess (*gusaba imbabazi*) before the courts, receive a reduction in sentence, and be released from prison is not the same as accepting moral responsibility and showing remorse (*kwicuza*). Both of these Kinyarwanda phrases, *gusaba imbabazi* and *kwicuza*, mean to ask for pardon, but *gusaba imbabazi* is used primarily in the legal arena, whereas *kwicuza* is used among Roman Catholics to refer to seeking pardon in the rite of reconciliation (confession). This distinction underlines the inherent conflict between justice's transcendental promises of peace, justice, healing, and reconciliation and its elision or silencing of alternative mechanisms or coping strategies (Dwyer 2010; Drexler 2010).

The second statement was made by a genocide widow in a focus group with two small women's groups from a very rural area of South province. The first group was comprised of genocide widows and the second, Hutu wives of prisoners. During the interview the Hutu women hardly spoke and gave very constrained responses, and the leader of the genocide widows' group did most of the talking. Her statement, especially given that she made it in front of her Hutu neighbors, was intended to underscore the continued distrust and suspicion among Tutsi genocide survivors. In response to a follow-up question, the same widow returned to the same theme by evoking the lasting trauma of genocide:

> We cannot forget the wounds that we have in our hearts, but the *gacaca* [process] has warned us to be patient and courageous. If you begin to feel trauma in the *gacaca* [trial], you cannot get anywhere. . . .
>
> I can't forget that I am left alone. When I don't have water in the house and night is falling, I think that I should have someone to go draw water. When there is no wood for the fire, that reminds me that there should be someone to go and collect wood. When I want this or that, I should have someone to help me. With everything that I do, I am reminded that I am alone. That's how it is. We go to *gacaca*, we try to be patient, but forget all that, it will never happen.

The fundamental message is that there can be no justice for genocide survivors. Whether in the *gacaca* process or any other judicial process, genocide survivors will never have justice because the gaping holes in their lives cannot be filled. No one can bring their dead family members back to life.

The statement from the third widow points to a disconnection between the official version of the *gacaca* process and the turmoil in which genocide survivors find themselves: they are forced to live among the people who killed their family members and to live in fear that these people may kill again.

Survivors have many different points of view concerning justice, the events of 1994, and the appropriate way to remember the genocide and their lost loved ones. All have been unanimous that dead family members can never be replaced or compensated, but many view justice through the courts (whether national or international) or through *gacaca* courts as an important duty—a way to recapture the dignity of those who died in ignominious ways. One genocide widow from South province has collaborated extensively over the years with investigators from the ICTR and from foreign governments. She has testified before foreign courts on several occasions at great emotional cost to herself. Yet she has undertaken all these activities quietly and discreetly to avoid attracting attention and potential revenge seeking. Also, she has not participated or volunteered to participate in investigations conducted by Rwandan authorities. When I asked her why, she said that she could not work with them because they "were not serious."

A second issue raised in several conversations and focus group interviews was the problem of new accusations against people who have been living in the community "peacefully" since 1994. While I was visiting a family in West province, the conversation turned to the topic of *gacaca*. Several neighbors and members of the patrilineage had gathered in the living room to welcome me with drinks in the customary fashion. The conversation eventually turned to local gossip. One woman asked, "Did you know that —— has become insane?" The others quickly began explaining:

> WOMAN 2: It's not surprising, because we just heard that he, too, killed during the genocide.
> MAN 1: It's someone who was released from prison thanks to the president of the republic who told us that. He said that —— had participated in the genocide.
> WOMAN 2: People asked the freed man why he didn't say anything sooner.
> MAN 2: He is ready to denounce him and give all the information if the *gacaca* court calls him.

While this gathering of family and friends was shocked to find out that this particular neighbor had participated in the genocide, they did not feel that the accusations were anything other than factual—the truth. For me, it was a relief to see them discussing *gacaca* and its complexities without fear and suspicion. In the group there were (Tutsi) genocide survivors, (Hutu) former prisoners and family members of former prisoners, (Hutu and Tutsi) members of the RPF who had joined during the civil war between 1990 and 1994, and (Hutu) supporters of President Habyarimana and the MRND. Yet the ties among them were strong enough to allow for what appeared to be unfettered discussion. The conversation then turned to the dark side of new accusations of genocide:

> WOMAN 2: I see that —— has been imprisoned again.
> VARIOUS OTHERS: This gentleman killed quite a lot of people in the genocide. He admitted it himself. Only after he was released from prison, that's when he began to lie, denouncing innocent people by saying they had participated in the genocide. After he had denounced a large number of these people, the population realized that he was lying. He himself said, "No one visited me or ever brought me something to eat when I was in prison. I will take my revenge." After that,

people realized that these others were innocent. The population is waiting patiently to see if the *inyangamugayo* are going to do something and if these people will be released from prison.

Confessions were the foundation of the *gacaca* process, with prisoners receiving reduced sentences in exchange for their testimony. Prisoners had many motivations to lie. As in the case cited above, some prisoners lied to seek revenge. The theme of revenge is a very strong one in *gacaca*, and its currents flow in many directions. Other prisoners lied because they did not make a full confession and wanted to cover up the atrocities they committed in the hopes of avoiding more severe punishment.

New accusations disrupted the social fabric that had been tenuously rewoven in certain communities. In a focus group in South province, a Tutsi genocide widow explained: "In *gacaca* not everything is going well. You see a husband and a wife who have stayed on the hill for thirteen years. We believe they are innocent, and all of a sudden you hear them denounced in *gacaca*; they did this or that. The family [the husband and wife] is shocked, discouraged, and gets angry saying that this [the accusations] is motivated by hate. There are interminable conflicts." Here the speaker leaves the question open whether the accusations are true or false; instead, she highlights that, regardless of whether they are true, the family of the accused perceives the accusations as unjust, as the seeking of revenge. To believe that accusations are motivated by revenge is not merely paranoia; these suspicions are often based on known cases of revenge seeking within the community. The problem is that the legitimacy of *gacaca* has been so undermined in some communities that residents dismiss all testimony as lies or half-truths.

In my research, numerous examples of revenge seeking in *gacaca* emerged. These cases appeared to fall into three main categories: revenge against particular individuals, revenge against particular individuals as representatives of a corporate group, and revenge against a corporate group.

In instances where people sought revenge against particular individuals, they were not necessarily seeking revenge for events that occurred during the genocide in 1994. Sometimes they appeared to be taking revenge for events in the distant past (e.g., previous periods of anti-Tutsi sentiment and violence such as 1959, 1962–63, and 1973). Most of these stories are difficult to describe in ethnographic detail because they risk endangering the tellers who are the victims of this revenge seeking. One Tutsi genocide survivor, Marie, who had been married to a Hutu, Janvier, explained to me the way that another Tutsi genocide survivor, Jeanne, constantly terrorized her during *gacaca* hearings.[5] Jeanne would frequently appear before the court and demand that Marie testify about what had happened during the genocide. Marie insisted that she did not witness anything because she spent several months in hiding along with her children, moving from house to house among her in-laws, who lived near each other on the hill. Jeanne insisted that Marie was lying, that she knew where victims' bodies were buried. Jeanne repeatedly threatened Marie: "Don't you know what the punishment for lying before the *gacaca* court is!?!" As Marie told her story to me, her body trembled, her voice quavered, and tears fell silently from her eyes.

Jeanne and her husband, Patrice (also a Tutsi who had survived the genocide), had long held a grudge against Marie and Janvier. Patrice had been the victim of Tutsi purges from higher education in 1973, and he blamed anti-Tutsi racism for the premature end of his education. Patrice eventually focused this anger on Janvier, who had been promoted to a leadership position in the regional government in the early 1990s. Jeanne and Patrice believed that Janvier received the promotion in lieu of Patrice because of his ethnicity. In the months following the genocide in 1994, Janvier continued to hold this position in the regional government and worked closely with the RPA officers stationed in the area. One day as he was walking on the main road into town, a truck transporting prisoners stopped. Without any explanation, Janvier was arrested by RPA soldiers accompanying the prisoners and taken away. It took Marie several weeks to find out what had happened to him. She eventually found him in a provincial prison. It took several months to find out that he stood accused of genocide, although he did not even have a judicial file.

With the loss of her husband's salary, Marie sought to have her children receive assistance from the genocide survivors' assistance fund (known by its French acronym, FARG), but Jeanne and Patrice, who headed the local genocide survivors' organization, blocked Marie's efforts by refusing to sign the necessary paperwork. Jeanne said to her, "The FARG does not help killers' children." Marie's husband spent seven years in prison under charges of genocide, although there was no evidence against him. Marie and her husband believed that Jeanne and Patrice were behind Janvier's arrest and imprisonment, but they had no proof of it.

When Janvier was finally released in 2001 because of the lack of evidence against him, many (Tutsi) genocide survivors in the community welcomed him back home, as they believed he was innocent. Patrice and Jeanne, on the other hand, harassed the family. On one occasion, Patrice tried to organize a mob to attack Janvier. On other occasions, they threatened that someday soon Janvier would be rearrested. Under great psychological strain, Janvier went to the capital city, Kigali, hoping to escape the harassment, but it still continued. The family he was staying with began to receive anonymous threatening phone calls. As a result of the harassment and the strains of adjusting to life outside prison, Janvier became pathologically paranoid, believing that he was constantly being watched and followed. One evening, he was hit by a dump truck as he was crossing the street. He died from his injuries. While Marie believed that Jeanne and Patrice had something to do with the accident, she had no proof. Police investigators labeled it an accident. A Roman Catholic priest familiar with the case explained: "With this sort of a death there are so many unanswered questions. Maybe it was a simple accident, but Marie will never believe it because of what came before." Trying to support her children alone, Marie hoped that Jeanne and Patrice would leave her in peace, but every time she attended *gacaca*, she faced Jeanne's accusations.[6]

The Rwandan government's genocide commemorations and national mourning practices have generated a polarizing discourse that defines all Tutsi as genocide victims and all Hutu as genocide perpetrators (Burnet 2009). Similar to efforts in Argentina and Chile (see Robben 2010), Rwandan government memorial practices created master narratives about Rwandan history, the civil war between 1990 and 1994, and the 1994 genocide. Under the logic of this discourse, certain Tutsi genocide survivors have sought revenge against individual Hutu as a scapegoat for Hutu as a corporate group.

Among women's groups in South province, several of the Hutu members faced accusations before the *gacaca* courts. In most cases, the association members, including genocide survivors, conducted investigations to assess the validity of the accusations. They then helped the member launch a defense before the court by locating witnesses and ensuring that the witnesses appeared to testify before the court. However, in a dramatic turn of events, one member, a Tutsi genocide widow, turned against another member, a Hutu widow whose husband had been killed by RPF soldiers in 1995.

> JENNIE BURNET: Has the *gacaca* process had any negative effects on you or your association?
> WOMAN: We mustn't lie to you; the *gacaca* process has had its negative effects. For example, our group leader was imprisoned. [*Whispering.*] There was an American researcher who came to interview women in the association on the topic of *gacaca*. In the meeting, Dancille said that there is injustice in *gacaca* because all the genocide survivors want to make certain that all the Hutu are imprisoned. After [the meeting] Rose [a woman in the association] went to see the *inyangamugayo* in ——— to denounce Dancille. She also wrote a letter saying that Dancille had engaged in divisionism.
>
> Dancille was arrested and imprisoned for four months. Because of the accusations of divisionism, the case went all the way to the office of the national prosecutor in the normal courts. When Dancille went before the *gacaca* court, our group members went to testify on her behalf and said that she hadn't participated in the genocide and that

she hadn't divided people and that she likes peace in the community. Afterward, the prosecutor also made inquiries. In the end, Dancille was released.

JENNIE: How has all this affected the association?

WOMAN: We had some trouble getting along during that period, but Rose asked forgiveness [kwicuza] from all the association leaders and also from Dancille. Now there aren't any more problems. Dancille forgave Rose, who is still remorseful. We try to show Rose that there is no problem.

Despite these statements, it was clear in my interactions with the members of the association that the story was far from over. Dancille, who had been a vibrant, smiling group leader when I first met her in 2000, had become a shadow of her former self. She walked with her head bent down and her eyes on the ground, and she did not say a word. The toll from her time in prison was evident in her gaunt face, worried eyes, and white hair. While she was imprisoned, her children had been forced to drop out of school to take care of the family farm and to bring her food and water in prison. Dancille did not say a word in any of the meetings and left the room any time the subject of her imprisonment and Rose's actions came up. She avoided having any conversations with me.

In a meeting the following week with all of the association leaders, I asked some questions about *gacaca*. After many women said that *gacaca* was working well, a Hutu genocide widow stood up and said that there was "justice for some in *gacaca*, but not justice for all." Immediately, Rose stood up and accused the woman of divisionism (a crime punishable by twenty-five years in prison under Rwandan law) in front of everyone. The meeting became very tense, and everyone was upset. Several women spoke in rapid succession, interrupting each other. In the end, a Tutsi genocide widow admonished Rose for "restarting her nonsense" and told her that she would be thrown out of the association if she continued.

The statement that had landed Dancille in prison, that some genocide survivors will not stop until all Hutu are in prison, was a sentiment that I heard in all three provinces that I visited in May and June 2007. These statements were only made in intimate groups where everyone trusted those who were listening. As illustrated by Dancille's case, making these statements is very risky. In a focus group with a women's association in North province, the members all said that *gacaca* was working well, that innocent prisoners were being released, and that the perpetrators were being found guilty and sentenced. Following the meeting, a few members lingered to chat. After one member, a (Tutsi) woman who had grown up in Burundi and returned to Rwanda after the genocide, left, the subject turned back to *gacaca*. The women (all of whom were Hutu) began speaking in low voices so that our conversation could not be overheard. They said that *gacaca* was not functioning well at all, that it was "profoundly dividing" the population along ethnic lines.

> MEMBER 1: Before, pastoralists and farmers in this region could talk to each other.[7] In 1998, 1999, and 2000, when conflicts arose between them, for instance, when someone's cattle grazed in someone's fields, we could bring them together, negotiate, and settle the problem. Since *gacaca* has started, all live in fear. They don't talk to each other. In front of each other, we don't say what we really think. That's why we couldn't say what was really happening [before the Tutsi returnee left].
>
> MEMBER 2: What we see now is that the *inyangamugayo* won't stop until all the educated Hutu are in prison with long sentences.
>
> JENNIE BURNET: Are all the *inyangamugayo* Tutsi?
>
> MEMBER 1: Not only Tutsi, they are '59ers.[8]
>
> MEMBER 3: I was an *inyangamugayo*. When I saw people giving false testimony and getting innocent people imprisoned, I denounced it. The other *inyangamugayo* told me to keep quiet, but I went to Kigali and told them [the Ministry of Justice] that the *inyangamugayo* here were not implementing the law correctly. They sent investigators here. Next thing you know, someone is denouncing me in *gacaca*. I got the message. I resigned, and I kept my mouth shut. No one sang my name in *gacaca* anymore.

Gacaca has been much touted as a reconciliation mechanism, and, indeed, its "traditional" purpose was as a conflict resolution mechanism. However, as it was implemented to try genocide suspects, *gacaca* deepened cleavages within communities and sowed mistrust on all sides. Ibuka, a national association of genocide survivors, noted the deepening of ethnic divisions in a report on *gacaca* that was mostly negative (Hirondelle News Agency 2007b).

Beyond these injustices, *gacaca* was also used to seek other gains. Stories of people denouncing others before *gacaca* to take their land are rampant in Rwanda; I heard them in all the communities I visited. Because these stories are ubiquitous, they strike me more as metaphorical statements about *gacaca* than as factual references to specific cases. Yet in rural North province, I encountered detailed statements about land usurping tied to *gacaca* in former Kinigi commune. After the RPF victory in 1994, a large number of Tutsi pastoralists moved into Kinigi with their cattle, which they grazed on the shoulders of the volcanoes. Between 1997 and 2001 Kinigi was seriously affected by an insurgency that entered Rwanda from Democratic Republic of Congo via the Birunga National Park. As part of its counterinsurgency operations, the Rwandan government forced the population of Kinigi to relocate into internally displaced persons camps. Many people were forced to destroy their houses, including modern brick houses with glass windows and metal doors, before moving into the camp. When I first met this women's group, they were living in deplorable conditions in small shelters made of sheeting that were crowded together at the foot of one of the volcanoes. Since the end of the insurgency, they had not been allowed to return to their houses or parcels. Instead, the government had forced them to settle in an *umudugudu* (agglomeration) under its policy of creating villages (Burnet and RISD 2003; Hilhorst and Leeuwen 1999; HRW 2001b; Laurent and Bugnion 2000; Musahara 1999; RISD 1999). In 2007, when I asked about prisoner integration, the women responded:

> Up until now, we have not yet seen any prisoner releases. On the contrary, many people are being imprisoned. What we see here is a problem of landholdings. Kinigi is inhabited by a lot of Tutsi, and the '59ers want all the land. So to get the land, the Tutsi and the '59ers who have money, they find Hutu and give them this money so that they can go and give false testimony. Those that they accuse directly are quickly put in prison, and the others take their land, saying that their grandparents lived in these places for a long time. The *inyangamugayo* just discovered this, and they said in a meeting that there are people with big bellies [*bafite inda nini*, meaning they are very poor, greedy, or wicked] and they give false testimony to get people arrested for nothing just because of money. They warned us not to start that again.

In other regions I encountered similar stories of people using *gacaca* to seek other gains, whether land or jobs, or to settle family disputes by getting someone else imprisoned. It is not surprising that some citizens used *gacaca* as a lever of power to get what they want. This phenomenon has a long tradition in the regular courts as well as in other bureaucratic venues in Rwanda. For instance, in his 1968 monograph, *Remera*, Gravel shows that cases brought before the tribal courts were trials of powers rather than trials of rights, meaning that the winner of a court case was not decided on whose rights had been violated but rather on whose power within the community was greater. In my own experience with the traditional form of *gacaca* to resolve a conflict with a neighbor in my rural field site in 2001, I encountered a similar result. Although the neighbor was found to be guilty by the hearing and assessed a list of restitutions to make to me, he did not complete any of the tasks meted out by the *gacaca*. As a permanent resident with kinship ties in the community and as a married man (*umugabo*), he had greater power within the community than I, so he was not forced to comply with the decisions. This outcome was a surprise to no one except me. From this historical perspective, the power plays in *gacaca* may be yet another example of the vernacularization of local justice in Rwanda (Merry 2006a, 2006b).

Gacaca appeared to operate in much the same way in communities around Rwanda. In places where *inyangamugayo* had legitimacy and power within the community, and when they had the will to carry out trials according to legal procedures, *gacaca* worked well. In conversations and interviews in 2009, residents of these communities recognized that, although imperfect, *gacaca* had at least returned many men to their homes. There was an improvement in the day-to-day life of people in the community, even if these improvements came with a lot of patience (*ubwihangane*) on the part of genocide survivors. However, in places where *inyangamugayo* did not have power or where the power brokers in the community sought ends other than fair genocide trials, *gacaca* served these other ends and led to many injustices.

Implications of Injustice

In the short term, *gacaca* destabilized Rwanda, and the *gacaca* courts became arenas where local power relations worked themselves out under the guise of national policy. The central government was well aware of these destabilizing effects, and President Kagame announced that all *gacaca* trials would conclude by the end of 2007. Yet in some communities the *gacaca courts* continued to work for several years to close their files, and the closing of the courts was postponed numerous times. In December 2011 the government announced that the official *gacaca* closing ceremony was scheduled for May 4, 2012 (Hirondelle News Agency 2011). According to the Rwandan government, the *gacaca* courts tried over 1.5 million people (ibid.), while Human Rights Watch put the figure at 1.2 million (HRW 2012).

Gacaca not only deepened the cleavages between Hutu and Tutsi but also made some Tutsi genocide survivors increasingly mistrustful of the current government and the RPF. In December 2007 Benoit Kaboyi, executive secretary of Ibuka, addressed an extraordinary congress of genocide survivors' associations: "The goal of the gacacas was not to parade people before the courts for form, but to try them well!" (Hirondelle News Agency 2007b). Despite such criticism, the government of Rwanda continued to support the *gacaca* process. In reaction to Kaboyi's statements, the minister of justice, Tharcisse Karugarama, vigorously defended the *gacaca* courts: "All Rwandans should be delighted. . . . Those who see things differently are people that are never satisfied" (Hirondelle News Agency 2007c).

Hutu who protected Tutsi during the genocide faced enormous difficulties during *gacaca*. In the hearings they found their acts of heroism met with suspicion. If they had hidden Tutsi in their homes for days or weeks but then left them behind in order to flee the advancing battle lines between the RPF and the FAR, they risked being deemed accomplices to the genocide, especially if the Tutsi they had tried to protect ended up dead. Furthermore, they endured discrimination in daily life where having connections to power (*un piston*) is a prerequisite for a job. On the other hand, they faced criticism among Hutu who supported the Hutu extremists and the genocide: "We told you they [the Tutsi] would subjugate Hutu as they did under the monarchy" (personal communication).

If these conditions were short-term problems, then *gacaca* could still be the basis for reconciliation, one of the government's key objectives as stated in the law and in speeches by government officials. Unfortunately, given local perceptions of widespread injustice in the *gacaca* process, the long-term prospects for a peaceful and just society are not positive. Similar to Drexler's (2010) findings on transitional justice in East Timor, *gacaca* delivered justice for some and established at least a partial truth, but it undermined the rule of law since it did not consider crimes committed by RPF soldiers. The "quest to establish 'the truth'" of the genocide through *gacaca* was "circumscribed by political considerations" that limited who was heard, what information was reported, and what the final verdict was (Hinton 2010, 14). Since the *gacaca* courts did not have legitimacy in the eyes of the population, they were often viewed as another imposition of the central government on local communities and as another venue in which local power conflicts worked themselves out while appearing to conform to central government policies.

Conclusion

Every Rwandan has a story to tell about the war, the genocide, or their aftermath. I heard one such story when I visited a friend's family in Kigali in July 2011. The brother, Olivier, worked in information technology for a large Rwandan company. He was married and had a young child. The youngest sibling, Marie, worked for the Kigali headquarters of an international company. They spoke fluent English, dressed in nice clothing, and had smart phones equipped with the Internet: they were young urban professionals firmly ensconced in the new middle class. They embodied the "high modernity" fetishized in Rwanda today (C. Newbury 2011, 224–26; Scott 1998, 4–5).

On my second visit to their home, they extolled the virtues of Rwanda under the leadership of President Paul Kagame and the RPF: "Rwanda is a secure country. There is no crime. It is very safe. So many foreigners come here to visit, to do business. The country is developing. We have nice buildings, we have nice streets. Look at our street [motioning to the road in

front of their house, which had been paved in cobblestones in the past year].
If you work hard, you can get ahead." I could not disagree with them. The
things they cited—personal security, foreign investors, business-friendly
policies, new buildings, and paved streets—were empirical realities I had
witnessed with my own eyes. But I was surprised by their positive attitude
given what I knew about the family. Their father had spent many years in
prison accused of genocide. An important figure in the Habyarimana
government, he died less than two years after he was found innocent and
released from prison. He spent his last years debilitated by illness aggravated
by years of poor conditions in prison. Only minutes before, Marie had asked
me for help applying to an American university so that she could leave
Rwanda. So I asked, "If Rwanda is so wonderful, why do so many Rwandans
leave if they find a chance?" They looked at each other, then laughed
nervously. They explained, "It's the things we lived through. It's not that we
want to leave forever. [pause] It's, it's, to have a way to get out if . . ." I understood what they left unsaid: every Rwandan wants an escape route in case
things go badly. A second citizenship in Europe, Canada, or the United States
is an insurance policy.

After an uncomfortable silence, Olivier tried to explain Marie's desire to
leave: "Did you know she was lost in the Congo for five years?" Stunned, I
replied, "No." Speaking in English, Marie recounted her survival story:

> Yeah. It's true. [*Nervous laugh.*] When they attacked the camp, I was lost. I
> was only six [years old]. The Red Cross found me and put me in a center [for
> unaccompanied minors]. Luckily, I knew my name, the names of my people,
> where I was from. So many of the other children didn't know anything. They
> had no way to be found. They were lost forever. At least I had some hope. My
> parents had taught me these things. Every day I looked at the lists, hoping to
> find a name I knew. After many months a family from Masisi adopted me
> and my cousin. They took us to their farm in the bush, the *real* bush.
>
> As the youngest and the only girl [among her siblings], I was *so* spoiled.
> Then, there I was in the bush, in the dirt, eating cassava every day. It was so
> hard for me because I wasn't used to working. [Before,] I went to school. I
> had nice clothes. I ate good food. I didn't do anything for myself.
>
> The family was nice, but they were so poor. They were farmers. They were
> not educated. Each girl had her own field to cultivate. That's how we bought
> clothes to wear and soap to wash. Every day we went to our fields together.
> We developed a way to share our work and help each other.
>
> At night we hid in the forest. We would sleep in the trees to hide [from
> the soldiers and militiamen] since we were girls, I mean . . . You know.
> [*Pause.*] Every night we slept there in the forest, hiding, cold, dirty. It was
> such a hard life. It was miserable.
>
> Every night for the first four years I prayed [*she closed her eyes and clasped
> her hands in front of her*], "God, please, I only ask you one thing. Please let

me see my mum and dad again. If not here on earth, then in heaven. If they are in heaven, then let me die so that I can see them again." I prayed the same prayer every night. I was lost for five years. I prayed the same prayer, "God, please, I only ask you one thing. Let me see my mum and dad again. If not here on earth, then in heaven," every night for four years. Then one day I woke up and I decided that I had to forget my old life and accept my new one. The old life was like a dream. I couldn't get it back, so I had to forget it.

Sometime in that fifth year, a man, a neighbor, he heard my name read from the list of missing people after mass. He came to me and asked if I was ——— from ———. I was afraid to respond. I was stunned to hear him say the name of my birthplace. He explained that he heard my name on the list, that my mother was looking for me. He went and spoke with my [adopted] parents and tried to convince them that they should send me back [to Rwanda]. At first they refused. They said, "We can't be sure it's her real parents. We can't send our daughters to live with strangers. It's too dangerous." The man eventually convinced them to let me go. They sent me to Goma to see if it was really my parents. My cousin stayed behind just in case.

When I got to Goma, I waited in the center for missing children. The other children told me it probably wasn't my real parents. They had all been waiting so long. No one came to get them. Then one day I saw a woman walking toward me. I recognized her immediately. It was my mother. I ran to her and jumped into her arms. Mum! She didn't hug me back. She didn't recognize me. When I left I was only a little girl, and then there I was, a young woman. I had grown so much. Then she looked in my eyes, and she saw that it was me. We hugged each other and hugged each other.

Marie continued her story, recounting what her mother had gone through to find her and how her brothers reacted when she returned. As she told her story, I had difficulty hiding my own emotional reaction to what she had survived as just a child. My own children were the same age Marie had been when she "lost" her parents. I pushed the thought of my own children in the same situation out of my mind.

More difficult to apprehend were Marie's shining face, happy demeanor, and constant smile, which belied her difficult past. When Marie paused, I was unsure what to say. After a few minutes, I said, "I don't know what to say. You've lived so many difficult things. How is it that you're always smiling?"

> MARIE: That's just it. God gave me back my life, so I have to enjoy it. Every minute of it. It's a miracle that I found my mum and dad. God answered my prayers. If I feel sad or discouraged, I think of the girls in Masisi. I know how hard life can be. Now, here I am. I went to school. I have a job. I have my family. Every day I thank God for giving me back my life.
>
> JENNIE BURNET: Have you seen or talked to your adoptive parents?

MARIE: I've never been to see them. I've never talked to them since the
day I left. I hope to someday. They were nice to me. [*Pause.*] That's
how life is. It's so hard. My life in Masisi, it's like a dream. Now I woke
up.

Marie's story illustrates two central phenomena related to the study of
war and genocide. First of all, human beings are incredibly resilient. They
can survive terrible things and find a way to go on living, to exercise their
agency, and to make meaning from their experiences. Second, the ways they
remember and make sense of their experiences of violence in the past affect
the decisions they make in their daily lives in the present as well as the goals
they pursue for the future. Marie used her difficult experiences as a foil to
minimize problems in the present. Few problems of quotidian life can
compete with sleeping in a tree in a rain forest to hide from potential rapists.
Yet as the stories of Rwandan women in this book illustrate, not all survivors
of genocide or war are able to make these same choices.

Rwandan women served many different roles in the civil war and
genocide and had varied explanations of the violent past and diverging views
of the future—some toward forgiveness, reconciliation, or peace, others
toward revenge, punitive justice, or renewed violent conflict. Both rural
peasant and urban elite women found mutual support and opportunities in
women's organizations. In these women's forums, they found emotional or
financial support to rebuild their lives and practiced using their voices to
advocate for social change. Furthermore, traditional Rwandan roles of
women as social mediators between households in the community and
between the patrilineages joined by their marriages gave women strategic
access to remake, or at least to challenge, divisions within communities
created or reinforced by violent conflict.

Yet the legacies of genocide continue to have repercussions in ordinary
women's daily lives. Violent landscapes that served as the backdrop of daily
life in Rwanda in the 1990s wrought rapid change in the meanings of ethnic
social classifications among Rwandans. The implications of ethnic categories
framed Rwandans' individual and collective experiences of the civil war and
genocide and structured their agency in the present. While gender has the
potential to unify Rwandans across the divisions of ethnicity in practice,
this goal is problematic because gender is imbricated with ethnicity and
other social categories.

Early in my research in 1997, I asked a genocide widow from a rural
community in southern Rwanda about reconciliation, whether it was
happening, whether it was possible. She responded angrily: "Why do you
foreigners [*abazungu*] ask such stupid questions?!? How can you ask me
about reconciling with my neighbors when I see their children wearing my

[dead] children's clothing, when they are in their house eating at my table, when they cook in my pots? Reconciliation!?! It's not possible." Over time it became clear that there was little consensus among Rwandans about what reconciliation might look like. Rwandan cultural traditions regarding reconciliation and revenge are contradictory and simultaneously promote forgiveness and revenge. While there was heterogeneity of views among Rwandans and even among survivors, many of them spoke of cohabitation (living together) instead of reconciliation. The national government's efforts to forge a new, nonethnic (nongenocidal) national identity through the removal of ethnicity from official bureaucratic life, the creation of the National Unity and Reconciliation Commission, the invention of solidarity camps, and the reinvention of national symbols have, on the one hand, shaped the beliefs and ideologies of younger generations. On the other hand, the Rwandan political economy and state policies have favored some Rwandans (survivors and old caseload refugees) and discriminated against others (new caseload refugees and prisoners' families). Thus, national-level reconciliation activities replicated the divisions of ethnic categories. Nonetheless, Rwandans "muddled through" the conflicts and tensions of post-genocide life out of necessity to achieve what they called "cohabitation." In this challenging ideological terrain, individual women and some women's organizations found their own paths to reconciliation in the early 2000s.

The social landscape has continued to evolve, as have the systems of social classification and their consequences. In trips to Rwanda in 2007, 2009, and 2011, I rarely heard Rwandans distinguish between old (primarily Tutsi) returnees (*abarutashye*), new (primarily Hutu) returnees (*abahungutse*), and Rwandans who stayed in the country (*abasopecya*), as they once regularly did between 1997 and 2002. The government's public education campaigns and especially its reconciliation activities among youth have had a significant effect. In 2011 a group of friends who had grown up in exile together invited me out for dinner. One man in the group had married a woman from his church. For several years, his family and friends shunned him because his wife was Hutu. Yet in 2011 he and his wife joined us. Everyone joked, laughed, and smiled as if nothing had ever been wrong. His parents had also come to accept his choice, tolerate his wife, and love their grandchildren.

In the *gacaca* process, over eight hundred thousand people were tried for genocide crimes, sentenced and punished, then released and returned to their home communities around the country. Communities and wives found a way to reintegrate them into the daily life of the community and family. Yet the past is not forgotten. It haunts ordinary women and men whose memories of violence remain submerged in the background only to reemerge from time to time, sometimes expectedly, like during the national mourning and commemoration activities, which now begin April 7 and continue until Liberation Day on July 4, and other times unexpectedly, like when genocide survivors face new tragedies. One family of genocide survivors I have known for many years recently faced one such tragedy. Their youngest sister went on a trip with classmates from the national university. During the trip she disappeared. A few days later, her body was found; it had been chopped with machetes. For this family, the symbolism could only be interpreted through the lens of genocide. They perceived their sister's murder as the genocide's continuation. Once again, they were afraid to leave the house. They wondered who might be following them, who wanted to kill them.

The legacy of the genocide continues to linger at the social level as well. In the mid-2000s a government policy mandated that all Rwandans must wear shoes. Couched in terms of a public health policy, the policy burdened the rural poor who went barefoot to spare money for other things such as food, school fees, and healthcare. The policy was enforced by local government administrators, police, and local defense, who fined citizens ten thousand Rwandan francs—an amount far exceeding the annual income of most subsistence farmers (Ingelaere 2010, 51). After the new policy was announced, the hills and streets of rural towns filled with men wearing cheap red or blue plastic clogs. Most of these men were workers—day laborers who carried merchandise at markets, loaded trucks in commercial districts, drove taxi bicycles, or transported large sacks of potatoes. The cheap plastic clogs became known as *Nta muhutu utarishe*, "No Hutu didn't kill." Used only in private places among those fortunate enough to have more expensive shoes, the nickname evoked the public presumption—no matter how untrue—that all Hutu participated in the genocide. The nickname was predicated on the reality that in today's Rwanda, the vast majority of poor people, whether rural farmers or day laborers, are Hutu. The nickname also fed into ethnic stereotypes: it was assumed that Tutsi could not accept the hard work done by the day laborers who wore these plastic clogs. Once the shoes had this nickname, they disappeared almost as quickly as they had appeared. Who, after all, could wear them? No one, Hutu or Tutsi, wanted to be associated with what their name symbolized. Many laborers who had spent two days' wages to buy the clogs destroyed them and bought less stigmatized, and stigmatizing, shoes.

Rwanda is frequently cited as the model for other African nations to follow for promoting economic growth, maintaining political stability, protecting the environment, fighting corruption, creating a "business-friendly environment," and establishing a rational taxation policy. The country has emerged as a leader on the continent of Africa. Its active participation in the African Union, its provision of troops for African Union and United Nations peacekeeping missions in Darfur, Sudan, its entry into the East African Economic Community, and its admission to the British Commonwealth have given Rwanda influence in international politics beyond the symbolic power of being the site of the twentieth century's last genocide. The country's impressive track record of economic growth highlights the RPF-led government's effective policies to promote growth and investment. In the past few years, Rwanda and President Kagame have received numerous international awards, including a Green Globe Award for Environmental Conservation, the Commonwealth Business Council's 2010 Africa Business Award for most improved investment climate, the Global Peace and Unity Services to Humanity Award 2010, the 2010 International Olympic Committee award for "Inspiring Young People," the Chello Foundation Humanitarian Award 2011 for President Kagame's "outstanding leadership of the Republic of Rwanda since 1994," and the 2007 African Gender Award.[1] Indeed, Rwanda has come a very long way since 1994.

Yet, in the shadow of this international spotlight, ordinary Rwandan women have struggled to rebuild their lives "from less than nothing," as one genocide widow described it. Few ordinary women have benefited from Rwanda's economic renaissance. These benefits have largely been concentrated in the hands of a few elites or in the small middle class of urban professionals. According to World Bank data, economic inequality in the country has increased in the last decade from a Gini coefficient of 46.68 in 2000 to 53.08 in 2005.[2] While some Rwandans, like Marie and Olivier, have benefited from the dramatic changes in the political economy in the past eighteen years, many rural farmers find themselves falling farther and farther behind. Rural women struggle to find the means to educate their children beyond primary school, as they see their children's education as the only hope of escaping from poverty.

Despite these challenges, ordinary Rwandan women have benefited from the overall improvement in gender equality. In 2008 the country elected a majority female parliament (52 percent in both houses and 56.25 percent in the Chamber of Deputies), and since 2003 there has been a minimum of 30 percent of women in all government decision-making bodies by constitutional mandate. All women have enjoyed increased legal protections and greater respect from kin and community members (Burnet 2011). These outcomes cannot be explained by dominant public policy, humanitarian, or development discourses that portray women in conflict zones either as innately disempowered victims of warfare and violence or as innate peacemakers who are fed up with male-dominated politics that brought war and conflict in the first place. Both these tendencies rely on stereotypical images of women as inherently nurturing and kind (di Leonardo 1991) and promote an idealized, "universal woman" (Malkki 1995). While these portraits are seductive, they oversimplify the complex and contradictory roles that women play in conflict and postconflict societies. Women's leading role in Rwanda's apparent renaissance was not a foregone conclusion. Instead, it resulted from the confluence of three primary factors.

First, the dire situation in the aftermath of the genocide required women to take on new roles in the family and society. Widows bereft of kin (the usual social safety net), single women with limited marriage prospects, women heads of household with full economic responsibility but little experience negotiating the public sphere alone, and child-headed households had to (re)invent a world that accommodated their unique circumstances. They learned self-reliance in the midst of material, emotional, and social realities unknown in living memory. Ordinary women broke cultural taboos and advocated for enhanced protection of women's rights not because they sought liberation from gender oppression but because they had no other choice.

Second, the Rwandan women's movement played a key role in advocating a place for women in rebuilding the country. Women leaders who survived the genocide revived and rebuilt women's organizations so that they could support their members who were in desperate need. They encouraged their exiled members to return home and join in the struggle to rebuild their country. Women who returned from long-term exile added valuable knowledge and new ideas gained in women's organizations in other countries. Women leaders joined together to lobby the transitional government to grant legal protection for women's inheritance rights. They advocated for the inclusion of women in the constitutional reform process. The constitutional commission's sole female member, Judith Kanakuze, a leader in the women's movement, convinced her male colleagues to guarantee women a voice in governance by creating gender quotas in every government body. In parliament, the Forum of Women Parliamentarians placed gender-based violence on the legislative agenda and pursued legislation to increase protection of children's rights.

Finally, mainstreaming women was a conscious strategy adopted by the Rwandan Patriotic Front while it was still a rebel movement. It continued to mainstream women after it came to power in 1994. The RPF's approach was modeled on the National Resistance Movement in Uganda (Burnet 2008a, 367; Longman 2006). Many leaders at the head of the RPF embraced gender equality in the hopes of improving society (Powley 2005, 159). The notable advances of women contributed to the perception of Rwanda as a postconflict success story (Burnet 2008a; Longman 2006; Powley 2003, 2005, 2008a, 2008b). From an empirical perspective, these women-friendly policies also helped the RPF maintain its hold on power and maintain a positive reception from the international community (Burnet 2008a, 2011; Longman

2006; Reyntjens 2011). Regardless of whether the RPF served its own ends, these policies helped transform ordinary Rwandan women's lives in positive ways, giving them greater economic autonomy, guaranteeing them equal access to education, and carving out new career paths for them. International funding for programs targeting women also played a significant role in supporting these transformations.

The challenges ordinary women faced in the aftermath of the genocide and war in Rwandan can help indicate paths to recovery in other conflict zones in the world and suggest interventions that could prevent genocide before it occurs. First, an end to violence and a restoration of basic security are fundamental. Reestablishing social relationships involves risk-taking and required trust. People need basic security to be willing to take steps toward reestablishing social relationships. Renewed social relationships are easily destroyed by new instances of violence. Second, as the experiences of the Hutu genocide widows' groups described in chapter 4 indicate, ordinary people must have their most basic needs—water, food, and shelter—met. When their basic needs are not met, people cannot invest in building social relationships and remain mired in their own misery. Third, as numerous examples from chapters 2 and 3 illustrate, ordinary men and women need space to mourn their lost loved ones in public. Without the space to mourn the dead publicly, people have trouble moving toward the future as their painful memories continue to haunt them. Fourth, interventions to help women should not assume a tabula rasa in the aftermath of conflict. Rather, they should build on women's activism dating from before the conflict. Fifth, ordinary women need to be given physical, emotional, and social spaces where they can share their stories of survival and be heard empathetically. Sixth, forging new experiences of cooperation through joint action can build the foundation of new relationships. Finally, government and international support for women's activism is vital.

Beyond the lessons that Rwandans can teach us about women's agency in the aftermath of conflict and about women's roles in reconstruction and peace building, understanding the aftermath of genocide can teach us about ourselves. As David Newbury writes, "Those most responsible for perpetrating [the genocide] . . . were not only a few isolated sociopaths, but often common people reacting to the conditions around them in horrifying fashion. In other words, with but few changes they could have been us, or family members to us, or people we know" (1998, 76). We are not as far removed from what happened in Rwanda as we may pretend. If genocide is truly a crime against humanity, then the 1994 Rwandan genocide—its origins, its conditions, and its aftermath—lives in all of us.

Glossary

ababyeyi. See *umubyeyi.*
abacengezi. See *umucengezi.*
abafasha. See *umufasha.*
abafunze. See *ufunze.*
abagabo. See *umugabo.*
abagore. See *umugore.*
abagore b'abafunze. See *umugore w'ufunze.*
abahungu. See *umuhungu.*
abahungutse. See *uhungutse.*
abakecuru. See *umukecuru.*
abakobwa. See *umukobwa.*
abana. See *umwana.*
abantu. See *umuntu.*
abapfakazi. See *umupfakazi.*
abapfakazi b'itsembabwoko. See *umupfakazi w'itsembabwoko.*
abari. See *umwari.*
abarokore. See *umurokore.*

abarokotse. See *uwarokotse.*

abarutashye. See *uwarutashye.*

abasaza. See *umusaza.*

abasopecya. See *umusopecya.*

abasore. See *umusore.*

abategarugori. See *umutegarugori.*

abatingitingi: People of Tingitingi, referring to Rwandans who went into exile in 1994 and returned in 1996 and 1997, presumed to be Hutu. Tingitingi was the place in the Congolese rainforest where many refugees gathered in an impromptu camp. Faced with vast Congolese rivers, the refugees decided to return to Rwanda instead of dying in the dense forest.

abaturage. See *umuturage.*

abaturutse hanze: Literally, "those who came from outside," referring to Rwandans who went into exile in 1959, 1963, or 1972 and returned to Rwanda after the RPF victory in 1994.

abatware. See *umutware.*

abazimu. See *umuzimu.*

abazungu. See *umuzungu.*

abicanyi. See *umwicanyi.*

akagari (sing.), *utugari* (pl.): Cell, the smallest administrative division. In most regions, it corresponds to a single hill.

Akazu: Literally, "little house," referring to the entourage of former president Habyarimana.

amatongo. See *itongo.*

Bakiga. *See* Mukiga.

Banyamulenge: Congolese ethnic group from the Mulenge region. Kinyarwanda speakers whose ancestors have lived in Mulenge since approximately the sixteenth century. Perceived to be Tutsi.

Banyanduga. *See* Munyanduga.

Banyarwanda: Rwandan people. The term can refer to citizens of Rwanda or to people of Rwandan cultural identity who speak Kinyarwanda.

Banyarwandakazi: Rwandan women.

ceceka. See *guceceka.*

demokarasi: Democracy.

foyers sociaux (French): Social centers.

gacaca: A traditional conflict resolution mechanism reappropriated and transformed by the Rwandan government to adjudicate genocide crimes.

gendarmerie (French): Police station.

génocidaires (French): Genocide perpetrators.

guceceka: To remain silent; to be silent.

gufashanya n'ukuzuzanya: To help each other and complement each other.

guhabura: To bring someone back into the proper path; to orient.

guhahamuka: To speak with a trembling voice; to be physically overcome by fear; to be breathless; to be psychologically traumatized.

gusaba imbabazi: To confess; to ask for pardon; used primarily in the legal arena.

guterekera: To divine the will of dead spirits; to offer gifts to dead spirits.

gutwika ahantu: To set a place on fire, the language used by the RPF to describe campaigns of indiscriminate killings in the months after the genocide.

icyitso (sing.), *ibyitso* (pl.): accomplice. Used by the Habyarimana government during the civil war and genocide to refer to citizens who supported or collaborated with the RPF.

ibibazo by'abagore (pl.): Women's problems.

ibikari. See *igikari*.

ibitero. See *igitero*.

ibyitso. See *icyitso*.

igikari (sing.), *ibikari* (pl.): Inner courtyard of a traditional homestead.

igikingi (sing.), *ibikingi* (pl.): Form of land tenure introduced in central Rwanda and spread to other regions.

igitabo kinini: Literally "big book." Used to refer to a thesis or dissertation.

igitero (sing.), *ibitero* (pl.): Hunting party; a group of men who attack. In the 1994 genocide, a killing squad or an attack by the army, a militia group, or group of men.

igitsinagabo: Masculine gender.

igitsinagore: Feminine gender.

imfura (sing. and pl.): Firstborn, as in the eldest son or daughter; person of integrity; noble, as in the elite during the time of the *mwami*.

imidugudu. See *umudugudu*.

imiganda. See *umuganda*.

imihoro. See *umuhoro*.

imirenge. See *umurenge*.

imiryango. See *umuryango*.

imisanzu. See *umusanzu*.

impinja. See *uruhinja*.

Impuzamugambi (sing. and pl.): Literally, "people who share values and goals." Began as the youth wing of the CDR political party and became one of the militia groups that killed Tutsi during the 1994 genocide.

indushyi (sing. and pl.): Abandoned wife; vulnerable woman; rejected wife; a widow who has not produced a son for her husband's lineage; a woman who never married and who stayed with her patrilineal kin while an adult.

ingabo z'umwami: Army of the king.

ingando (sing. and pl.): Literally, camp. In the postgenocide period, used to refer to solidarity camps or reeducation camps designed to teach civics to returning refugees, young people admitted to higher learning institutions, government officials, released prisoners, or surrendered combatants.

inkokokazi (sing. and pl.): Hen.

Inkotanyi (sing. and pl.): The RPF's name for its armed wing. The original Inkotanyi belonged to Mwami Rwabugiri (1853–95) and was considered one of the best armies the nation ever had.

Interahamwe (sing. and pl.): Literally, "those who work together." Began as the youth wing of the MRND political party and became one of the militia groups that killed Tutsi during the 1994 genocide.

inyangamugayo (sing. and pl.): Literally, "people of integrity," who were usually respected elders on a hill. In postgenocide Rwanda, *gacaca* judges.

inyenzi (sing. and pl.): Cockroach. Originally, the term was used by the Kayibanda government to refer to small armed groups of Tutsi who attacked the country from Burundi after its 1962 independence. Hutu extremists used the same name to refer to the RPF in the 1990s. During the genocide Hutu extremists used the term to refer to Tutsi and to RPF supporters.

inzirakarengane (sing. and pl.): Victims of the genocide, synonymous with Tutsi.

inzoka (sing. and pl.): Snake or worm, the standard Kinyarwanda term for intestinal worms. During the genocide Hutu extremists used the term to refer to Tutsis, portraying them as "snakes," meaning dishonest, like the serpent in the book of Genesis.

inzu (sing. and pl.): House, referring to the physical structure as well as to the conjugal household comprised of husband, wife, and children.

isangano: A place where people feel comfortable expressing themselves.

itongo (sing.), *amatongo* (pl.): Abandoned house, or remains of houses, in particular when the owner is dead.

itsembabwoko (sing.): Literally, "killing an ethnic group." Term used for genocide until 2008.

itsembabwoko n'itsembatsemba (sing.): Genocide and massacre.

itsembatsemba (sing. and pl.): Massacre.

jenoside yakorewe abatutsi: Genocide against Tutsi; replaced *itsembabwoko* as the official name of the genocide by a constitutional amendment in 2008 (Amendment no. 3 of 13/08/2008).

Kangura: Literally, "to wake up others." Name of a Hutu extremist newspaper in the early 1990s.

Kinyamateka: A monthly news magazine published by the Roman Catholic Church in Rwanda.

Kinyarwanda: The language or culture of the Rwandan people.

kubana: To live together.

kubohoza: To liberate. In the early 1990s *kubohoza* was used to force someone to join a political party. During the genocide it was used to mean rape as a form of liberation of Tutsi women from their "Tutsiness." In the period after the RPF victory it was used to refer to seizing and occupying someone else's property (house, land).

kuzuzanya: To complement or complete each other.

kwicuza: To ask to be pardoned. Accepting moral responsibility and showing remorse, used among Roman Catholics to refer to seeking pardon in the rite of reconciliation.

kwinjira: To enter; to marry a woman (especially a widow) from outside the family and go live in her house; to live with a woman (especially a widow) in her house and fulfill the role of husband. See also *umwinjira*.

kwiyunga: To reconcile.

mama, nyoko, nyina: My mother; your mother; his or her mother.

muchaka muchaka: Soldiers' early-morning run, part of the RPA's training for new recruits at military camps.

mugondo (sing. and pl.): Nylon sports shorts or boxer shorts worn under pants or skirts.

Mukiga (sing.), Bakiga (pl.): Person from Rukiga, a mountainous region in northern Rwanda. A Northerner. When used in opposition to Munyanduga, the term can refer to Rwandans born in northern Rwanda.

Munyanduga (sing.), Banyanduga (pl.): Person from Nduga, a region in central Rwanda. When used in opposition to Mukiga, the term can refer to Rwandans born in central or southern Rwanda, former Gitarama or Butare prefectures.

mwami: King; monarch; traditional ruler of Rwanda.

Nta muhutu utarishe: Literally, "No Hutu didn't kill," meaning all Hutu killed in the genocide.

nyumbakumi: "Ten houses" in Swahili; the local official responsible for ten households.

piston (French): Literally, "piston," referring in colloquial language to the support of a family member or friend inside a company or government administration.

radio trottoir (French): Literally, "sidewalk radio," meaning rumors heard from friends, neighbors, and coworkers.

ubuhake: Cattle clientage.

ubumwe: Unity.

ubumwe n'ubwiyunge: Unity and reconciliation, the phrase used by the postgenocide government to refer to the national reconciliation campaign.

uburetwa: Compulsory labor required of all Hutu in the late precolonial and colonial periods.

ubuyanja: Renewal; rebirth.

ubwihangane: Patience; concealment of suffering; forbearance.

ubwiyunge: Reconciliation.

ubwoko: Genre; sort; or type. When applied to humans, social identity or ethnicity.

ufunze (sing.), *abafunze* (pl.): A person in prison; prisoner.

uhungutse (sing.), *abahungutse* (pl): Literally, "someone who came from exile"; Rwandans who went into exile in 1994 and returned in 1996 and 1997; new returnees, presumed to be Hutu.

umubyeyi (sing.), *ababyeyi* (pl.): Parent; mother; father.

umucengezi (sing.), *abacengezi* (pl.): Infiltrator. Commonly applied to the insurgents who were fighting to overthrow the RPF-led regime in the late 1990s and early 2000s.

umudugudu (sing.), *imidugudu* (pl.): Agglomeration; used to refer to a village.

umufasha (sing.), *abafasha* (pl.): Literally, "helper," meaning wife.

umugabo (sing.), *abagabo* (pl.): Husband; man; father.

umuganda (sing.), *imiganda* (pl.): Communal labor required of all Rwandan citizens for community projects.

umugore (sing.), *abagore* (pl.): Wife; woman; mother.

umugore w'ufunze (sing.), *abagore b'abafunze* (pl.): Prisoner's wife.

umuhoro (sing.), *imihoro* (pl.): Traditional machete.

umuhungu (sing.), *abahungu* (pl.): Son; boy.

umukecuru (sing.), *abakecuru* (pl.): Old woman; female elder.

umukobwa (sing.), *abakobwa* (pl.): Daughter; girl.

umuntu (sing.), *abantu* (pl.): Person; human being.

umupfakazi (sing.), *abapfakazi* (pl.): Widow; widower.

umupfakazi w'itsembabwoko (sing.), *abapfakazi b'itsembabwoko* (pl.): Genocide widow.

umurenge (sing.), *imirenge* (pl.): Sector, the level of government administration below the district and above the cell.

umurokore (sing.), *abarokore* (pl.): Born-again Christian; "saved person."

umuryango (sing.), *imiryango* (pl.): Lineage.

umusanzu (sing.), *imisanzu* (pl.): A contribution to the war effort.

umusaza (sing.), *abasaza* (pl.): Old man, male elder.

umusopecya (sing.), *abasopecya* (pl.): Literally, "Sopecya people," meaning Rwandans who lived in Rwanda before the 1994 genocide. Refers to the gas station at a major intersection in Kigali known as Société de Pétrol de Cyangugu (SOPECYA) before the genocide and renamed Sopetrad when it reopened in 1995.

umusore (sing.), *abasore* (pl.): Bachelor; young man.

umutegarugori (sing.), *abategarugori* (pl.): Literally, "person who wears the *urogori*," meaning a wife and mother.

umuturage (sing.), *abaturage* (pl.): Peasant; resident of a rural area; compatriot (non-pejorative).

umutware (sing.), *abatware* (pl.): Chief (of a county).

umuzimu (sing.), *abazimu* (pl.): Spirit; ghost; ancestor spirit.

umuzungu (sing.), *abazungu* (pl.): White person.

umuzungukazi: White woman.

umwana (sing.), *abana* (pl.): Child.

umwari (sing.), *abari* (pl.): Maiden; young woman.

umwicanyi (sing.), *abicanyi* (pl.): Killer. In postgenocide Rwanda, a genocide perpetrator.

umwinjira (sing.): A man who enters the home of a woman (especially a widow) and fulfills the roles of a husband.

urugo (sing.), *ingo* (pl.): Compound; homestead; wall around a homestead. The term can also refer to the conjugal household comprised of husband, wife, and children.

urugori: A crown made from a sorghum stalk, bamboo, banana leaves, or ivory that a woman who is married and who has given birth to a son wears around her head just above her ear.

uruhinja (sing.), *impinja* (pl.): Newborn; baby.

utugari. See *akagari*.

uwarokotse (sing.), *abarokotse* (pl.): Survivor, meaning a genocide survivor.

uwarutashye (sing.), *abarutashye* (pl.): Literally, "those who came back home," referring to a Rwandan who returned from long-term exile after the RPF victory in 1994 and who is presumed to be Tutsi.

Notes

Introduction

1. Estimates over how many people died in the 1994 genocide vary widely. The most conservative estimate of "at least a half a million" comes from Human Rights Watch and is based on a study conducted by demographer William Seltzer (Des Forges 1999, 15). A UN expert estimated that 800,000 Rwandans had died between April and July 1994, but this number included those who died from causes other than genocide (quoted in ibid.). Gérard Prunier (1997) estimates that around 800,000 Tutsi lost their lives between April and July 1994. In 2001 the Rwandan government's Ministry of Local Affairs conducted a census of victims and arrived at an estimate of over 1 million "killed in massacres and genocide between 1 October 1991 and 31 December 1994" (IRIN 2001b). The report estimated that 97.3 percent of these victims were Tutsi, or approximately 1.04 million. Although the government report includes all Rwandans who died due to massacres and genocide from 1991 through 1994, it is likely that the Rwandan government estimates are high given that the 1991 census estimated the Tutsi population within the country at 700,000.

2. The genocide planners relied on the use of hunting language and metaphors to organize civilian participation in the genocide: "Those people called to participate in the genocide transformed themselves into hunters in pursuit of dangerous animals" (Mironko 2004, 52–53). This dehumanization made it psychologically possible for ordinary people to believe their actions were for the good of the wider society and sanctioned by the highest government authorities.

3. To distinguish between the waves of Rwandan refugee movements in the region, the UNHCR began to refer to the primarily Tutsi refugees who left Rwanda in 1959, 1962–64, or 1972 as "old caseload refugees," in that they had long-standing refugee status in UNHCR databases. The more than one million primarily Hutu refugees who fled the country in 1994 were referred to as "new caseload refugees" because their refugee status claims were more recent.

4. Begoña Aretxaga (1997) calls memory "cultural repositories" of discourses, images, representations, and symbols.

5. See Liisa Malkki's (1995) examination of Burundian Hutu in refugee camps in Tanzania.

6. I borrow the term "mythico-historical" from Malkki (1995).

7. Donatia spoke in French: "Oui, c'est comme ça. Le génocide nous habite." My translation into English does not fully capture the poetry or imagery of her statement. An alternate translation, "The genocide inhabits us," comes closer to a literal translation, but the English word "inhabit," despite its common root, is not quite a synonym of the French *habiter*.

8. As Bruno Latour stated it, "If you stop making and remaking groups, you stop having groups" (2005, 35). In other words, there are no groups; there is only group making. My approach draws on actor-network theory as elaborated by Latour (2005), Callon (1986), Law (1986), and others.

9. See Prunier (1997, 5) for these statistics. These statistics were also reported in the CIA Factbook up until 2010 (ethnicity was dropped in the 2011 edition of the CIA Factbook online), https://www.cia.gov/library/publications/the-world-factbook/geos/rw.html.

10. Lemarchand (1970, 172) estimates that 130,000 (mostly Tutsi) Rwandans fled the country, while Reyntjens (1985, 455) estimates more than 300,000. These waves of Rwandan refugees later proved important in the emergence of the Rwandan Patriotic Front and the evolution of the civil war from 1990 through 1994.

11. In Rwanda, as in many other African countries, the state remained the principal employer in the country. In addition, state employment gave access to economic and social resources in the form of land, capital, and government contracts.

12. Under Habyarimana's ethnic equilibrium policy, 9 percent of appointments were "reserved" for Tutsi. However, an estimated 14 percent of the population was Tutsi. Thus, this questionable policy did not reflect the ethnic composition of the country's population as it purported to do.

13. Development projects launched in the country "succeeded," at least according to the measure established by the aid community. Both Uvin (1998) and C. Newbury (1992) have critiqued this perception of development success. Uvin even argues that the development industry in Rwanda helped make the genocide possible.

14. For more on this period, see Chrétien (1995, 1997), Prunier (1997), Reyntjens (1994), C. Newbury (1995, 1998), Lemarchand (1995), D. Newbury (1998), D. Newbury and C. Newbury (2000), Longman (1995, 1997, 1998, 1999), Des Forges (1999), de Lame (1996), Jefremovas (2002), and Umutesi (2000).

15. I borrow the phrase "consensual dictatorship" from a Hutu intellectual I interviewed in 2001. He explained that, tired of genocide and massacres, the political elite of all parties accepted RPF dominance during the transition period.

16. In April and May 1995 two large-scale killings occurred at camps of internally displaced persons (IDP) when soldiers opened fire on people in the camp without discriminating between armed Interahamwe or FAR soldiers and unarmed civilians, including women, children, and the elderly. Smaller-scale killings of civilians and extrajudiciary executions took place in late 1994 and throughout 1995.

17. FAR soldiers participated widely in the genocide by providing tactical support to the Interahamwe militias and other civilians in attacks on large gatherings of Tutsi. Tutsi members of the FAR were executed very early in the genocide. During the genocide, the FAR was simultaneously fighting a war against members of the RPF, who were attempting to seize the country.

18. The RPF eventually extended the transitional period by four years. National elections to elect members of Parliament and a president were held in 2003.

19. The term "Hutu Power" was used to designate the coalition of extremist Hutu politicians and political parties that supported the genocide, including the Mouvement républicain national pour la démocratie et le développement (MRND[D]), the Coalition pour la défense de la république (CDR), and the Mouvement démocratique républicain—Power (MDR—Power), led by Frodauld Karamira, which broke off from the more moderate Mouvement démocratique républicain (MDR), led by Faustin Twagiramungu (Des Forges 1999, 202).

20. The airport would later be renamed the Kigali International Airport.

21. The Rwandan administrative districts changed in 2001 and 2006. The prefectures listed here are for the administrative divisions in place from 1996 to 2001.

22. For a few examples of this criticism, see d'Hertefelt, Trouwbourst, and Scherer (1962); D. Newbury (1991, 2001); Des Forges (2011); and C. Newbury (1988).

23. The reporting on Rwanda of African Rights, the organization responsible for the report, has often appeared partisan and slanted in favor of the RPF-led government. African Rights seldom reported on the human rights violations committed by the RPF, the RPA, or the new government.

24. The man spoke in English and Kinyarwanda. "Northerner" refers to people from the northwestern prefectures of Gisenyi and Ruhengeri, a region perceived to be predominantly Hutu and a seedbed of the Hutu extremism responsible for the genocide. "Mountain dweller" is my translation of Mukiga (person from Rukiga), which refers to Rwandans inhabiting the mountainous regions of northern Rwanda, including parts of Gisenyi, Ruhengeri, and Byumba. "That peasant" is my translation of *umuturage*, which can have a positive connotation, but in this context it carries the negative sense of an uneducated "country bumpkin," less civilized and sophisticated than the speaker.

25. Population figures and economic growth data appear in the World Bank's World Databank of World Development Indicators and Global Development Finance, http://databank.worldbank.org/.

Chapter 1. Social Classifications, State Power, and Violence

1. The word *indushyi* was also applied to daughters who "divorced" their husbands (i.e., who returned home from failed marriages). In cases of divorce, a wife would leave with children perceived as being too young to be separated from their mothers (below the age of eight or nine). Older children remained with their father or his patrilineage.

2. Today in Rwanda, the standard translation for this proverb is "wives have no ethnicity." However, the Kinyarwanda word translated here as "ethnicity," *ubwoko*, means "sort" or "type" and can be applied to monkeys, trees, or bananas as easily as to people. Prior to the 1950s, ethnicity was not the primary way that Rwandans classified each other. At that time, the word *ubwoko*, when referring to human beings, meant the combination of a person's social attributes relevant to a given context; hence, I translate *ubwoko* in this proverb as "identity."

3. In the field I worked principally with two research assistants. On previous occasions when I had asked similar questions I had not encountered these difficulties, probably because I was with the other research assistant, who was a married woman of about forty with four children.

4. This figure is based on my field research gathering life histories of women. According to official statistics, in 1991 the reported fertility rate was 8.4 (Réseau des femmes œuvrant pour le développement rural 1991). In 1993 Ford reported that the average Rwandan woman had 8.9 live births in her lifetime. In 1998 the National Population Office reported the mean number of children born to a woman was 7.11 (based on crude birthrates) (ONAPO 1998). In life history interviews, most women I spoke with indicated that they had had two to three miscarriages in their lifetimes. Combining these lower fertility rates with my interview data, I estimate that Rwandan women average ten pregnancies in their lifetimes.

5. See Chrétien (1995), Des Forges (1999), Fujii (2009), Lemarchand (1995), Longman (2009), Prunier (1997), and Straus (2006) for a detailed discussion.

6. See D. Newbury and C. Newbury (2000) for the specifics on the Rwandan case and Wolf (1982), Obeyesekere (1997), Chidester (1996), Prakash (1992), and Comaroff and Comaroff (1991) for a more general discussion of the construction of knowledge in the colonial context.

7. Jefremovas (2002), Schoenbrun (1998), and Vansina (2004) have recently made some notable contributions that include women and gender in Rwandan history.

8. C. Newbury (1988) has documented the transformation in the categories "Hutu" and "Tutsi" during the late precolonial and colonial periods.

9. For example, in Kinyaga, where C. Newbury (1988) conducted her research, "Tutsi" identity was a reflection of differences in power and wealth rather than merely a function of descent.

10. Cattle clientage is a socioeconomic relationship whereby a patron loans a client a cow. The client then must regularly give gifts to the patron, demonstrate his loyalty to the patron, and provide labor to the patron.

11. See, for example, "Havila and the Tutsi Hebrews" on the Kulanu website at http://www.kulanu.org/tutsi/havila.php. The New World Encyclopedia website recapitulates the Hamitic hypothesis in the entry for Bujumbura (http://www.new worldencyclopedia.org/entry/Bujumbura) but not for Rwanda (http://www.new worldencyclopedia.org/entry/Rwanda) or Kigali (http://www.newworldencyclopedia .org/entry/Kigali).

12. See d'Hertefelt (1971) and D. Newbury (1980) for more on clans.

13. See C. Newbury (1988) for a detailed discussion of these new institutions and their effects on the rural population and ethnic politics.

14. To say that a woman has "cow's eyes" in Rwanda is a high compliment.

15. Meaning it was a trick by the RPA or the AFDL to lure refugees to a location to be slaughtered.

16. Before returnees could find employment in Rwanda, the government required them to participate in "solidarity camps" (ingando). In the camps participants were (re)taught Rwandan history, the details of the genocide, and the ideologies of the "new Rwanda." Although these reeducation camps were criticized by international human rights organizations for many valid reasons, some participants viewed the camps' lessons as beneficial, as they helped to counteract the genocide-denying propaganda that had been spread in the refugee camps.

17. For more on this period, see Chrétien (1995, 1997), Prunier (1997), Reyntjens (1994), C. Newbury (1995, 1998), Lemarchand (1995), D. Newbury (1998), D. Newbury and C. Newbury (2000), Longman (1995, 1997, 1998, 1999), Des Forges (1999), de Lame (1996), Jefremovas (2002), and Umutesi (2000).

18. This conception of democracy continued to influence Rwandans' perceptions in the postgenocide period. In the early 2000s, many Rwandans feared the reintroduction of elections and "democracy." For more on Rwandan politics and democracy, see Reyntjens (2004, 2011), Longman (2006), and Burnet (2008a, 2011).

19. Theories abound as to who shot down the plane and why. For more, see Straus (2006, 44–46), Prunier (1997, 213–29), and Ruzibiza (2005). Regardless of who shot down the plane, the Hutu Power elements in Rwanda used the event to mobilize the population to commit genocide.

20. Presidential Guard soldiers were handpicked from Habyarimana's native region, Ruhengeri, and were very loyal to the president.

21. See the work of Christopher Taylor (1999) for an analysis of the symbolic discourse of sexual violence in extremist Hutu rhetoric leading up to the genocide and in certain practices of sexual violence during the genocide.

22. During the political liberalization of the early 1990s, forced recruitment of party members by the state party (MRND) was also called kubohoza in an inversion of the term's literal meaning.

23. I defined "adult" as over twenty years of age. The actual percentages for all these studies could be even higher, as many women with husbands in prison report their husbands as members of the household in surveys. Similarly, women are often reluctant to indicate that they are heads of household even when their husbands are

not present (whether because they are dead, in prison, missing, or polygamous and residing with another wife). Polygamy is illegal in Rwanda, but it is socially recognized and accepted in some regions.

24. See the introduction for an explanation of the term "old caseload refugee."

25. See, for example, "Press Communiqué of the Government of Rwanda," issued by the Ministry of Foreign Affairs on August 21, 1996, http://reliefweb.int/node/26805.

26. The meanings of Hutu, Tutsi, Banyarwanda, and Banyamulenge changed dramatically in Zaire (Democratic Republic of the Congo) beginning in the early 1990s during the liberalization of the political system in Mobutu's Zaire. For details, see Willame (1997), Reyntjens (2009), Lemarchand (2008), and Prunier (2009).

Chapter 2. Remembering Genocide

1. Although I employ the notion differently, my use of "amnesia" as the diagnosis for Rwandan's collective condition was inspired by Lessie Jo Frazier's "Amnesia as Agency," part of the Colloquium series of the Department of Anthropology at the University of North Carolina at Chapel Hill, January 25, 2002. Buckley-Zistel (2006) has written about "chosen amnesia" as a strategy for local coexistence in Rwanda. Buckley-Zistel's analysis focuses on Rwandans' choice to forget social cleavages from before the genocide to facilitate coexistence.

2. Here I use the archaic word "remembrances" deliberately to evoke *Remembrance of Things Past*, the English title of the original translation of Marcel Proust's *À la recherche du temps perdu*. A more recent translation, called *In Search of Lost Time*, more closely reproduces the original French title. In addition, I intend to evoke the word's double meaning: "memory or recollection in relation to a particular object, fact, etc." and the "operation of the mind which is involved in recalling a thing or fact" (*OED*, 2nd ed., online).

3. For more on the gendered political economy and women's property rights, see Jefremovas (1991, 2002) and Burnet and RISD (2003).

4. For more details on the practice and meanings of *kwinjira*, see Musabyimana (2006, 129).

5. For more on how the Rwandan government manages its image in the international media, see Pottier (2002).

6. Muhabura is the name of a volcano in northwestern Rwanda, but the name comes from the verb *guhabura*, "to bring someone back into the proper path, to orient."

7. A Rwandan proverb, "Akebo kajya iwamungarurire" (The [gift] basket must be returned), is frequently invoked to describe this cultural notion that all favors must be returned. Literally, the proverb refers to Rwandan gift exchange practices. Pottier (2002, 154–56) discusses the application of this notion to international diplomacy in postgenocide Rwanda and the RPF's implication of the international community in the (re)writing of history surrounding the RPF-perpetrated massacre at Kibeho in April 1995.

8. I hyphenate "remembering" here to emphasize the fact that remembering by the state is a political project whereby the "members" (i.e., "the constituent portions

of a complex structure," *OED*, 2nd ed., online) or memories are reincorporated into a subjective system that is structured and structuring (see Lawless 2000; Stewart 1996).

9. See, for example, Des Forges (1999), Fujii (2009), Longman (1995, 1998, 2009), Straus (2006), and Vidal (1998).

10. Interviews conducted by the author between 1997 and 2002. See also Des Forges (1999), Longman (1995, 1999, 2009), Vidal (1998).

11. On genocide perpetrators' motivations, see Straus (2006) and Fujii (2009).

12. Kagame's 2001 speech recorded from the live broadcast on national radio and translated by a research assistant.

13. See, for example, the "Murambi" article on the Genocide Archive Rwanda website, http://www.genocidearchiverwanda.org.rw/index.php?title=Murambi, accessed September 9, 2011.

14. For more on the symbolism and treatment of bodies during the genocide, see Taylor (1999, 2002).

15. See Linke (2009) for more on how the symbolic violence of displayed bodies replicates genocidal ideologies.

16. Accusations against Bishop Misago continued in the Rwandan state media until 1999, when President Pasteur Bizimungu accused the bishop, who was seated on the dais among honored guests, during the national commemoration ceremony held at Kibeho in southern Rwanda. Shortly after the 1999 ceremony, Bishop Misago was arrested and put on trial for genocide. He was eventually found not guilty. For a more complete exploration of the complex layering of mythico-histories and memory in the 1996 ceremonies and at the Kibeho site in Gikongoro, see Burnet (2005).

17. In 2000 Ibuka, the national genocide survivors' association, published its list of genocide victims in cooperation with the Rwandan government.

18. My translation of the original sign in Kinyarwanda. Kabgayi is a major center of the Catholic Church with many different missionary congregations. Many Rwandans sought refuge at religious centers during the genocide. The *génocidaires* took advantage of their concentration at these places to massacre them more easily.

19. Based on a photo of work at the site taken in October 2010 and archived on the Genocide Archive Rwanda website, http://www.genocidearchiverwanda.org .rw/index.php/Image:Ibuka_photo_01062.jpg, accessed September 15, 2011.

Chapter 3. Amplified Silence

1. See Gready (2010) for a discussion of the ways the RPF maintained control over civil society organizations.

2. Public secrets are the things that everybody knows but nobody talks about (Taussig 1999, 50).

3. These arbitrary arrests continued through at least 1999.

4. "Bizimungu Jailed 15 Years," *New Vision* (Uganda), June 8, 2004.

5. For more on the massacres at the Kibeho internally displaced persons camp, see Brisset-Foucault (1995), Médecins sans frontières (1995), and UNDHA (1995a, 1995b, 1995c).

6. It resembles the practices Linda Green (1999, 6) observed in the highlands of Guatemala.

7. As reported in the biography of his official website, http://www.benjah-rutabana .com/biographie.htm, accessed March 11, 2011.

8. An important exception was if they had family members living in Rwanda because the family members could be punished as proxies.

9. In French she used the expression "passer une nuit blanche," which means to stay up all night for negative reasons such as insomnia, hunger, and so on. Many women used this phrase in recounting their memories of war, exile, or return either to mean "to spend the night outdoors, unsheltered" or "to go to sleep without eating."

10. On all Rwandan identity cards, an individual's commune of origin is noted. The commune of origin is generally where a person was born and grew up, although for many urban Rwandans it can be their parents' commune of origin, a place where they never even lived.

11. Upon return all refugees were required to report to their communes of origin in order to get new identity cards. To receive an identity card in Rwanda, an individual must first seek affidavits from the grassroots authorities all the way down to the level of *nyumbakumi* (the local official in charge of ten houses). After following the chain of command, all the affidavits are presented at the commune office. At the time of repatriation this process was also used to verify whether a person had participated in the genocide. Nonetheless, this system did not always succeed. As in the case of Revocata, many Rwandans did not live in their communes of origin before the war, and thus any crimes they might have committed were unknown by local officials. Often those genocide perpetrators purposefully avoided returning to places where they had committed genocide in hopes of avoiding arrest or prosecution for their crimes. Many genocide survivors in Rwanda today complain that the northwest is full of intellectuals pretending to be peasant farmers to avoid arrest. Although I have found no concrete data to support this hypothesis, it is certainly possible.

12. If his statements were accurate, the stool was at least one hundred years old and could have been older.

13. "Mutama" is Kirundi for "old man," a term of respect for older men and the local, respectful nickname for our neighbor, who was the oldest man in the area.

14. Traditionally, *gacaca* (pronounced ga-cha-cha) was a mechanism of conflict resolution in communities. When a conflict arose, whether over land, livestock, or a harm done, the families involved would call wise people. The meetings took place in the most private part of the home, a back court covered with short grass, called *gacaca*, hence the name. Although *gacaca* varied significantly by region, some basic tenets remained more or less the same. One of the purposes of *gacaca* was to establish the "truth" or facts of what exactly had happened. Each witness was asked to explain what he or she had seen happen. As different witnesses "testified," the "wise people" asked questions in order to explain discrepancies between the different witnesses' accounts. In 1995 efforts began to reinvent *gacaca* as a mechanism for adjudicating the massive number of cases of people accused of genocide. After several internationally funded studies, the Rwandan parliament passed a new law establishing formal *gacaca* jurisdictions to try lower categories of genocide crimes.

In 2001 the courts began operating on a pilot basis. By 2003 more than one hundred thousand Rwandans had been imprisoned on charges of genocide. *Gacaca* jurisdictions began operating nationwide in 2005. As will be discussed in chapter 7, many genocide survivors gained some kind of justice, no matter how dissatisfactory, through *gacaca*, but victims of RPF-perpetrated violence were left without public acknowledgment of what had happened, much less precise information about who had killed their loved ones.

Chapter 4. Sorting and Suffering

1. This taboo against discussing ethnicity created great difficulties in asking questions about coexistence and reconciliation. As a researcher arriving in the country in April 1997, I had to learn the new vernacular for discussing these questions. The Twa constitute less than 1 percent of the population. As the consequences of the genocide and of state policies for Twa have varied widely, I do not discuss them in this chapter. Finally, the phrase "politically incorrect" has become so trivialized in the United States that it is inadequate to express the level of emotional and political peril discussions of ethnicity and the genocide entail in Rwanda. Nonetheless, I use the phrase because it succinctly communicates the actual situation.

2. Uli Linke's (2002, 2009) work on public memory and symbolic violence in Germany after 1945 is relevant to the themes I consider in this chapter.

3. The terms *abaturutse hanze* and *abarutashye* denote the same thing: people who returned from outside. The two phrases have very different connotations. *Abaturutse hanze* is more commonly used by the Rwandan population and does not carry a special connotation. *Abarutashye* is used by old returnees when talking about themselves; the phrase sounds arrogant because it implies that they returned from outside *victoriously*. In other words, they see themselves as synonymous with members of the RPF, which won the war.

4. The Kinyarwanda term *abicanyi* means "killers," but in postgenocide Rwanda the word has become synonymous with perpetrators. The Kinyarwanda term *abacengezi* means "infiltrators." Ironically, the same term was used by the Habyarimana regime and especially the Hutu Power extremists to label the RPA soldiers hiding in the population.

5. *Le Soir*, April 7, 1995 (quoted in Vidal 2001, 8), my translation.

6. The phrase "heart of the household" comes from a Kinyarwanda proverb, "Umugore n'umutima w'urugo" (The wife is the heart of the house).

7. Yohani's wife was a triple outsider, since she was born outside the community, she was "Hutu," and she had grown up in Congo.

8. The designation "widow of the genocide" is semiofficial. There are genocide widows' organizations throughout the country associated under a national organization known by its French acronym, AVEGA.

9. At the time this interview was conducted in 2001, over 130,000 Rwandans were imprisoned, accused of genocide. In general, prisoners depended on family members to bring them food and drinking water several times a week.

10. In the course of my interviews with women in Rwanda, I found that frequently they would smile or laugh softly when recounting heart-wrenching stories. I came

to understand these actions as culturally appropriate expressions of grief. Rwandan society does not encourage expressions of emotion.

11. *Gacaca* is the reinvented form of a traditional conflict resolution mechanism that the Rwandan government has used to adjudicate most cases of genocide. *Gacaca* is discussed at length in chapter 7 of this volume.

12. Danielle de Lame has written in great detail on secrecy in rural Rwanda and the difficulty for outsiders (whether foreign anthropologists or Rwandans from the next hill) to gain access to the "'terribly closed' rural world" (2005a, 14).

13. After independence in 1962, armed groups of exiled Tutsi, called *inyenzi* by the Kayibanda regime, launched periodic attacks on the border regions in Rwanda. In December 1963 one such attack from Burundi penetrated to within twenty kilometers or so of Kigali (Kimonyo 2008, 53). Following this attack, the Kayibanda regime launched a campaign of repression against Tutsi political leaders, and local officials in some communities launched attacks on Tutsi. See Kimonyo (2008, 52–55), Lemarchand (1970, 217–24), and Reyntjens (1985, 463).

14. The RPF recruiters asked families to send their second sons because first-born sons, *imfura*, held an important place as the head of the lineage for the next generation.

Chapter 5. Defining Coexistence and Reconciliation in the New Rwanda

1. These works include Crépeau (1985), Crépeau and Bizimana (1978), and Ntampaka (1997), among others.

2. Although Ntampaka states that this is a literal translation, it is not. A literal translation would be "Instead of lying over the truth, you'd rather lie over the blade of an axe."

3. In 2001 the government criminalized "having genocidal ideology" and "spreading divisionism" with the passage of Law No. 47/2001, "On Prevention, Suppression and Punishment of the Crime of Discrimination and Sectarianism."

4. At this time, government administration began at the level of "ten houses" (*nyumbakumi*), then cell (roughly equivalent to a hill), then sector, then commune, and then prefecture.

5. In 1999 I was inscribed in the registry of the Rwandan family I lived with in Kigali and went to visit the *nyumbakumi* to inform him of my presence. He asked to see my passport, visa, and research authorizations from the government. I left copies of these documents with him.

6. Law No. 2/1998.

7. Republic of Rwanda, National Policy for Orphans and Other Vulnerable Children in Rwanda, http://www.youth-policy.com/Policies/Rwanda_National_Policy_for_OVC.cfm, accessed April 13, 2005.

8. The father was later exonerated and released from prison.

9. Interviewees used the French term *ethnism*, which I have translated here as "institutionalized ethnic preference." The term is analogous to the word "racism" in English.

10. Law No. 03/1999 of March 12, 1999.

11. Articles 24 and 88 of the Arusha Peace Agreement on power sharing.

12. *Kinyamateka* is a monthly news magazine published by the Roman Catholic Church in Rwanda. During the period before independence, it criticized abuses of power by the monarchy and called for a democracy to replace colonialism. In the years leading up to the genocide, it was one of the few newspapers that confronted Hutu extremist rhetoric. After the genocide, it tried to take a balanced approach to postgenocide politics, criticizing human rights abuses by the interim government responsible for the genocide as well as the RPF until its editor, Father Andé Sibomana, died from a serious illness.

13. Reuters, "Rwanda Adopts New Flag to Bury Genocide Memories," Kigali, October 1, 1999, http://www.cnn.com/WORLD/africa/9910/01/BC-RWANDA-FLAG.reut/index.html (no longer available).

Chapter 6. Paths to Reconciliation

1. For example, communities experienced communal conflicts centered on the social identities "Hutu," "Tutsi," and "Twa" in 1959, 1961, 1963–64, and 1973.

2. During the genocide families who were believed to have sons among the RPF rebels were among the first targeted for killing.

3. Grace's husband had been killed on the second day of the genocide when the Presidential Guard conducted a house-by-house search of their neighborhood looking for people on their death lists.

4. Often they would know about the searches in advance thanks to tips.

5. Association des femmes pour le développement rural (AFDR) is a pseudonym. I have used a pseudonym to protect the anonymity of the organization's leaders and comply with the research protocol approved by the Institutional Review Board for the Use of Human Subjects in Research.

6. As Paul Gready writes: "The government employs various strategies of management and control in relation to civil society" (2010, 641). Filip Reyntjens (2004, 184–85) and Timothy Longman (2011, 27–28) both describe the RPF strategy of co-opting civil society organizations by forcing organizations to accept pro-RPF leaders at their heads. Danielle Beswick (2010) outlines a variety of "shadow methods" used by the government to control civil society organizations.

7. To distinguish themselves from genocide widows, many members would call themselves "widows from life," meaning that their husbands had died from illness or old age.

8. Although this translation remains faithful to the timing indicated by the speaker (e.g., "a few days"), it should be noted that in this narrative the women compressed the events of more than a year.

Chapter 7. Reconciliation, Justice, and Amplified Silence

1. Organic Law No. 08/96 of August 30, 1996, on the organization of prosecutions for offences constituting the crime of genocide or crimes against humanity committed since October 1, 1990.

2. Organic Law No. 40/2000 of January 26, 2001, setting up *gacaca* jurisdictions and organizing prosecutions for offenses constituting the crime of genocide or crimes against humanity committed between October 1, 1990, and December 31, 1994; Organic Law No. 16/2004 of June 19, 2004, establishing the organization, competence, and functioning of *gacaca* courts charged with prosecuting and trying the perpetrators of the crime of genocide and other crimes against humanity committed between October 1, 1990, and December 31, 1994; Organic Law No. 10/2007 of March 1, 2007, modifying Law No. 16/2004; Organic Law No. 28/2006 of June 27, 2006, modifying Law No. 16/2004; and Organic Law No. 08/2004 of April 28, 2004, on the establishment, organization, duties, and functioning of the National Service in charge of the follow-up, supervision, and coordination of the activities of *gacaca* jurisdictions.

3. See chapter 4, articles 72–75 of Organic Law No. 16/2004 of June 19, 2004, and chapter 4, articles 68–71 of Organic Law No. 40/2000 of January 26, 2001.

4. In an ironic twist of fate, those who are innocent and have no crimes to which to confess remain incarcerated while the *gacaca* process continues.

5. All names have been changed to hide the identities of informants.

6. Attendance at *gacaca* is a compulsory civic duty. On days that *gacaca* is held, all businesses, schools, and offices close so that everyone can attend. Citizens who are absent from *gacaca* face fines and even imprisonment.

7. In this statement "pastoralists" can be read as "Tutsi" and "farmers" as "Hutu." Many of the Tutsi living in rural areas of North province are predominantly cattle herders with only small garden plots, while the Hutu usually have comparatively large fields and only one or two cows and smaller livestock. Many of these Tutsi pastoralists are actually Bagogwe, who historically were distinct from Tutsi but were considered Tutsi by the late 1980s.

8. In this context "'59ers" refers to the predominantly Tutsi refugees who returned to Rwanda following the RPF victory in 1994. Many of these refugees had left Rwanda in 1959, when mass violence targeted members of the Tutsi nobility, or they were the descendants of those who had left in 1959.

Conclusion

1. African Conservation Foundation, "Rwanda Awarded Green Globe Award for Environmental Conservation," http://www.africanconservation.org/201011021986/conservation-news-section/rwanda-awarded-green-globe-award-for-environmental-conservation, accessed September 21, 2011; Rwanda Embassy in Japan, "Rwanda Wins C'wealth Award," http://www.rwandaembassy-japan.org/en/modules/wordpress/index.php?p=173, accessed September 21, 2011; "Rwanda: Kagame Receives Global Peace Award," *New Times*, October 30, 2010, http://www.bridge2rwanda.org/2010/10/rwanda-kagame-receives-global-peace-award/, accessed September 21, 2011; "Kagame Receives IOC Award," *New Times*, September 1, 2011, http://allafrica.com/stories/201109020772.html, accessed September 21, 2011; Rwanda Focus, "President Kagame Receives Award from Chello Foundation," http://focus.rw/wp/2011/07/president-kagame-receives-award-from-chello-foundation/, accessed September 21, 2011; African Gender Forum and Award,

"Award 2007—Laureates' Achievement in Gender Mainstreaming," http://www
.africangenderaward.org/award1.html, accessed February 14, 2012.

2. World DataBank, http://databank.worldbank.org, accessed September 21,
2011.

Works Cited

African Rights. 1994. *Rwanda: Who Is Killing? Who Is Dying? What Is to Be Done?* London: African Rights.

———. 1995a. *Rwanda: Death, Despair, and Defiance.* 2nd ed. London: African Rights.

———. 1995b. *Rwanda Not So Innocent: When Women Become Killers.* London: African Rights.

———. 1996. *Rwanda Killing the Evidence: Murder, Attacks, Arrests and Intimidation of Survivors and Witnesses.* London: African Rights.

Aghion, Anne. 2002. *Gacaca: Living Together Again in Rwanda?* Brooklyn, NY: First Run/Icarus Films.

Amnesty International. 1994. *Rwanda: Reports of Killings and Abductions by the Rwandese Patriotic Army, April–August 1994.* New York: Amnesty International.

———. 1998. *Rwanda, the Hidden Violence: "Disappearances" and Killings Continue.* London: Amnesty International.

Anderson, Benedict. 1991. *Imagined Communities.* London: Verso.

Ansoms, An. 2008. Striving for Growth, Bypassing the Poor? A Critical Review of Rwanda's Rural Sector Policies. *Journal of Modern African Studies* 46 (1): 1–32.

———. 2010. Views from Below on the Pro-poor Growth Challenge: The Case of Rural Rwanda. *African Studies Review* 53 (2): 97–123.

Ansoms, An, and Andrew McKay. 2010. A Quantitative Analysis of Poverty and Livelihood Profiles: The Case of Rural Rwanda. *Food Policy* 35 (6): 584–98.

Aretxaga, Begoña. 1997. *Shattering Silence: Women, Nationalism, and Political Subjectivity in Northern Ireland.* Princeton, NJ: Princeton University Press.

Article 19. 1996. *Broadcasting Genocide: Censorship, Propaganda & State-Sponsored Violence in Rwanda 1990–1994.* London: Article 19.

Babbit, Eileen F., Rebecca Dale, Brian Ganson, Ivana Vuco, Branka Peuraca, Holly Benner, and Odette Nyirakabyare. 2002. Imagine Coexistence: Assessing Refugee Reintegration Efforts in Divided Communities. Fletcher School of Law and Diplomacy, Tufts University, July.

Behar, Ruth. 1996. *The Vulnerable Observer: Anthropology That Breaks Your Heart.* Boston: Beacon Press.

Beswick, Danielle. 2010. Managing Dissent in a Post-genocide Environment: The Challenge of Political Space in Rwanda. *Development and Change* 41 (2): 225–51.

Bourdieu, Pierre. 1977. *Outline of a Theory of Practice.* Translated by R. Nice. Cambridge: Cambridge University Press.

———. 2003. Participant Objectivation. *Journal of the Royal Anthropological Institute* 9 (2): 281–94.

Bowker, Geoffrey C., and Susan Leigh Star. 1999. *Sorting Things Out: Classification and Its Consequences.* Cambridge, MA: MIT Press.

Brauman, Rony, Stephen Smith, and Claudine Vidal. 2000. Rwanda: Politique de terreur, privilège d'impunité. *Esprit* 267 (August/September): 147–61.

Brisset-Foucault, Marc. 1995. Report of the Independent International Commission of Inquiry on the Events at Kibeho, April.

Buckley-Zistel, Susanne. 2006. Remembering to Forget: Chosen Amnesia as a Strategy for Local Coexistence in Post-Genocide Rwanda. *Africa* 76 (2): 131–50.

Burnet, Jennie E. 2005. Genocide Lives in Us: Amplified Silence and the Politics of Memory in Rwanda. PhD diss., University of North Carolina at Chapel Hill.

———. 2008a. Gender Balance and the Meanings of Women in Governance in Post-genocide Rwanda. *African Affairs* 107 (428): 361–86.

———. 2008b. The Injustice of Local Justice: Truth, Reconciliation, and Revenge in Rwanda. *Genocide Studies and Prevention* 3 (2): 173–93.

———. 2009. Whose Genocide? Whose Truth? Representations of Victim and Perpetrator in Rwanda. In *Genocide: Truth, Memory, and Representation*, edited by Alexander Laban Hinton and Kevin Lewis O'Neill, 80–110. Durham, NC: Duke University Press.

———. 2010. (In)justice: Truth, Reconciliation, and Revenge in Rwanda's *Gacaca*. In *Transitional Justice: Global Mechanisms and Local Realities after Genocide and Mass Violence*, edited by A. L. Hinton, 95–118. New Brunswick, NJ: Rutgers University Press.

———. 2011. Women Have Found Respect: Gender Quotas, Symbolic Representation and Female Empowerment in Rwanda. *Politics & Gender* 7 (3): 303–34.

Burnet, Jennie E., and RISD (Rwanda Initiative for Sustainable Development). 2003. Culture, Practice, and Law: Women's Access to Land in Rwanda. In *Women and Land in Africa: Culture, Religion and Realizing Women's Rights*, edited by L. M. Wanyeki, 176–206. New York: Zed Books.

Butler, Judith. 1990. *Gender Trouble: Feminism and the Subversion of Identity*. New York: Routledge.

Callon, Michel. 1986. Some Elements of a Sociology of Translation: Domestication of the Scallops and the Fishermen of St Brieuc Bay. In *Power, Action, and Belief: A New Sociology of Knowledge?*, edited by J. Law, 196–229. London: Routledge.

Carroll, Christina M. 2000. An Assessment of the Role and Effectiveness of the International Criminal Tribunal for Rwanda and the Rwandan National Justice System in Dealing with the Mass Attrocities of 1994. *Boston University International Law Journal* 18 (2): 163–200.

Chakravarty, Anuradha. 2006. Local Dynamics of Contention around Genocide Trials in Rwanda. Paper presented at the African Studies Association Annual Meeting, San Francisco, November 16–19.

Chidester, David. 1996. *Savage Systems: Colonialism and Comparative Religion in Southern Africa*. Charlottesville: University of Virginia Press.

Chrétien, Jean-Pierre. 1995. *Rwanda: Les médias du génocide*. Paris: Éditions Karthala.

———. 1997. *Le défi de l'ethnisme: Rwanda et Burundi 1990–1996*. Paris: Éditions Karthala.

———. 2000. *L'Afrique des Grands Lacs: Deux mille ans d'histoire*. Paris: Aubier.

———. 2006. *The Great Lakes of Africa: Two Thousand Years of History*. Translated by Scott Straus. New York: Zone.

Chubaka, Bishikwabo, and David Newbury. 1980. Recent Historical Research in the Area of Lake Kivu: Rwanda and Zaire. *History in Africa* 7:23–45.

Clifford, James. 1988. *The Predicament of Culture*. Cambridge, MA: Harvard University Press.

Codere, Helen. (1970) 1986. Field Work in Rwanda, 1959–1960. In *Women in the Field: Anthropological Experiences*, edited by P. Golde, 143–66. Berkeley: University of California Press.

———. 1973. *The Biography of an African Society: Rwanda 1900–1960*. Tervuren, Belg.: Musée royal de l'Afrique centrale.

Comaroff, Jean, and John Comaroff. 1991. *Of Revelation and Revolution: Christianity, Colonialism, and Consciousness in South Africa*. Chicago: University of Chicago Press.

Crépeau, Pierre. 1985. *Parole et sagesse: Valeurs sociales dans les proverbes du Rwanda*. Annales sciences humaines 118. Tervuren, Belg.: Musée royal de l'Afrique centrale.

Crépeau, Pierre, and Simon Bizimana. 1978. *Proverbes du Rwanda*. Tervuren, Belg.: Musée royal de l'Afrique centrale.

Das, Veena. 1995. National Honour and Practical Kinship: Of Unwanted Women and Children. In *Critical Events: An Anthropological Perspective on Contemporary India*, edited by Veena Das, 55–83. New York: Oxford University Press.

de Certeau, Michel. 1984. *The Practice of Everyday Life*. Translated by S. Rendall. Berkeley: University of California Press.

Degni-Segui, Rene. 1996. Report on the Situation of Human Rights in Rwanda. United Nations Human Rights Commission, Geneva, 52nd Session, January 29.

de Lame, Danielle. 1996. *Une colline entre mille, ou, Le calme avant la tempête: Transformations et blocages du Rwanda rural*. Annales sciences humaines 154. Tervuren, Belg.: Musée royal de l'Afrique centrale.

————. 1997. Le génocide rwandaise et le vaste monde, les liens du sang. In *L'Afrique des Grands Lacs: Annuaire 1996–1997*, edited by S. Marysse and Filip Reyntjens, 157–77. Paris: L'Harmattan.

————. 2005a. *A Hill among a Thousand: Transformations and Ruptures in Rural Rwanda*. Translated by Helen Arnold. Madison: University of Wisconsin Press. Originally published as *Une colline entre mille, ou, Le calme avant la tempête*. Tervuren, Belg.: Musée royal de l'Afrique centrale, 1996.

————. 2005b. (Im)possible Belgian Mourning for Rwanda. *African Studies Review* 48 (2): 33–43.

Des Forges, Alison. 1995. The Ideology of Genocide. *Issue: A Journal of Opinion* 23 (2): 44–47.

————. 1999. *"Leave None to Tell the Story": Genocide in Rwanda*. New York: Human Rights Watch.

————. 2003. The Striking Force: Military and Militia in the Rwandan Genocide. Paper presented at the conference "The Unfolding of Genocide in Rwanda: Evidence from Micro-level Studies," Kigali and Butare, Rwanda, November 17–21.

————. 2005. Origins of Rwandan Genocide. *Journal of African History* 46 (3): 550–51.

————. 2006. Land in Rwanda: Winnowing out the Chaff. In *L'Afrique des Grands Lacs: Annuaire 2005–2006*, edited by Filip Reyntjens and S. Marysse, 353–71. Paris: L'Harmattan.

————. 2011. *Defeat Is the Only Bad News: Rwanda under Musinga, 1896–1931*. Edited by David Newbury. Madison: University of Wisconsin Press.

Destexhe, Alain. 1994. *Rwanda: Essai sur le génocide*. Brussels: Éditions Complexe.

————. 1995. *Rwanda and Genocide in the Twentieth Century*. New York: New York University Press.

d'Hertefelt, Marcel. 1964. Mythes et Ideologies dans le Rwanda Ancien et Contemporain. In *The Historian in Tropical Africa*, edited by Jan Vansina, 219–38. London: Published for the International African Institute by the Oxford University Press.

————. 1971. *Les clans du Rwanda ancien*. Tervuren, Belg.: Musée royal d'Afrique centrale.

d'Hertefelt, Marcel, A. Trouwbourst, and J. Scherer. 1962. *Les anciens royaumes de la zone interlacustre méridionale*. London: International African Institute.

Dialogue. 1995a. Carnet du 1er août au 31 septembre 1995. *Dialogue* 186:137–48.

————. 1995b. Carnet du 1er decembre au 31 decembre 1994. *Dialogue* 180:131–36.

————. 1995c. Carnet du 1er juin au 31 juillet 1995. *Dialogue* 185:79–90.

————. 1995d. Carnet du 1er mai au 31 mai 1995. *Dialogue* 184:99–110.

————. 1995e. Carnet du 1er mars au 30 avril 1995. *Dialogue* 183:99–108.

————. 1995f. Carnet du 1er octobre au 31 octobre 1995. *Dialogue* 187:67–78.

di Leonardo, Micaela. 1991. *Gender at the Crossroads of Knowledge: Feminist Anthropology and the Postmodern Era*. Berkeley: University of California Press.

Drexler, Elizabeth F. 2010. The Failure of International Justice in East Timor and Indonesia. In *Transitional Justice: Global Mechanisms and Local Realities after Genocide and Mass Violence*, edited by Alexander Laban Hinton, 49–66. New Brunswick, NJ: Rutgers University Press.

Drumtra, Jeff. 1998. *Life after Death: Suspicion and Reintegration in Post-genocide Rwanda*. Washington, DC: U.S. Committee for Refugees.

Dwyer, Leslie. 2010. Building a Monument: Intimate Politics of "Reconciliation" in Post-1965 Bali. In *Transitional Justice: Global Mechanisms and Local Realities after Genocide and Mass Violence*, edited by by Alexander Laban Hinton, 227–48. New Brunswick, NJ: Rutgers University Press.

Ekoko, François, Mel Holt, Henri Maire, and Moustapha Tall. 2001. Report of the Panel of Experts on the Illegal Exploitation of Natural Resources and Other Forms of Wealth of the Democratic Republic of the Congo. New York: United Nations Security Council.

Fein, Helen. 1990. Genocide: A Sociological Perspective. *Current Sociology* 38 (1): v–126.

Feldman, Allen. 1991. *Formations of Violence: The Narrative of Body and Political Terror in Northern Ireland*. Chicago: University of Chicago Press.

Ford, Robert E. 1993. Marginal Coping in Extreme Land Pressures: Ruhengeri, Rwanda. In *Population Growth and Agricultural Change in Africa*, 145–86. Gainesville: University Press of Florida.

Franche, Dominique. 1997. *Rwanda: Généalogie d'un génocide*. Paris: Éditions mille et une nuits.

Fujii, Lee Ann. 2009. *Killing Neighbors: Webs of Violence in Rwanda*. Ithaca, NY: Cornell University Press.

Gakwaya, Felin. 2007. Inkiko za Gacaca zimaze guca imanza zirenga ibihumbi 700. BBC, December 3. http://www.bbc.co.uk/greatlakes/news/story/2007/12/071203_gacacacourts.shtml.

Geertz, Clifford. 1973. The Integrative Revolution: Primordial Sentiments and Civil Politics in the New States. In *The Interpretation of Cultures: Selected Essays by Clifford Geertz*, 255–310. New York: Basic Books.

Gravel, Pierre Bettez. 1968. *Remera: A Community in Eastern Ruanda*. The Hague, Netherlands: Mouton.

Gready, Paul. 2010. "You're Either with Us or against Us": Civil Society and Policy Making in Post-genocide Rwanda. *African Affairs* 109 (437): 637–57.

Green, Linda. 1999. *Fear as a Way of Life: Mayan Widows in Rural Guatemala*. New York: Columbia University Press.

Hagengimana, Athanase, and Devon E. Hinton. 2009. "Ihahamuka," a Rwandan Syndrome of Response to the Genocide. In *Culture and Panic Disorder*, edited by Devon E. Hinton and B. Good, 205–29. Stanford, CA: Stanford University Press.

Haraway, Donna J. 1991. *Simians, Cyborgs, and Women: The Reinvention of Nature*. New York: Routledge.

Harff, Barbara, and Ted Robert Gurr. 1998. Systematic Early Warning of Humanitarian Emergencies. *Journal of Peace Research* 35 (5): 551–79.

Herzfeld, Michael. 1991. Silence, Submission, Subversion: Toward a Poetics of Womanhood. In *Contest Identities: Gender and Kinship in Modern Greece*, edited by Peter Loizos and Evthymios Papataxiarchis, 79–97. Princeton, NJ: Princeton University Press.

Hilhorst, Dorothea, and Mathijs van Leeuwen. 1999. *Imidugudu*, Villagisation in Rwanda: A Case of Emergency Development? *Disaster Sites*, no. 2.

Hinton, Alexander Laban. 2002. The Dark Side of Modernity: Toward an Anthropology of Genocide. In *Annihilating Difference: The Anthropology of Genocide*, edited by Alexander Laban Hinton, 1–42. Berkeley: University of California Press.

———. 2005. *Why Did They Kill? Cambodia in the Shadow of Genocide*. Berkeley: University of California Press.

———. 2010. Introduction: Toward an Anthropology of Transitional Justice. In *Transitional Justice: Global Mechanisms and Local Realities after Genocide and Mass Violence*, edited by Alexander Laban Hinton, 1–24. New Brunswick, NJ: Rutgers University Press.

Hirondelle News Agency. 2007a. Rwanda/Prisons—Rwanda Wants to Relieve Congestion in Its Prisons. December 4. http://tinyurl.com/6mcyo5w.

———. 2007b. Rwanda/Gacaca—Ibuka Draws Up a Negative Assessment of the Gacaca Courts. December 7. http://tinyurl.com/86rheyt.

———. 2007c. Rwanda/Gacaca—The Rwandan Government Refutes Criticism by Ibuka. December 12. http://tinyurl.com/7ncdo6h.

———. 2011. Rwanda/Gacaca—Official Closing Ceremony for Gacaca Courts to be Held May 4. December 23. http://tinyurl.com/7y9bgn3.

HRW (Human Rights Watch). 1993. *Beyond the Rhetoric: Continuing Human Rights Abuses in Rwanda*. New York: Human Rights Watch.

———. 1995. *World Report 1995*. New York: Human Rights Watch.

———. 1996a. *Shattered Lives: Sexual Violence during the Rwandan Genocide and Its Aftermath*. New York: Human Rights Watch.

———. 1996b. *World Report 1996*. New York: Human Rights Watch.

———. 1997. *What Kabila Is Hiding: Civilian Killings and Impunity in Congo*. New York: Human Rights Watch.

———. 2000. *Rwanda: The Search for Security and Human Rights Abuses*. New York: Human Rights Watch.

———. 2001a. Rwanda—President Paul Kagame's Washington Visit. Human Rights Watch, February 1. http://www.hrw.org/news/2001/02/01/rwanda-president-paul-kagames-washington-visit.

———. 2001b. *Uprooting the Rural Poor in Rwanda*. New York: Human Rights Watch.

———. 2002a. Rwanda. In *World Report 2002*. New York: Human Rights Watch.

———. 2002b. *Rwanda: Activists in Detention*. New York: Human Rights Watch.

———. 2002c. Rwanda: Opposition Politician Shot, Others Detained. Human Rights Watch, January 10. http://www.hrw.org/fr/news/2002/01/09/rwanda-opposition-politician-shot-others-detained.

———. 2003a. Preparing for Elections: Tightening Control in the Name of Unity. Human Rights Watch, May 8. http://www.hrw.org/reports/2003/05/08/preparing-elections.

———. 2003b. *Rwanda, Lasting Wounds: Consequences of Genocide and War on Rwanda's Children.* New York: Human Rights Watch.

———. 2004a. Rwanda: Parliament Seeks to Abolish Rights Group. Human Rights Watch, July 2. http://www.hrw.org/news/2004/07/02/rwanda-parliament-seeks-abolish-rights-group.

———. 2004b. *Struggling to Survive: Barriers to Justice for Rape Victims in Rwanda.* New York: Human Rights Watch.

———. 2005. Rwanda—Human Rights Overview. In *World Report 2005.* New York: Human Rights Watch.

———. 2006a. Rwanda—Human Rights Overview. In *Human Rights Watch 2006.* New York: Human Rights Watch. http://hrw.org/english/docs/2006/01/18/rwanda 12286.htm.

———. 2006b. *Swept Away: Street Children Illegally Detained in Kigali, Rwanda.* New York: Human Rights Watch.

———. 2007a. *Killings in Eastern Rwanda.* New York: Human Rights Watch.

———. 2007b. Rwanda—Events of 2006. In *Human Rights Watch 2007.* New York: Human Rights Watch. http://hrw.org/englishwrk7/docs/2007/01/11/rwanda 14782.htm.

———. 2007c. Rwanda—Human Rights Overview. In *World Report 2007.* New York: Human Rights Watch.

———. 2008a. *Law and Reality: Progress in Judicial Reform in Rwanda.* New York: Human Rights Watch.

———. 2008b. Rwanda—Human Rights Overview. In *World Report 2008.* New York: Human Rights Watch.

———. 2012. Rwanda—Human Rights Overview. In *World Report 2012.* New York: Human Rights Watch.

HRW (Human Rights Watch) and FIDH (La Fédération internationale des ligues des droits de l'Homme). 1996. *Rwanda—Trials Applauded and Criticized.* New York and Paris: Human Rights Watch and La Fédération internationale des ligues des droits de l'Homme.

Ingelaere, Bert. 2010. Peasants, Power and Ethnicity: A Bottom-Up Perspective on Rwanda's Political Transition. *African Affairs* 109 (435): 273–92.

International Committee of the Red Cross. 2002–10. *Annual Report.* Geneva: International Committee of the Red Cross.

IRIN (Integrated Regional Information Networks). 1996. Weekly Round-Up of Main Events in the Great Lakes Region, 15–22 June. http://reliefweb.int/node/26005.

———. 2000. Rwanda: Focus on the National Unity and Reconciliation Commission. Integrated Regional Information Network, February 24. http://www.irinnews.org/printreport.aspx?reportid=14028.

———. 2001a. IRIN Update 1152 for the Great Lakes. Integrated Regional Information Network, April 9. http://reliefweb.int/node/79551.

———. 2001b. Rwanda: Government Puts Genocide Victims at 1.07 Million. Integrated Regional Information Network, December 19. http://www.irinnews.org/Report/29236/RWANDA-Government-puts-genocide-victims-at-1-07-million.

———. 2004a. Rwanda: Chronology for 2003. Integrated Regional Information Network, January 9. http://www.irinnews.org/Report/47982/RWANDA-Chronology-for-2003.

———. 2004b. Rwanda: Government Justifies Civil Society Probe. Integrated Regional Information Network, October 12. http://www.irinnews.org/Report/51673/RWANDA-Government-justifies-civil-society-probe.

———. 2004c. Rwanda: Kigali Directs Attorney General to Probe "Genocidal" Groups. Integrated Regional Information Network, September 24. http://www.irinnews.org/Report/51476/RWANDA-Kigali-directs-attorney-general-to-probe-genocidal-groups.

———. 2005. Rwanda: Release of Suspects in the 1994 Genocide Angers Survivors. Integrated Regional Information Network, August 9. http://www.irinnews.org/Report/55758/RWANDA-Release-of-suspects-in-the-1994-genocide-angers-survivors.

Jacob, Irénée. 1984. *Dictionnaire rwandais–français en 3 volumes*. Vol. 1 (A–H). Kigali: Imprimerie scolaire.

———. 1985. *Dictionnaire rwandais–français de l'Institut national de recherche scientifique*. 3 vols. Vol. 3 (S–Z). Kigali: Imprimerie scolaire.

———. 1988. *Dictionnaire rwandais–français en 3 volumes*. Vol. 2 (I–R). Kigali: Imprimerie scolaire.

Jefremovas, Villia. 1991. Loose Women, Virtuous Wives and Timid Virgins: Gender and Control of Resources in Rwanda. *Canadian Journal of African Studies* 25 (3): 378–95.

———. 2000. Treacherous Waters: The Politics of History and the Politics of Genocide in Rwanda and Burundi. *Africa* 70 (2): 298–308.

———. 2002. *Brickyards to Graveyards: From Production to Genocide in Rwanda*. Albany: State University of New York Press.

Kanakuze, Judithe. 2004. Le rôle de la femme dans le processus de démocratisation au rwanda. Paper presented at the "Séminaire sur l'observation électorale par la société civile rwandaise / POER," Kigali, Rwanda, August 5.

Kaplan, Robert D. 1992. Continental Drift. *New Republic* 207 (27): 15.

———. 1994. The Coming Anarchy. *Atlantic Monthly* 273 (2): 22.

Karega, Jyoni wa, Philbert Kagabo, Abbe Smaragde Mbonyintege, Jean Chrisostome Munyampirwa, and Ladislas Twahirwa. 1996. *Gacaca: Le droit coutumier au rwanda*. Kigali: Nations Unis Haut Commissaire aux Droits de L'Homme Operation sur le terrain au Rwanda.

Kimonyo, Jean-Paul. 2001. La relation identitaire hutu/tutsi. In *Ruptures socioculturelles et conflit au Rwanda*, edited by Centre de Gestion des Conflits-Université National du Rwanda, 62–93. Butare: Centre for Conflict Management, National University of Rwanda.

———. 2008. *Rwanda: Un génocide populaire*. Paris: Karthala.

Kriesberg, Louis. 2001. Changing Forms of Coexistence. In *Reconciliation, Justice, and Coexistence: Theory & Practice*, edited by M. Abu-Nimer, 47–64. Lanham, MD: Lexington Books.

Kumar, Krishna, ed. 2001. *Women and Civil War: Impact, Organizations, and Action*. Boulder, CO: Lynne Rienner.

Kumar, Krishna, David Tardif-Douglin, Kim Maynard, Peter Manikas, Annette Sheckler, and Carolyn Knapp. 1996. *Rebuilding Post-War Rwanda (Study 4).* Joint Evaluation of Emergency Assistance to Rwanda, March. http://www.grandslacs .net/doc/0744.pdf.

Kuper, Leo. 1981. *Genocide: Its Political Use in the Twentieth Century.* New Haven, CT: Yale University Press.

Latour, Bruno. 2005. *Reassembling the Social: An Introduction to Actor-Network-Theory.* Oxford: Oxford University Press.

Laurent, Chantal, and Christian Bugnion. 2000. External Evaluation of the UNHCR Shelter Program in Rwanda 1994–1999. UNHCR, Reintegration and Local Settlement Section. http://www.alnap.org/resource/2871.aspx.

Law, John. 1986. *Power, Action, and Belief: A New Sociology of Knowledge?* London: Routledge.

Lawless, Elaine J. 2000. Transformative Re-membering: De-scribing the Unspeakable in Battered Women's Narratives. *Southern Folklore* 57 (1): 65–79.

Lemarchand, René. 1970. *Rwanda and Burundi.* London: Pall Mall Publishers.

———. 1994. Managing Transition Anarchies: Rwanda, Burundi, and South Africa in Comparative Perspective. *Journal of Modern African Studies* 32 (4): 581–604.

———. 1995. Rwanda: The Rationality of Genocide. *Issue: A Journal of Opinion* 23 (2): 8–11.

———. 1998. Genocide in the Great Lakes: Which Genocide? Whose Genocide? *African Studies Review* 41 (1): 3–16.

———. 2007. Consociationalism and Power Sharing in Africa: Rwanda, Burundi, and the Democratic Republic of the Congo. *African Affairs* 106 (422): 1–20.

———. 2008. *The Dynamics of Violence in Central Africa.* Philadelphia: University of Pennsylvania Press.

Lemkin, Ralph. 1944. *Axis Rule in Occupied Europe.* Washington, DC: Carnegie Endowment for International Peace.

Linke, Uli. 2002. Archives of Violence: The Holocaust and the German Politics of Memory. In *Annihilating Difference: The Anthropology of Genocide,* ed. Alexander Laban Hinton, 229–70. Berkeley: University of California Press.

———. 2009. The Limits of Empathy: Emotional Anesthesia and the Museum of Corpses in Post-Holocaust Germany. In *Genocide: Truth, Memory and Representation,* edited by Alexander Laban Hinton and Kevin Lewis O'Neill, 147–91. Durham, NC: Duke University Press.

Longman, Timothy. 1995. Genocide and Socio-Political Change: Massacres in Two Rwandan Villages. *Issue: A Journal of Opinion* 23 (2): 18–21.

———. 1997. Rwanda: Democratization and Disorder: Political Transformation and Social Deterioration. In *Political Reform in Francophone Africa,* edited by John F. Clark and David E. Gardinier, 287–306. Boulder: Westview Press.

———. 1998. Rwanda: Chaos from Above. In *The African State at a Critical Juncture: Between Disintegration and Reconfiguration,* edited by Leonardo A. Villalon and Phillip A. Huxtable, 75–92. Boulder, CO: Lynne Rienner Publishers.

———. 1999. State, Civil Society, and Genocide in Rwanda. In *State, Conflict and Democracy in Africa,* edited by Richard A. Joseph, 339–58. Boulder: Lynne Rienner.

———. 2006. Rwanda: Achieving Equality or Serving an Authoritarian State? In *Women in African Parliaments*, edited by Gretchen Bauer and Hannah Evelyn Britton, 133–50. Boulder, CO: Lynne Rienner.

———. 2009. *Christianity and Genocide in Rwanda*. New York: Cambridge University Press.

———. 2011. Limitations to Political Reform: The Undemocratic Nature of Transition in Rwanda. In *Remaking Rwanda: State Building and Human Rights after Mass Violence*, edited by Scott Straus and Lars Waldorf, 25–47. Madison: University of Wisconsin Press.

Lorch, Donatella. 1995. Rwandan Killings Set Back Effort to Provide Foreign Aid. *New York Times*, April 26, A3.

Malkki, Liisa. 1995. *Purity and Exile: Violence, Memory, and National Cosmology among Hutu Refugees in Tanzania*. Chicago: University of Chicago Press.

Maquet, Jacques J. 1954. *Le système des relations sociales dans le Ruanda ancien*. Tervuren, Belg.: Musée royal d'Afrique centrale.

———. 1961. *The Premise of Inequality in Rwanda: A Study of Political Relations in a Central African Kingdom*. London: Oxford University Press.

McNeil, Donald G., Jr. 1995. Ntarama Journal: At Church, Testament to Horror. *New York Times*, August 4.

Médecins sans frontières. 1995. Report on Events in Kibeho Camp, April 1995. MSF, May 16. http://www.msf.fr/sites/www.msf.fr/files/1995-05-16-MSF.pdf.

Merry, Sally Engle. 2006a. *Human Rights and Gender Violence: Translating International Law into Local Justice*. Chicago: University of Chicago Press.

———. 2006b. Anthropology, Law, and Transational Processes. *Annual Review of Anthropology* 35:99–116.

Mgbako, Chi. 2005. *Ingando* Solidarity Camps: Reconciliation and Political Indoctrination in Post-genocide Rwanda. *Harvard Human Rights Journal* 18 (Spring): 201–24.

Minow, Martha. 1998. *Between Vengeance and Forgiveness: Facing History after Genocide and Mass Violence*. Boston: Beacon Press.

Mironko, Charles. 2004. Igitero: Means and Motive in the Rwandan Genocide. *Journal of Genocide Research* 6 (1): 47–60.

Mironko, Charles, and Susan Cook. 1995. Broadcasting Racism, Reaping Genocide: Radio Télévision des Mille Collines (RTLM) and the Rwandan Genocide. Paper presented at the Annual Conference of the American Anthropological Association, Washington, DC, November 16.

———. 1996. The Linguistic Formulation of Emotion in Rwanda. Paper presented at Symposium About Language and Society—Austin (SALSA) IV, Austin, TX, April 12–14.

Musabyimana, Gaspard. 2006. *Pratiques et rites sexuels au Rwanda*. Paris: L'Harmattan.

Musahara, Herman. 1999. Villagisation and Land Use in the Context of the Rwandan Economy. Paper read at Land Use and Villagisation Workshop, Mille Collines Hotel, Kigali, September 20–21.

Newbury, Catharine. 1988. *The Cohesion of Oppression*. New York: Columbia University Press.

——. 1992. Rwanda: Recent Debates Over Governance and Rural Development. In *Governance and Politics in Africa*, edited by Goran Hyden and Michael Bratton, 193–219. Boulder, CO: Lynne Rienner.

——. 1995. Background to Genocide: Rwanda. *Issue: A Journal of Opinion* 23 (2): 12–17.

——. 1998. Ethnicity and the Politics of History in Rwanda. *Africa Today* 45 (1): 7–24.

——. 2002. States at War: Confronting Conflict in Africa. *African Studies Review* 45 (1): 1–20.

——. 2004. Mourning. Possibility or Impasse? *Cahiers d'études africaines* 44 (173/174): 428–30.

——. 2005. Suffering and Survival in Central Africa. *African Studies Review* 48 (3): 121–32.

——. 2011. High Modernism at the Ground Level: The Imidugudu Policy in Rwanda. In *Remaking Rwanda: State Building and Human Rights after Mass Violence*, edited by Scott Straus and Lars Waldorf, 223–39. Madison: University of Wisconsin Press.

Newbury, Catharine, and Hannah Baldwin. 2000. Aftermath: Women's Organizations in Postconflict Rwanda. Working paper no. 304. Washington, DC: Center for Development Information and Evaluation, US Agency for International Development. http://pdf.usaid.gov/pdf_docs/PNACJ324.pdf.

——. 2001a. Confronting the Aftermath of Conflict: Women's Organizations in Postgenocide Rwanda. In *Women and Civil War: Impact, Organizations, and Action*, edited by Krishna Kumar, 97–128. Boulder, CO: Lynne Rienner.

——. 2001b. Profile: Rwanda. In *Women and Civil War: Impact, Organizations, and Action*, edited by Krishna Kumar, 27–38. Boulder, CO: Lynne Rienner.

Newbury, Catharine, and David Newbury. 1999. A Catholic Mass in Kigali: Contested Views of the Genocide in Rwanda. *Canadian Journal of African Studies* 33 (2–3): 292–328.

Newbury, David. 1980. The Clans of Rwanda: An Historical Hypothesis. *Africa* 50 (4): 389–403.

——. 1991. *Kings and Clans: Ijwi Island and the Lake Kivu Rift, 1780–1840*. Madison: University of Wisconsin Press.

——. 1994. Trick Cyclists? Recontextualizing Rwandan Dynastic Chronology. *History in Africa* 21:191–217.

——. 1997. Irredentist Rwanda: Ethnic and Territorial Frontiers in Central Africa. *Africa Today* 44 (2): 211–21.

——. 1998. Understanding Genocide. *African Studies Review* 41 (1): 73–97.

——. 2001. Precolonial Burundi and Rwanda: Local Loyalties, Regional Royalties. *International Journal of African Historical Studies* 34 (2): 255–314.

——. 2003. The Path of a Genocide: The Rwanda Crisis from Uganda to Zaire. *Holocaust and Genocide Studies* 17 (1): 202–4.

——. 2004. Engaging with the Past to Engage with the Future: Two Visions of History. *Cahiers d'études africaines* 44 (173/174): 430–31.

——. 2005. Returning Refugees: Four Historical Patterns of "Coming Home" to Rwanda. *Comparative Studies in Society and History* 47 (2): 252–85.

Newbury, David, and Catharine Newbury. 2000. Bringing the Peasants Back In: Agrarian Themes in the Construction and Corrosion of Statist Historiography in Rwanda. *American Historical Review* 105 (3): 832–77.

Nordstrom, Carolyn. 1997. *A Different Kind of War Story.* Philadelphia: University of Pennsylvania Press.

Ntampaka, Charles. 1997. Le rôle des règles issues de la culture rwandaise dans la promotion de la justice et de la démocratie. *Dialogue* 197:7–17.

NURC (National Unity and Reconciliation Commission). 2000. *Annual Report: February 1999–June 2000.* Kigali: National Unity and Reconciliation Commission.

———. 2004. Reconciliation Is a Long-Term Painful Process. Report on IJR workshop. http://www.nurc.gov.rw/eng/ijrworkshop.htm. Accessed March 2, 2005 (no longer available).

Obeyesekere, Gananath. 1997. *The Apotheosis of Captain Cook: European Mythmaking in the Pacific.* 2nd ed. Princeton, NJ: Princeton University Press.

ONAPO (Office national de la population). 1998. Socio-Demographic Survey 1996: Final report. Kigali: Ministry of Finance and Economic Planning. http://snap3 .uas.mx/RECURSO1/unfpa/data/docs/unpf0015.pdf.

Oyewumi, Oyeronke. 1997. *The Invention of Women: Making an African Sense of Western Gender Discourses.* Minneapolis: University of Minnesota Press.

Penal Reform International. 2003. PRI Research on *Gacaca* Report 4: The Guilty Plea Procedure, Cornerstone of the Rwandan Justice System. London: Penal Reform International. http://www.penalreform.org/files/rep-ga4-2003-guilty-plea-en_0.pdf.

———. 2006. Monitoring and Research Report on the *Gacaca*: Information-Gathering during the National Phase. London: Penal Reform International. http://www .penalreform.org/files/rep-ga8-2006-info-gathering-en_0.pdf.

Pottier, Johan. 1996. Relief and Repatriation: Views by Rwandan Refugees; Lessons for Humanitarian Aid Workers. *African Affairs* 95:403–29.

———. 2002. *Re-imagining Rwanda: Conflict, Survival and Disinformation in the Late Twentieth Century.* New York: Cambridge University Press.

———. 2006. Land Reform for Peace? Rwanda's 2005 Land Law in Context. *Journal of Agrarian Change* 6 (4): 509–37.

Powley, Elizabeth. 2003. Strengthening Governance: The Role of Women in Rwanda's Transition. Washington, DC: Hunt Alternatives Fund. http://www .huntalternatives.org/download/10_strengthening_governance_the_role_of_ women_in_rwanda_s_transition.pdf.

———. 2005. Rwanda: Women Hold up Half the Parliament. In *Women in Parliament: Beyond Numbers,* rev. ed., edited by Julie Ballington and Azza Karam, 154–63. Stockholm, Sweden: International Institute for Democracy and Electoral Assistance.

———. 2008a. Engendering Rwanda's Decentralization: Supporting Women Candidates for Local Office. Washington, DC: Hunt Alternatives Fund. http://www .huntalternatives.org/download/1091_engendering_rwandas_decentralization .pdf.

———. 2008b. Defending Children's Rights: The Legislative Priorities of Rwandan Women Parliamentarians. Washington, DC: Hunt Alternatives Fund. http:// www.huntalternatives.org/download/1077_defending_childrens_rights.pdf.

Powley, Elizabeth, and Elizabeth Pearson. 2007. "Gender Is Society": Inclusive Lawmaking in Rwanda's Parliament. *Critical Half* (Winter): 17–21. http://www.huntalternatives.org/download/525_winter_2007_critical_half.pdf.

Prakash, Gyan. 1992. Writing Post-Orientalist Histories of the Third World: Indian Historiography Is Good to Think. In *Colonialism and Culture*, edited by Nicholas B. Dirks, 353–88. Ann Arbor: University of Michigan Press.

Prendergast, John, and David Smock. 1999. Postgenocidal Reconstruction: Building Peace in Rwanda and Burundi. Washington, DC: United States Institute of Peace (USIP). http://www.usip.org/publications/post-genocidal-reconstruction-building-peace-rwanda-and-burundi.

Prunier, Gérard. 1997. *The Rwanda Crisis: History of a Genocide.* 2nd ed. New York: Columbia University Press.

———. 1998. The Rwandan Patriotic Front. In *African Guerrillas*, edited by Christopher Clapham, 119–33. Bloomington: Indiana University Press.

———. 2009. *Africa's World War: Congo, the Rwandan Genocide, and the Making of a Continental Catastrophe.* New York: Oxford University Press.

Republic of Rwanda, Ministry of Finance and Economic Planning, and National Census Commission. 2003. *Report on the Preliminary Results: The General Census of Population and Housing: 16–30 August 2002.* Kigali: Government of Rwanda.

Réseau des femmes œuvrant pour le développement rural. 1991. *Profil socio-économique de la femme rwandaise.* Kigali: Réseau des femmes œuvrant pour le développement rural.

Reyntjens, Filip. 1985. *Pouvoir et droit au Rwanda: Droit public et évolution politique, 1916–1973.* Tervuren, Belg.: Musée royal de l'Afrique centrale.

———. 1990. Le *gacaca* ou la justice du gazon au Rwanda. *Politique africaine* 40:31–41.

———. 1994. *L'Afrique des Grands Lacs en crise: Rwanda, Burundi 1988–1994.* Paris: Karthala.

———. 1995. Subjects of Concern: October 1994. *Issue: A Journal of Opinion* 23 (2): 39–43.

———. 2004. Rwanda, Ten Years On: From Genocide to Dictatorship. *African Affairs* 103 (411): 177–210.

———. 2005. Chronique politique du Rwanda et du Burundi, 2003–2005. In *L'Afrique des Grands Lacs: Annuaire 2004–2005*, edited by Filip Reyntjens and Stefaan Marysse, 1–26. Paris: L'Harmattan.

———. 2006. Post-1994 Politics in Rwanda: Problematising "Liberation" and "Democratisation." *Third World Quarterly* 27 (6): 1103–17.

———. 2009. *The Great African War: Congo and Regional Geopolitics, 1996–2006.* Cambridge: Cambridge University Press.

———. 2011. Constructing the Truth, Dealing with Dissent, Domesticating the World: Governance in Post-genocide Rwanda. *African Affairs* 110 (438): 1–34.

RISD (Rwanda Initiative for Sustainable Development). 1999. Land Use and Villagisation in Rwanda. Paper read at Land Use and Villagisation Workshop, Mille Collines Hotel, Kigali, September 20–21.

Robben, Antonius C. G. M. 2010. Testimonies, Truths, and Transitions of Justice in Argentina and Chile. In *Transitional Justice: Global Mechanisms and Local*

Realities after Genocide and Mass Violence, edited by Alexander Laban Hinton, 179–205. New Brunswick, NJ: Rutgers University Press.

Ruzibiza, Abdul Joshua, and Claudine Vidal. 2005. *Rwanda, l'histoire secrète*. Paris: Éditions du Panama.

Rwanda Newsline. 2000. More Students Leave for Exile. *Rwanda Newsline*, December 24–January 2, 32.

Sanders, Edith R. 1969. The Hamitic Hypothesis: Its Origin and Functions in Time Perspective. *Journal of African History* 10 (4): 521–32.

Scarry, Elaine. 1985. *The Body in Pain: The Making and Unmaking of the World*. Oxford: Oxford University Press.

Schoenbrun, David Lee. 1998. *A Green Place, a Good Place: Agrarian Change, Gender and Social Identity in the Great Lakes Region to the 15th Century*. Portsmouth, NH: Heinemann.

Schotsman, Martien. 2000. À l'écoute des rescapés: Recherche sur la perception par les rescapés de leur situation actuelle. Kigali: GTZ (Deutsche Gesellschaft für Technische Zusammenarbeit).

Scott, James C. 1998. *Seeing Like a State: How Certain Schemes to Improve the Human Condition Have Failed*. New Haven, CT: Yale University Press.

Simpson, Chris. 1998. Rwandans Execute 22. Transcript of National Public Radio broadcast, April 24.

Southall, Aidan W. 1970. The Illusion of Tribe. *Journal of Asian and African Studies* 5:28–50.

Stearns, Jason, and Federico Borello. 2011. Bad Karma: Accountability for Rwandan Crimes in the Congo. In *Remaking Rwanda: State Building and Human Rights after Mass Violence*, edited by Scott Straus and Lars Waldorf, 152–69. Madison: University of Wisconsin Press.

Stewart, Kathleen. 1996. *A Space on the Side of the Road*. Princeton, NJ: Princeton University Press.

Straus, Scott. 2006. *The Order of Genocide: Race, Power, and War in Rwanda*. Ithaca, NY: Cornell University Press.

Straus, Scott, and Lars Waldorf, eds. 2011. *Remaking Rwanda: State Building and Human Rights after Mass Violence*. Madison: University of Wisconsin Press.

Taussig, Michael. 1992. Tactility and Distraction. In *The Nervous System*, 141–48. New York: Routledge.

———. 1999. *Defacement: Public Secrecy and the Labor of the Negative*. Stanford: Stanford University Press.

Taylor, Christopher C. 1999. *Sacrifice as Terror: The Rwandan Genocide of 1994*. London: Berg Publishers.

———. 2002. The Cultural Face of Terror in the Rwandan Genocide of 1994. In *Annihilating Difference: The Anthropology of Genocide*, edited by Alexander Laban Hinton, 137–78. Berkeley: University of California Press.

———. 2003. Kings and Chaos in Rwanda: On the Order of Disorder. *Anthropos* 98 (1): 41–58.

Thomson, Susan. 2009. Resisting Reconciliation: State Power and Everyday life in Post-genocide Rwanda. PhD diss., Dalhousie University, Halifax, Nova Scotia.

———. 2011. Reeducation for Reconciliation: Participant Observations on *Ingando*. In *Remaking Rwanda: State Building and Human Rights after Mass Violence*, edited by Scott Straus and Lars Waldorf, 331–42. Madison: University of Wisconsin Press.

Tsing, Anna. 2004. *Friction: An Ethnography of Global Connection*. Princeton, NJ: Princeton University Press.

Turshen, Meredeth. 2001. The Political Economy of Rape: An Analysis of Systematic Rape and Sexual Abuse of Women During Armed Conflict in Africa. In *Victims, Perpetrators or Actors?: Gender, Armed Conflict and Political Violence*, edited by Caroline O. N. Moser and Fiona C. Clark, 55–68. London: Zed Books.

Twagiramariya, Clotilde, and Meredeth Turshen. 1998. The Sexual Politics of Survival in Rwanda. In *What Women Do in Wartime: Gender and Conflict in Africa*, edited by Meredeth Turshen and Clotilde Twagiramariya, 101–21. New York: Zed Books.

Umutesi, Marie Beatrice. 2000. *Fuir ou mourir au Zaïre: Le vécu d'une réfugiée rwandaise*. Paris: L'Harmattan.

United Nations. 1948. Convention on the Prevention and Punishment of the Crime of Genocide. http://www.hrweb.org/legal/genocide.html.

UNDHA (United Nations Department of Humanitarian Affairs). 1995a. Humanitarian Situation in Rwanda No. 2: Update on the April 21/22 Killings in Rwanda. UN Rwanda Emergency Office, Kigali.

———. 1995b. Humanitarian Situation in Rwanda No. 8: Update on the April 21/22 Killings in Rwanda. UN Rwanda Emergency Office, Kigali.

———. 1995c. Humanitarian Situation in Rwanda No. 9: Update on the April 21/22 Killings in Rwanda. UN Rwanda Emergency Office, Kigali.

UNDP (United Nations Development Program). 2010. Millennium Development Goals Progress Report: Rwanda Country Report 2010. Kigali, Rwanda. http://www.devinforwanda.gov.rw/sites/default/files/MDG%20Progress%20Report_Rwanda%20Country%20Report%202010.pdf.

UNHCHR (United Nations High Commission for Human Rights). 1997a. Human Rights Field Operation in Rwanda: Report of the United Nations High Commissioner for Human Rights. United Nations General Assembly, 54th Session. http://www.unhcr.org/refworld/docid/3ae6b0e84.html.

———. 1997b. Report of the Joint Mission Charged with Investigating Allegations of Massacres and other Human Rights Violations Occurring in Eastern Zaire (Now Democratic Republic Of Congo) since September 1996. United Nations General Assembly, 52nd Session. http://www.unhcr.org/refworld/docid/3ae6aec24.html.

———. 2010. Democratic Republic of the Congo, 1993–2003: Report of the Mapping Exercise Documenting the Most Serious Violations of Human Rights and International Humanitarian Law Committed within the Territory of the Democratic Republic of the Congo between March 1993 and June 2003. Geneva, Switz.: Office of the United Nations High Commission for Human Rights. http://www.ohchr.org/en/Countries/AfricaRegion/Pages/RDCProjetMapping.aspx.

UNHCR (United Nations High Commission for Refugees). 2001. Imagine Coexistence white paper. United Nations High Commission for Refugees, Kigali. Original edition, description of the Imagine Coexistence project.

UNHRFOR (United Nations High Commission for Human Rights Field Operation in Rwanda). 1997a. Deterioration of the Security and Human Rights Situation in Ruhengeri Prefecture, Including Killings of Civilians during Military Operations, May–June 1997. Kigali: United Nations High Commission for Human Rights Field Operation in Rwanda. http://reliefweb.int/node/32185.

———. 1997b. *Killings and Other Attacks against Genocide Survivors and Persons Associated with Them from January through December 1996.* Kigali: United Nations High Commission for Human Rights Field Operation in Rwanda.

———. 1997c. *Killings and Other Attacks against Genocide Survivors and Persons Associated with Them from January to Mid-February 1997.* Kigali: United Nations High Commission for Human Rights Field Operation in Rwanda.

———. 1997d. Rwanda: Report on the Human Rights Situation and the Activities of HRFOR, Jul–Aug 1997. Kigali: United Nations High Commission for Human Rights Field Operation in Rwanda. http://reliefweb.int/node/32902.

US Department of State. 2006. Rwanda Country Report on Human Rights Practices, 2005. June 11. http://www.state.gov/g/drl/rls/hrrpt/2005/61587.htm.

Uvin, Peter. 1998. *Aiding Violence: The Development Enterprise in Rwanda.* West Hartford, CT: Kumarian Press.

Uvin, Peter, and Charles Mironko. 2003. Western and Local Approaches to Justice in Rwanda. *Global Governance* 9:219–31.

Vansina, Jan. 1962. L'évolution du royaume Rwanda des origines à 1900. Thesis, Académie royale des Sciences d'Outre-Mer, Bruxelles.

———. 2001. *Le Rwanda ancien.* Paris: Karthala.

———. 2004. *Antecedents to Modern Rwanda: The Nyiginya Kingdom.* Madison: University of Wisconsin Press.

Vesperini, Helen. 2001. "Rwanda Unveils New Flag and Anthem." BBC, December 31. http://news.bbc.co.uk/2/hi/africa/1735405.stm.

Vidal, Claudine. 1998. Questions sur le rôle des paysans durant le génocide des Rwandais tutsi. *Cahiers d'études africaines* 38 (2–4): 331–45.

———. 2001. Les commémorations du génocide au Rwanda. *Les temps modernes* 613:1–46.

———. 2004. Humanitarian Workers as Witness of History: Human Rights Watch Report on the Aftermath of Genocide in Rwanda. *Temps Modernes* 59 (627): 92–107.

Wagner, Michele D. 1998. All the *Bourgmestre's* Men: Making Sense of Genocide in Rwanda. *Africa Today* 45 (1): 25–36.

Weiner, Eugene. 1998. Coexistence Work: A New Profession. In *The Handbook of Interethnic Coexistence,* edited by Eugene Weiner, 13–26. New York: Continuum.

Willame, Jean-Claude. 1997. *Banyarwanda et Banyamulenge: Violences ethniques et gestion de l'identitaire au Kivu.* Paris: L'Harmattan.

Wolf, Eric R. 1982. *Europe and the People without History.* Berkeley: University of California Press.

Index

Page numbers in italics indicate illustrations, figures, tables, and maps.

abacengezi, umucengezi (infiltrators). *See* infiltrators (*abacengezi, umucengezi*)

abafunze (prisoners). *See* prisoners (*abafunze*)

abagore b'abafunze (wives of prisoners), 130, 134, 136–40, 169, 190–91

abagore, abategarugori (wives). *See* marriage; wives (*abagore, abategarugori*); women

abantu (people), 132, 162, 200

abapfakazi (widows). *See* widows (*abapfakazi*)

abapfakazi b'itsembabwoko (genocide widows). *See* genocide widows (*abapfakazi b'itsembabwoko*); women

abari, umwari (maidens), 42–45, *43*, 130, 134–36, 228, 237n6

abarokotse, uwarokotse (survivors). *See* survivors (*abarokotse*)

abatingitingi, abatahutse, abahungutse, uhungutse (new returnees). *See* new returnees (*abatingitingi, abatahutse, abahungutse, uhungutse*); refugees

abaturutse hanze, abarutashye (old caseload returnees). *See* old caseload returnees (*abaturutse hanze, abarutashye*); refugees

abicanyi, umwicanyi (perpetrators). *See* perpetrators (*abicanyi, umwicanyi*)

accomplice/s (*icyitso, ibyitso*), 4–5, 20, 59, 138, 195, 211, 225, 234n4

AFDL (Alliance des forces démocratiques pour la libération du Congo-Zaïre), 56, 70, 233n15

259

Gossip, Markets, and Gender: How Dialogue Constructs Moral Value in Post-Socialist Kilimanjaro
Tuulikki Pietilä

Surviving the Slaughter: The Ordeal of a Rwandan Refugee in Zaire
Marie Béatrice Umutesi; translated by Julia Emerson